Curious Stories

Stories

from

The Bible

ROBERT F. SIMMS

ALSO BY ROBERT F. SIMMS

Hosea
Spokesman of Heavenly Love (Commentary)

Malachi
The Last Message Before the Messiah (Commentary)

The Evangelist
A Story of John Mark (A Novel)

The Letter of the Apostle Paul to the Church at Laodicea
(A Novel)

Christianity Made Simple
The Message of Paul's Letter to the Romans

Walking the Walk, Not Just Talking the Talk
A Commentary on James

Where Did I Come From: Your
Spiritual Nature and What it Means to You

7 Days: Seven-Day Waiting
Periods in the Bible and a Plan for
Spiritual Renewal

Ponder, Pray, Practice: 366 Daily
Devotions for Thinking Christians

Sacred Subversion
How Some Churches Defeat Their Pastors
and Destroy Themselves

Living Life for the Highest Purpose

Ventures in Stewardship

The Challenge of Cooperation

To Dr. Walter Johnson,
who cursed this perfectionist with
the obsession of getting all
footnotes and bibliography
entries right.
Not that they are.

CURIOUS STORIES

from

The Bible

ROBERT F. SIMMS

Contents

INTRODUCTION

The Bible is an old, old book. As such, its documents contain some accounts that are anything from slightly odd to downright perplexing to modern readers. Often, an account makes a readily understood point in context; it's just the cultural setting or something else history hasn't preserved for us that makes the account stand out as strange or remarkable.

But some stories remain bizarre to the average reader. And their relevance and significance to their individual Bible books and to the scripture as a whole are sometimes up in the air because of multiple interpretations from competent scholars and exegetes.

The multiplicity of curious and offbeat stories is not lost on anyone, especially critics of Judaism or Christianity, who delight in lampooning scripture as they condemn its believers. Lists can be found of the stories the enemies of Christianity describe as absurd. Often, however, their assessment of the story is absent any sense of its genuine meaning. In most cases, they haven't done their homework before caricaturing.

As an example, consider a recent book by Kristen Swenson, *A Most Peculiar Book: The Inherent Strangeness of the Bible* (Oxford University Press, 2021). Swenson is among those who fail to apply even common sense to their perusal of curious Bible accounts and sayings. She observes that "in the Gospel of Luke, Jesus has an unusual requirement for his disciples: that they have to hate their own family," and she just about leaves the matter there, as if nobody really knows what Jesus meant. The saying of Jesus, however, is hardly difficult. He was using the common element of

9

hyperbole—apparently more common then than now—and meant simply that where choosing Jesus over one's family, one had better choose following Jesus as if family meant nothing.

In another place Swenson recounts the story of Balaam's talking donkey—the subject of one of our chapters in this book—and she betrays an astonishing lack of Bible knowledge in several of her statements about the account, implying that we modern readers should be as baffled as she says Balaam was over the Angel of the Lord's opposing his intention to curse Israel.

Another modern critic of Christianity thinks Ezekiel's vision of God with the wheel within a wheel is utterly bizarre, by which he doesn't mean merely astounding and glorious, but fundamentally unbelievable, something with which to entertain the credulous.

We think that some of the so-called "scholars" who constantly pooh-pooh the Bible for its ancient tales give away their own folly in spades.

This book will try not to leave the reader believing that the odd accounts and statements found in the Bible are impenetrable. This author's belief—consistent with that of orthodox Christians around the world through the ages—is that the Bible's curious stories are intended by their writers, as well as the Holy Spirit who inspired them, to be understood and to teach us. Our purpose, in other words, is not merely to enumerate them and express our surprise or confusion over them, but instead to dig into their significance at the time they were written and their lessons in the larger picture of scripture. This significance and application lie in detailed and thorough exegesis.

It should be noted that this book is not simply about accounts of miracles. In fact, most of the chapters don't have to do with miracles, except perhaps supernatural appearances. Nor is this book about Bible stories that are merely difficult for modern worshipers of science to believe. For instance, we have *not* included:

- The account of the great flood, which most devotees of Darwin believe is simply not true;
- Any of the ten plagues God brought upon Egypt through Moses in order to free the Hebrews from slavery;
- The passage of the Israelites through the Red Sea on dry ground;
- The short battle of David with Goliath the giant;
- The odd theatrics of some of Israel's prophets;
- Most of Jesus' miracles;
- Any of the visions in the Revelation to John.

Some of these passages of scripture we haven't included are popular targets of Bible critics. Many modern readers who have no interest in taking the Bible seriously don't think much of the Bible makes sense. Their disapprobation is not our interest in this book.

What we're interested in is the accounts, statements or teachings which, even if you believe in the truth of the scriptures, seem suddenly out of place, or hard to reckon with, or unsettlingly abrupt, or unnecessarily extreme.

Not all the accounts we've chosen are actually stories. One is simply a verse that strikes the reader as odd because of its placement, introducing a quirky subject for reasons not immediately obvious. A couple are not curious overall, but only in one part.

Most of these curious stories are in the Old Testament. In part, that's because the Old Testament is much older than the New Testament. And the earliest written books contain some accounts that were even older and had been passed down by oral tradition. Context sometimes gets lost in such stories, compression may occur as they are retold, and sayings and symbolic language that were readily understood by those who originally told the stories may have been lost to history.

Curious stories in the New Testament are fewer, but we have included a few accounts that still have people—even scholars— scratching their heads.

We admit there is nothing novel about the subject of this book.

As we said above, many others have made lists of bizarre stories and some have written books about them. What may make this present work a bit different from the rest of the pack is our purpose. We propose to take the stories most often identified as curious or bizarre, and to discover why they are where they are in the book we call the word of God. Because we're convinced that nothing—no matter how curious or strange to one reader or another—is in the Bible by accident.

It may just be that one of these curious Bible stories will leap several millennia into this day and time and speak to one of our readers in a very personal way. That's the way the Bible works—curiously enough.

Sons of God, Daughters of Men
Genesis 6:1-6

This chapter just about wasn't included in the book. Another chapter would have begun the book—something less controversial, less debated. One has only to survey Internet based studies that allow readers to comment, to realize that proponents of various viewpoints can be vociferous and even belligerent. There is, in particular, animus against a "supernatural" reading of this story, though it is the majority view today. And to be sure, this account about "the sons of God and the daughters of men" is one of the more fantastical tales in the whole Bible.

By using the word "fantastical" we are not implying in any way that the story is not factual. We're saying that the story is of the kind that most people today, immersed as they are in restrictively scientific thinking, would reject as being fantasy. Granted, many outsiders to biblical revelation think the Bible is fantasy altogether. And those who would accord some basic factual content to the overall history of the Bible usually treat stories of miracles with modernistic contempt. Never mind the fact that for atheistic evolutionists to be right, one of the most fantastical miracles ever to take place would have to have happened when out of a pond of primordial chemicals suddenly a fully formed strand of DNA appeared, without any help from a nonexistent God. Here, we agree with Norman Geisler and Frank Turek: "I don't have enough faith to be an atheist."[1]

This fantastical tale, with which we begin this book of curious Bible stories, is found early in Genesis, at the beginning of the sixth chapter:

> [1]When human beings began to increase in number on the earth and daughters were born to them, [2]the sons of God saw that the daughters of humans were beautiful, and they married any of them they chose. [3]Then the LORD said, "My Spirit will not contend with humans forever, for they are mortal; their days will be a hundred and twenty years."
> [4]The Nephilim were on the earth in those days—and also afterward—when the sons of God went to the daughters of humans and had children by them. They were the heroes of old, men of renown" (Genesis 6:1-4 NIV).

Scholars across the board agree that, however this passage is to be interpreted, it constitutes "an approaching crisis"[2] that would bring the Lord's destruction of earthly life by flood. The pivotal nature of this story is one reason we are compelled to see it as sufficiently provocative of divine wrath.

Our challenge is to decide what the various terms in the passage mean, and thereby discover what the passage means as a whole.

---

[1] Norman L. Geisler and Frank Turek, *I Don't Have Enough Faith to Be an Atheist* (Wheaton, Illinois, Crossway, 2004).

[2] Derek Kidner, *Genesis*, The Tyndale Old Testament Commentaries (Downers Grove, Illinois, Inter-Varsity Press, 1967) 83.

Discovering the Text

Sons of God

As our story opens, we are told that human beings have been doing what God commissioned them to do, being fruitful and multiplying. No controversy is here, nothing to interpret that causes any debate. There's just the little literary spotlight that ends the phrase: "and daughters were born to them." The focus is now on these daughters. Because, in addition to these daughters routinely attracting the attention of the sons of men, they have drawn the notice of "the sons of God."

Bible translators and scholars have debated the identity of these "sons of God" for many years. The meaning of the entirety of the passage hangs on who these persons were.

We should recognize first that the oldest interpretation is that the "sons of God" were heavenly beings, sometimes called "angels" specifically. Much later in history there developed two other strains of interpretation, one holding that these "sons of God" were descendants of Seth, while the daughters of men were descendants of Cain, supposedly casting the Sethite men as godly and the Cainite women as ungodly. The other interpretive strain was the concept that the "sons of God" were prominent, and perhaps despotic, dynastic rulers of the era.

Few people attempt to promote either the "Cainite" view or the "dynastic rulers" view today, for the chief reason that there is little to support either view and plenty to refute them.

In the Cainite view, the sin "is a forbidden union, a yoking of what God intended to keep apart, the intermarriage of believer with unbeliever. ...But ...nowhere in the OT are Sethites identified as the sons of God."[3] Nor can supporters find any scriptures that

_____

[3] Victor P. Hamilton, *The Book of Genesis, Chapters 1-17,* The New International Commentary on the Old Testament (Grand Rapids, Michigan, William B. Eerdmans

15

suggest in any way that Seth's descendants were characteristically godly or that Cain's descendants were contrastingly ungodly. It is a view coming from an inference about Seth and Cain themselves, not any evidence about their progeny. We reject this view entirely.

In the dynastic-rulers view, proponents say that powerful, ruling men who took whatever women they liked to be part of their harems constitute the offense of Genesis 6:2. As to the name "sons of God," "...while both within the OT and in other ancient Near Eastern texts individual kings were sometimes called God's son, there is no evidence that groups of kings were so styled"[4] as "sons of God." Sometimes supporters of this view point to Psalm 82 and interpret its references to "sons of God" and "judges" as meaning human beings accorded great status to represent God Almighty in ruling the earth. But this interpretation is plagued with difficulties.[5] A substantial number of theologians regard Psalm 82's term "sons of the Most High" and "the gods" as actually referring to the heavenly beings who had been given a heavenly, administrative role over nations other than Israel, and had been unfaithful in carrying out that role.

We join most scholars in rejecting the "dynastic-rulers" view.

That brings us back to the "supernatural view," the view held by the church and by Jews in the intertestamental period (the "second Temple" period), that the "sons of God" were supernatural beings. The Word Biblical Commentary documents that it is the view held by the earliest Jewish exegesis—1 Enoch, Jubilees, the Septuagint, Philo, Josephus and the Dead Sea Scrolls, and that the NT books of 2 Peter and Jude and the early Christian writers Justin, Irenaeus, Clement of Alexandria, Tertullian, and Origen, also take this line.[6]

Publishing Company, 1990) 264.

[4] Hamilton, 264.

[5] We will not attempt to interpret Psalm 82 as part of this chapter.

[6] Gordon J. Wenham, *Genesis*, The Word Biblical Commentary (Waco, Texas, Word Books, 1987) 139.

In concurring with this view, this author is in good company. The view may not be ultimately incontrovertible, but it is strongly persuasive.

Most writers will call these "sons of God" "angelic" beings or simply "angels." We're not certain that this term is adequate or particularly descriptive. We prefer "heavenly beings," though we may depart from it now and then and resort to "angelic beings" or some such term.

The Hebrew term in v2 is $b^e n\bar{e}$ $h\bar{a}$ '$\breve{e}l\bar{o}h\hat{i}m$ (בני־ האלהים). The NIV, which we've used as our text above, and all other translations render it, "sons of God." In the Hebrew, $\breve{e}l\bar{o}h\hat{i}m$ has the definite article, $h\bar{a}$, meaning "the," and it identifies God Almighty, Yahweh. This term appears again in Job 1:6, 2:1, and 38:7 (there in the plural) where it speaks of what is today called "the heavenly council," heavenly beings created by God who are "members of the Lord's court and who expedite his bidding."[7]

Angels are certainly heavenly (or celestial) beings, but there are heavenly beings other than angels. The seraphim (Isaiah 6:2,6) are one kind, and cherubim (2 Samuel 22:11) are another, neither of whom are referred to as angels. We know little about these non-angelic beings. Angels proper (both the Hebrew and Greek terms mean "messengers") probably constitute the vast majority of heavenly beings, and they are the beings who appear to people and speak and act for the Lord. A good Old Testament example would be the three men who appeared to Abraham (Genesis 18:2ff), two of whom were certainly angels, while the third turns out to have been the Angel of the Lord, a theophany. A New Testament example of the appearance of an angel would be the Angel Gabriel (Luke 1:19 and 1:28).

In our story, according to the most ancient interpretation, the "sons of God" are angelic or heavenly beings who took on human

---

[7] Hamilton, 262.

form and then mated with human women.

Opposition to this view consists principally of the argument that sexual union between an angel and a human being would be impossible. Opponents quote Jesus, who said, **"At the resurrection people will neither marry nor be given in marriage; they will be like the angels in heaven"** (Matthew 22:30). But the contention that angels can't have sex is a superficial argument. Jesus' statement that people will be like angels in heaven specifically referred to sexual/marital status and he was unquestionably referring to the angels who were not involved in any primordial rebellion, who had not sinned, and who were still allowed to come and go from the presence of God in heaven as they did their work for him. While angels *could* take on fully functioning human bodies, only those who rebelled against God had done so.

In fact, what Genesis 6 is describing is an event that substantially *defines* the kind of rebellion that *some* angels or heavenly beings participated in, for which God's wrath then came on the earth in the deluge.

Those who would still argue against the supernatural view of this verse retort: why would God destroy human life (and all life) in the Flood if it was angels who sinned? This is a strange argument, akin to the Pharisees' argument in front of Jesus when they brought the woman caught in the act of adultery and insisted she should be stoned. —Where was the man? Was the woman alone culpable? In Genesis 6, the genders are reversed, but the same situation inheres: The sons of God were only half of the evil involved.

Furthermore, the situation was apparently pervasive. And most of all, it constituted a pollution of the human race with an angel-human half-breed. This was a totally unacceptable development in God's creative plan, here near the beginning of the human race.

Some read Genesis 6:2 as reflecting rape or forcible marriage. The dynastic or despotic-ruler view virtually assumes such. But the language in Genesis is indicative of the opposite. Of the Hebrew word translated "married" in our text above, the New International

Commentary notes that it "commonly describes marital transactions, including taking a wife for oneself" and that "furthermore, in the OT (Gen. 36:2; 2 Sam. 1:20,24; Isa. 3:16) $b^e n\bar{o}t$ ("daughters") followed by a gentilic or a place name normally designates those who are eligible for marriage, another indication that we are dealing here with marriage rather than rape."[8] All the major translations render the word "married" or "took wives," except the Good News Translation, which says colloquially, **"they took the ones they liked."**

Consequently, this was a bilateral event. "The obvious avoidance of any terms suggesting lack of consent makes the girls and their parents culpable, the more so when the previous chapter has demonstrated that mankind was breeding very successfully on its own."[9] We cannot know the ultimate depth of the punishment these sons of God received, are receiving and will receive for their sins, but what happened as a result of these angelic-human unions certainly justified God's judgment in the Flood.

The lingering argument of those who oppose the supernatural view is simply a rational one, an insistence that angels are not human beings and that human beings have sex and angels don't. As we've outlined above, this is not a biblical argument. It is an assumption. And it doesn't even take into account the implications of, first of all, the ability that angels have shown repeatedly in the Bible to take human form, and secondly, the implications of a passage such as Genesis 19, where angels lodge at Lot's house and the men of the city crowd at the door demanding that he send them outside so they can have sex with them.

Angels apparently have the ability to take on fully human form: they eat (Genesis 18:8); they typically appear as young men (Mark 16:5); and they may disguise themselves as ordinary people

---

[8] Hamilton, 265.
[9] Wenham, 141.

encountered in a Christian's daily life (Hebrews 13:2). From Genesis 6, it appears that these angelic or heavenly entities were able to take on human-like flesh, complete with all the typical body parts and the genetic composition of human beings, enabling them to have sexual intercourse with women brought into the world in the normal course of reproduction since creation—the daughters of men.

In other words, the evidence is overwhelmingly on the side of taking "sons of God" to mean heavenly beings, and the statement of Genesis 6:2 as to what they did means we may understand them to have the power to take on fully human form.

To further establish this interpretation, consider what Peter said in the New Testament, referring to **"the spirits in prison; Which sometime were disobedient"** (1 Peter 3:19-20), and saying, **"God spared not the angels that sinned, but cast them down to hell"** (2 Peter 2:4). These were references to Genesis 6. And then there's Jude 6, where **"the angels who did not keep their positions of authority but abandoned their proper dwelling—these he has kept in darkness, bound with everlasting chains for judgment on the great Day"** (Jude 6 NIV). These passages reflect the familiarity of Peter, Jude, the other apostles, and indeed all Jews of Jesus' day, with such works as 1 Enoch and other writings of the period between the end of the Jewish captivity and the coming of Christ. They *all* believed Genesis 6 referred to heavenly beings violating God's intended role for them, desiring to have a bodily experience including sexual union.

Here, then, we stake out our position firmly:

1. We fully accept the supernatural view of "sons of God." Let's make that very, very clear.

2. It follows then, as we have demonstrated, that the "daughters of men" were normal, human women and the pairings were consensual marriages.

Now, *why* did the sons of God want to do what they did? We've said it was because they wanted bodily experience. And the implication of 6:2 is certainly that. They "saw that the daughters of humans were beautiful." This is one of dozens of obvious and predictable biblical descriptions of the attraction of the sexes—both licit and illicit. Men and women get themselves in trouble for no more reason than that they find each other irresistible! One of the more memorable stories is David's spying on Bathsheba as she took a bath on her roof (2 Samuel 11:2ff). So, we could simply stop there and take Genesis 6:1-6 as a story about the monumental result of simply not being able to exercise self-control.

But is that all? Would a few angel-men mating with a few fully human women make the destruction of the human race—and the world with it—necessary in God's justice?

Well, for one thing, we don't know exactly how extensive this mating/marrying was, but it appears to have been more than just "a few" unions. The rest of the passage suggests that quite a few offspring of these unions changed the shape of developing cultures in those early historic times.

What could the greater motive for this heavenly-earthly pairing have been?

The Word Biblical Commentary offers that "...the divine-human intercourse was, like eating the tree of life, intended to procure eternal life for man. This attempt to usurp what belongs to God alone is therefore condemned."[10] This view is possible, if the heavenly beings who took on flesh and took women as wives *knew* or had good reason to *believe* that their children would overcome the fact of death that had entered the human experience with the first sin. But we have no reason to believe they thought that, and at any rate, their progeny didn't take on everlasting *physical* life. So God didn't have to destroy the world to thwart this supposed plan to

---

[10] Wenham, 141.

procure eternal life for man. We don't think this was the ultimate goal.

We stand with a growing number of scholars who believe that "The corporate divine rebellion of Genesis 6 was a horrific event aimed at the destruction of the people of God and humanity at large."[11] He had already given the first prophecy of a deliverer to come through the Adam and Eve's offspring (Genesis 3:15). Corrupting that seed beyond repair would put a kink in God's plan. The reader has only to consider the number of times the unseen enemy has inspired megalomaniacs in totalitarian positions to attempt to wipe out the Jews, to convince him that even as early as a few generations after Adam, the fallen ones of heaven were conspiring to eliminate the possibility of a Messiah who would defeat them eternally.

The question arises whether the women involved in these heaven-earth unions were aware or unaware of the ulterior motives of the sons of God. Either is possible, but it may be likely that the human women involved—which would imply their families as well and thus humanity in general—were very definitely aware of the plans of the sons of God, and went along with them because they wanted to achieve immortality, to "be like gods."

We will shortly be discussing the offspring of these heavenly-human unions, who are called "Nephilim." Of these, Michael Heiser writes, "The fallen sons of God…corrupted humanity and turned them toward idolatry. The Nephilim and their descendants wreaked physical destruction and, through their disembodied spirits, ongoing physical and spiritual devastation." Re-reading Genesis 1-5, one can see the path on which humanity was treading, and realize that the opening verses of Genesis 6 suggest that the fallen heavenly beings were intent on ruining God's plans.

---

[11] Michael S. Heiser, *Demons* (Bellingham, Washington, Lexham Press, 2020) 141.

God's rapid response

The mating of angelic men and human women produced offspring, and we're told about it in v4. But oddly, first the writer of Genesis gives us a statement about God's rapid and determined response to the interference of the sons of God with exclusively human reproduction: **"Then the LORD said, "My Spirit will not contend with humans forever, for they are mortal; their days will be a hundred and twenty years"** (v3). This verse lets us know that it wasn't just the kind of children produced by these marriages that mattered to God, but the fact of the unions in the first place, the mingling of the nature of heavenly beings with human beings.[12] Jude would later describe **"the angels who did not keep their positions of authority but abandoned their proper dwelling"** (Jude 6).

Apparently between the first rebellion in Eden and this second intrusion of sons of God into the sphere of human reproduction, the situation had gotten dangerously destructive to man's fundamental qualification to produce offspring who could become God's people. If the infection were total, there could not be a qualified line of humanity or indeed a single qualified woman from whom the unique Son of God—the Messiah—could be born.

God's response had to be drastic. But he didn't plan on starting *all* over again, only *mostly*—he saved eight souls, Noah and his family. He would judge the rampant sin and almost entirely eliminate the intrusion of rebellious angels, through a flood of global proportions.

"My Spirit" refers, of course, to the presence of God in his world, moving among humanity to inspire and direct. However, the state of humanity by the time of Genesis 6 was horribly wrong, due to the entrance of sin and then the further interference of fallen heavenly beings. So God did not intend to "strive" (KJV) or "contend" (CSB) with man **forever.** The Hebrew word *yadown*

---

[12] Hamilton, 266.

normally means one of these two words, though the NIC translates it "remain," for which we see little support. God didn't intend to fight man continually, because apart from full fellowship with God—lost in Eden—man was **mortal** (HCSB). This word is *basar*, which normally means flesh. Some translations, including our HCSB choice, render it "mortal," apparently to suggest that the word is used here to indicate that everybody dies. We take it as most other translations do, to mean sinful flesh, prone to disobedience and rebellion.[13] This was the reading of the Amplified Bible (1965). Given that God granted man the freedom to choose his path, God did not plan to force him into obedience. Instead, he would "reboot" creation, starting the human race over with one family, that of Noah.

The question is then what the writer of Genesis meant by **"their days shall be a hundred and twenty years."** The average Bible reader and student probably thinks that God was announcing an age limit on human beings to 120. And indeed, an inspection of Genesis shows the amazing ages of Adam and many of his early descendants decreasing generation by generation until people didn't live past 120. But God's statement that man's days would be 120 years was made as the "therefore" to his premise that he wouldn't strive or contend with man forever. Limiting *individual's* lives to 120 years would hardly solve that problem. That's why some scholars believe he was declaring a grace period of 120 years from the time of Genesis 6:1 until the Flood, when he would indeed stop contending with the world gone mad following the fall and the perverse influence of the fallen angels.[14] However, Kidner points out that either of these meanings is "consonant with what follows in Genesis."[15]

---

[13] The NLT, to be inclusive, renders the single word *basar* as "mortal flesh."

[14] See e.g. Hamilton, 269.

[15] Kidner, 85.

That leads us to the other fascinating language of this curious story: the offspring of the unions of heavenly beings with earthly ones.

The Nephilim

Who were the **Nephilim?** The word is almost always transliterated these days in Bible translations, though the KJV, GNT and a few others have "giants." It is widely believed that the Nephilim were, indeed, giants, and both the translations of the Septuagint and the Latin Vulgate and the information given us in Numbers 13:33 support the view. The Septuagint has γιγαντες (*gigantes*) which means simply "giants."

Translating the Hebrew word *n^epilîm* is the critical issue at this point. Hamilton in the New International Commentary says that it should be translated "fallen ones," believing that it comes from a word also found in Deuteronomy 22:4 (a fallen donkey), Psalm 145:14 ("the Lord upholds all who fall"), and Ezekiel 32:22 ("fallen by the sword"). But the matter is not settled. Wenham says the "etymology of 'Nephilim' is obscure."[16] Heiser argues quite cogently that spelling variants in the original language suggest that Nephilim does *not* come from the word meaning "fallen," and he further says that many who choose to believe it does come from that root are looking for reasons to believe that the "sons of God" and thus their progeny were fully human (as in one of the rejected interpretations above).

But Heiser concludes, "In reality, it doesn't matter whether 'fallen ones' is the translation. In both the Mesopotamian context and the context of later Second Temple Jewish thought, their fathers are divine and the nephilim (however translated) are still

---

[16] Wenham, 143.

described as giants."[17]

Further, they are described as **"heroes of old, men of renown."** As many commentators put it, they were warrior-giants.

Readers will think, as they should, of the very common and ancient descriptions of early historic giants who interacted with humanity. Some of those characters loom out of the mythology of ancient civilizations and reappear in successive civilizations as part of their pantheons. The Greek gods and goddesses were sometimes described as being like human beings in form but much larger and more powerful. The question has been asked many times whether these early myths have their basis in the historical appearance of these "heroes of old, men of renown," described in the Bible.

Beings with direct parallels to the characters of Genesis 6 (both the sons of God and the Nephilim) appear in stories preserved in various Mesopotamian texts and other middle eastern texts. Devoted Bible scholars believe that common experiences of the ancients were described with some variation (sometimes significant variation) by differing cultures, with coloration and interpretation fitting their own religious views.

Bible scholarship, however, holds that the writer of Genesis—whose account in Genesis 6:1-6 was astoundingly brief where some other cultures' accounts were effusive—was using his terse and blunt summary as a polemic against these other cultures. Non-Israelite cultures uniformly held the contrasting view that these spiritual entities who mated with human women were benevolent and that their children, the warrior-giants, were as well. But to the ancient follower of Yahweh, these divine and quasi-divine beings had done little but get humanity into deeper trouble than it had already gotten itself.

Can we say anything else about the Nephilim? We note that the terse, summary statement in v4 is that they **"were on the earth in**

---

[17] Michael S. Heiser, *The Unseen Realm* (Bellingham, Washington, Lexham Press, 2015) 105.

those days—and also afterward"—which surely must mean after the Flood, the description of which comes just after this story. But, the reader will ask, weren't all creatures destroyed in the Flood? The Bible says so. How could the Nephilim have survived?

We have no direct evidence to go on in answering this question. The tentative conclusion would be that they didn't survive, but that the sons of God weren't finished coming from the spiritual realm, taking on human form, and mating with human women. If this is so, apparently some of that activity took place after the Flood as well. The Flood was a comprehensive reset of life on earth, but nothing is said in the Bible about Yahweh's subsequently keeping the sons of God from doing what they had done. If they did, they continued until—obviously—they were then denied such access. Otherwise, there would have been no Nephilim on the earth "afterward."

We run into these Nephilim—chiefly through their descendants —in the Rephaim (Deuteronomy 2:20 *et al.*), whom the King James Version calls "giants," and the "sons of Anak" (Numbers 13:33), but which most other translations, as we noted above, call Nephilim. They continued to be extremely large in size, with comparable strength, which contributed to the difficulty the Israelites had in conquering some parts of the Promised Land. It wasn't until sometime during the wars conducted by King David that the problem of these descendants of the Nephilim was eliminated. By that time, presumably some genetic modification of the grand and great grandchildren, etc., of the post-Flood Nephilim had taken place and they had become oddly tall but not gargantuan. Some estimates of the original Nephilim derived admittedly from non-biblical sources were that they were twice or more than twice the height of normal human beings. But by David's time one of the few remaining descendants, Goliath, was probably only nine feet tall, and commensurately strong.[18]

_____

[18] Some scholars believe that the imposing enemies Moses and Joshua encountered, while very large, were not what the scared Israelite armies thought they

Demons

One other thing we should note about the Nephilim, both before and after the Flood, has to do with what happened to their spiritual natures. While the sons of God themselves were spiritual in their original nature, their children, the Nephilim, had spiritual natures more like human beings, and upon their deaths they did not ascend or become like the Nephilim.

The Bible itself does not give us this information, but Jews during the second Temple era (the intertestamental period) interpreted both the scriptures and their other sacred writings to mean that the disembodied spirits of the Nephilim (upon their deaths) were confined to the regions of the dead and became the demons.[19] These were the malevolent spiritual beings that plagued Jews prior to the coming of Christ and whom Jesus was so famous for casting out. Their first fathers, the sons of God, had wanted badly to have human form and experience sexual union with women. The children thus produced were no less crazed by this craving for flesh, leading these demons to seek to possess human beings when and where they found opportunity. From various Bible descriptions we might infer that this "opportunity" may have consisted of a person's pursuing spiritism or witchcraft, but it's impossible for us to be certain about all reasons for demon possession.

Summing up the story

Putting together our interpretations from the four verses of this story, what we have is this:

> Some spirit beings God created rebelled against him. These embittered *elohim*, or "sons of God," with the ultimate goal

---

were, but only that they brought to mind the cultural memory of the Nephilim. The matter is probably beyond our knowing, this side of heaven.

[19] See Heiser, *Demons*, 12.

of sabotaging Yahweh's creation, pursued their already intense desire to have sexual experience with beautiful human women. Finding humanity receptive to this interference from divine beings, they fathered children who came to be known as Nephilim, which were typically giants in stature and strength. An unknown number of these giants became renowned warriors, inspiring probably many ancient stories from other cultures about gods or demigods who influenced their respective early histories. As these bastardized beings died out, their spirits—not like normal human souls—became the demons of New Testament times (and possibly have been experienced since).

To use the expression of the New International Commentary in ruminating about the identity of the Nephilim, "It's impossible to be dogmatic"[20] about our interpretation of the whole story. But we're confident this is what the Bible is telling us in Genesis 6:1-4.

Learning the Lessons

The lessons of this story about sons of God and giants to the lives of Christians (and others) are difficult to derive. As in some other chapters in this book, we caution the reader about merely "spiritualizing" the text and making direct applications where they aren't warranted. But it's difficult even to spiritualize Genesis 6:1-4.

The main points of this story are facts that we should believe as part of the background of our faith. Even so, there are practical applications. One of the life lessons can be stated simply:

1. Be holy
A Teaching to Obey ☑

God intended for his called and saved people to be separated

---

[20] Hamilton, 265.

unto him, people who live holy lives apart from the ways of the world.

The great evil of Genesis 6:2 was that beings God created set about to become something they were not made to be, thus corrupting humanity itself, and endangering the plan of salvation already revealed. If God hadn't then performed a major reset in the Great Flood, humanity would have been doomed.

These perilous times in remote human history demonstrated in the largest scale what should be learned and applied in the smallest scale of every individual Christian life today: be holy unto God. God called a people to be his own, commanding them to be holy as he was holy (Leviticus 19:2, 1 Peter 1:16). The concept of holiness in the Bible involves morality and ethics to be certain, but its chief meaning is to be set apart, to be separate. Holiness is a concept of being the property of the Lord and being reserved for his use, not being up for anything the world has to offer. The Christian who daily—moment by moment continually—will give himself to be the dwelling place and the instrument of God's Spirit, will be someone who will obey the Lord's commands, follow the Lord's leading, and be filled with the Lord's presence.

2. Do not tamper   A Teaching to Obey ☑

Humanity must not tamper, through science or anything else, with God's created order to pervert its purposes.

The lustful intrusion of the "sons of God" may be seen as a parallel for what one writer calls "the hubris of unrestrained science."[21] They took on human-like existence with the purpose of altering the very nature of humanity, using their already inflamed

---

[21] "Church My Way." Accessed June 30, 2024. https://churchmyway.org/the-origins-and-lessons-of- the-nephilim/.

lust for sexual experience.

We don't have any "sons of God" running about in the world today, but we do have some outrageously unprincipled scientists. Not all science is good. Just because we reach a level of knowledge that enables us to do something doesn't mean it should be done. One of the classic evils of mid 20th century Germany was its experimentation on prisoners, most of whom were Jews. A catalog of horrors took place for the purpose of testing drugs and medical procedures, most of which were done to improve military success or to perfect humanity, but they uniformly involved torture of various forms.

The end of WW2 didn't mean the end of unethical experiments, however. Numerous examples could be cited of medical or military experiments in the years since. And in today's topsy turvy world of nonsensical, perverse concepts—which are diametrically opposed to everything we've ever known about human life—medical "experts" are performing operations and therapies to try to change women into men and men into women. In doing so they are mutilating children as well as accommodating adults in their inordinate desires and delusions of mental illness. Almost unbelievably, innumerable businesses, corporations, and government entities are going along with this immoral madness, and making life difficult for people who hold to God's truth.

Studying such Bible passages as Genesis 6:1-6 makes one wonder how long God will allow such perversion of his creative purposes to continue on a mass scale before he steps in—again—to call a halt to it. Certainly right now Christians can be engaged in speaking and acting to influence their communities, culture and government for God's truth, calling for repentance and obedience to him.

NOAH AND THE SIN OF HAM
Genesis 9:20-27

Among the stranger stories to be found in early Bible records is that of Noah's curse of Canaan. Understanding this story can be a difficult challenge. For certain, however, if we don't understand this account Moses included in the first of his five books, deriving some applicable truth for Christian living from it could be an even more problematic task.

The scripture records the dramatic salvation of Noah and his family by means of an immense ark, which bore them and hundreds of animals upon flood waters for a year before coming to rest on a mountain. Once they disembarked, as the surviving members of the human race they began its history again. And here's what Genesis 9:20-27 says about Noah and his three sons, from the King James Version:

> [20] And Noah began *to be* an husbandman, and he planted a vineyard: [21] And he drank of the wine, and was drunken; and he was uncovered within his tent. [22] And Ham, the father of Canaan, saw the nakedness of his father, and told his two brethren without. [23] And Shem and Japheth took a garment, and laid *it* upon both their shoulders, and went backward, and covered the nakedness of their father; and their faces *were* backward, and they saw not their father's nakedness. [24] And Noah awoke from his wine, and knew what his younger son had done unto him.
> [25] And he said, Cursed *be* Canaan; a servant of servants

shall he be unto his brethren.

²⁶ And he said, Blessed *be* the LORD God of Shem; and Canaan shall be his servant.

²⁷ God shall enlarge Japheth, and he shall dwell in the tents of Shem; and Canaan shall be his servant.

This is a curious and strange story. Most Christians reading their Bibles encounter it and think it's about a snickering son who runs afoul of his father's temper for a breach of basic privacy. But it's about much more than that, and if we're to get anything out of it, we have to do our due diligence, biblically speaking, digging into Hebrew language, culture and storytelling.

Discovering the Text

The main problem we have in determining what is going on is the suspiciously simple interpretation of the passage that has long been the most popular. Traditionally the story has been read in this way:

> Ham accidentally happened on his father when he was drunk, passed out and unclothed in his tent; Ham then enjoyed himself a bit, being a voyeur, and then went out and told his brothers, probably laughing about it; the brothers covered up Noah; eventually Noah woke up, found out about Ham's incursion on his privacy, and pronounced a curse on Ham's son, Canaan. End of story.

Since many well-respected commentators of the past and present hold to this view, which we might call the "voyeurism view," maintaining a more complex view tends to be an uphill battle. But the problems with the voyeurism view are multiple. First of all, there's a gross disconnect between the offense and the punishment. There's no warning in the Bible—or any other ancient near-eastern laws—against accidentally seeing someone without his clothes on, or for that matter, looking on purpose. If it happened unintentionally, it was embarrassing for certain, but it wasn't something God revealed any legal charge or punishment for. So why, if Ham just happened to come into his father's tent at the wrong time, did Noah later drop such an extreme curse on Ham's *son?*

In spite of these problems, which basically render the voyeurism view doubtful, many commentators go with the view, though they don't always agree among themselves on the details. The interpretation presented here has the support of a number of scholars, it's based on the Hebrew text, and it's a sort of "no holds barred" look at what Moses wrote.

The keys to understanding the meaning of this ancient story, which tends to be arcane, abbreviated and somewhat ambiguous, lie in the idioms or euphemisms it employs. Those are the things we must uncover, to get at the historical event that comes down to us in a strange way.

See or uncover nakedness

To begin with, both "to see the nakedness of" and "to uncover the nakedness of" are often idioms for having sex.

That ancient peoples used idioms or euphemisms for having sex should not come as a surprise to any of us. In fact, "having sex" is somewhat euphemistic, itself. We have a word that explicitly means "having sex:" coitus. However, that word comes directly from the Latin, and almost no one uses the term except in scientific discussions. Instead, we employ various euphemisms depending on the mood we're in, the implications we want to leave with our readers or listeners, or, more relevant to the current subject, how comfortable we are talking about "having sex" in the first place. We say: "They went to bed," "they slept together," "they made love," or one of probably hundreds of evasive terms including some that we wouldn't print here. Perhaps the simplest would be, "They did it."

As for terms in the Hebrew, most of us are already familiar with the verb "to know" as a euphemism for sex: "Adam knew Eve his wife, and she conceived" (Genesis 4:1). To "uncover" or "see" nakedness is another such idiom. To uncover someone's nakedness is both literal and suggestive: one typically takes off another's clothes for the purpose of having sex. Multiple Old Testament passages demonstrate the idiomatic use of the words clearly:

Leviticus 20:17 equates "seeing" with "uncovering" nakedness, and the passage is without question about having a forbidden sexual encounter.

Ezekiel 16:35-37 makes clear that a prostitute's "uncovering nakedness" and her "whoring" are the same thing: having sex.

Ezekiel 22:10 refers to men having uncovered (or KJV, "*dis*covered") their fathers' nakedness, and the passage demonstrably is about illicit sexual activity.

Exekiel 23:10 likewise refers to the Syrians' uncovering the nakedness of Judah, a metaphorical passage describing the nation in terms of illicit sexual conduct.

So, to "see" or to "uncover" nakedness often simply means "to have sex."

Nakedness of...

Not only is "uncovering nakedness" or "seeing nakedness" an idiom for having sex, but "the nakedness of (someone)" is idiomatic, as well. In other words, whom a person is having sex with may be expressed in an idiomatic way.

One of the longer passages illustrating this idiom is in Leviticus 18, and it makes the case conclusively that "the nakedness of someone" is often an idiom for *someone else related to them*:

[6] **None of you shall approach to any that is near of kin to him, to uncover their nakedness: I am the LORD.** [7] **The nakedness of thy father, or the nakedness of thy mother,**

shalt thou not uncover: she is thy mother; thou shalt not uncover her nakedness. [8] The nakedness of thy father's wife shalt thou not uncover: it is thy father's nakedness. [9] The nakedness of thy sister, the daughter of thy father, or daughter of thy mother, whether she be born at home, or born abroad, even their nakedness thou shalt not uncover. [10] The nakedness of thy son's daughter, or of thy daughter's daughter, even their nakedness thou shalt not uncover: for theirs is thine own nakedness (Lev 18:6-10 KJV).

Numerous other versions clarify further the meaning of these verses. The King James is fine but the connections of the phrases in the Hebrew can be somewhat obscured by that translation. The ESV, NIV, NASB, HCSB, CSB, CEV, and AMP all render the verses such that it is clear that the Hebrew means that between spouses *either* person's nakedness is the *other* person's. In fact, as verse 10 says plainly, any father's nakedness is synonymous with that of his children or grandchildren.

Again, note what verse 8 says: "The nakedness of thy father's wife …is thy *father's* nakedness."

All this is a way of saying that in the ancient Hebrew culture one might euphemistically or idiomatically refer to the nakedness of someone's spouse by his own. It's sort of an extension of the idea that husband and wife become one flesh. In Hebrew and other near-eastern cultures, any woman who "belongs to" a man is that man's nakedness. (And don't be offended by "belongs to," because we still say with relish of our spouses, "You belong to me!")

That means we are strongly obligated to consider the idiomatic use of the term "nakedness of their father" in this passage as a reference to Noah's *wife,* not more literally his own nudity.

In fact, in the story in Genesis 9, the words "see nakedness" are used *both* idiomatically and literally: the brothers of Ham went backwards into their father's tent and covered the "nakedness of their father," which meant "their mother," and they covered her up and "saw not" their mother unclothed.

The bottom line is that if one wished to tell a story about an illicit sexual union, he might both use a euphemism for having sex *and also* use an idiom to refer to the forbidden person to have sex with. That leaves it to the context of Genesis 9:20-25 to help us determine whether Moses was using such circumlocutions here. Of course, it's entirely likely that Moses was making use of written sources that had been preserved and passed down about this already-ancient story about Noah. The question is, did the writer couch his meaning in idiomatic language, even if only for purposes of delicacy? The answer is plainly that he did.

Further, it is significant that Moses gave these instructions to the people just before they began to take over "the land of Canaan," which was named after Canaan the son of Ham. They were not to do as the people of Canaan did, "neither shall ye walk in their ordinances." The Canaanites celebrated all manner of sexual profligacy, certainly after the manner of their named father. That Moses should repeatedly use the term "the nakedness of his father" is no accident. He was referencing by implication the incestuous behavior of Ham, the father of Canaan.

The gloating report

Furthermore, Ham "told his two brethren without." The text doesn't directly tell us what the timing was, but the suggestion of "without," or "outside the tent" is that Ham came out, his brothers were already there, perhaps by a fire, and that he told them what he had done. In the voyeurism view, Ham's report would have been a snickering tale, an immature account of his secret exploits of seeing his father drunk and without clothes on. But if we're right about the nature of what Ham actually *did* to his mother—we're convinced we are—his report to his brothers was probably not meant to promote laughter, but instead intended to assert his superiority or his usurpation of their status as the elder sons. It seems likely that there was, and had been, serious rivalry among these men, and Ham's informing them of his deed would have been gloating about his new advantage over them.

Whose tent?

There is still another issue for us to investigate, namely where did the action of this story take place? Nearly all translations, including the KJV, render the Hebrew word *'āholōh* as "his tent." A few, however, including the respected Amplified Bible, the Aramaic Bible and the Literal Standard Version, translate it "*the tent.*" These latter do so mostly to split the difference between two possibilities. For reasons of Hebrew grammar not necessary to explain in depth for the reader, the Hebrew word "tent" has a suffix normally meaning "her." In the end, it may not matter, since it was common for the tent of a man to have many compartments, and it is entirely possible, if not likely, that Noah's tent had a connected "room" that was his wife's, more or less exclusively. If Ham entered her part of the tent, it was intentional. If we have discovered accurately that Ham intended to take advantage of his mother, it's very possible that he entered her "room," so to speak. Perhaps we don't have enough information to speculate.

In any event, this, then, would be a condensed summary of what took place in Genesis 9:20-24:

> Noah and his wife enjoyed a night of drinking and were in their tent passed out. Ham entered the tent and, taking advantage of his mother's being dead to the world (and possibly partly or fully unclothed), he had sex with her. Then he left and told his brothers about it. His brothers went into the tent and covered up their mother (remember, "their *father's* nakedness"). Later in the morning somehow, perhaps being told by his other two sons, Noah found out what Ham had *done,* which was to have sex with his own mother, *Noah's wife.* The deed was done *to Noah* ("to him") because

38

a sin against his wife was a sin against him.

This story, then, is not about voyeurism, or homosexuality or anything else but incest. *That* is why Noah was so provoked.

The maternal-incest view of this story not only avoids the weaknesses of the voyeurism view (and the paternal-incest/ homosexual-conduct view, which we have not covered here) but it fully explains the profound impact of Ham's deed provoking Noah's curse. When we get to the curse itself, you will see further why it took the form it did.

At this point, though, if you're not only shocked by this but you also question how things could be so bad in Noah's own family, remember that the scripture says that "*Noah* found grace in the eyes of the Lord" (Genesis 6:8). It doesn't say anything about his children, especially Ham, or even about Noah's wife. We'd like to believe that all of Noah's family was equally as righteous as he, but we all know how family life can be, don't we? And this was in a time when, as the Bible says only three verses before that remark about Noah, "And GOD saw that the wickedness of man was great in the earth, and that every imagination of the thoughts of his heart was only evil continually" (Genesis 6:5). Noah's family was not entirely unaffected by the absolute and extreme depravity of the world around them.

The honor of the brothers

Before we leave the incident of Ham's sin, we should comment on what Shem and Japheth did when Ham boasted of what *he* had done in the tent. They backed into the tent and covered up their mother—their *father's nakedness*— as we have noted. Some scholars even believe the garment they used was their mother's own: "[Ham] exits and informs his brothers of his grasp at familial power (v22b), perhaps producing an article of clothing as proof of his claim. The brothers, in turn, act with excessive filial deference and piety in returning 'the garment'"[22] From this we gather very obviously that they were far more honorable than Ham, that they did not share his pride in what he had done but were appalled by it, and that they were intent on mitigating in some way their brother's wrongdoing. It was perhaps a token act at best, but it was all they could do at that point. We can only imagine the relationship the three brothers had, both before and after Ham's disgraceful behavior. It probably further underwrote Noah's pronouncements when the details of that night became known to him.

The curse of Canaan: when, why and what

Now that we are clear on what went on in Noah's tent, let's address what came next: the curse of Canaan. For quite a long time many people reading this passage have referred to the curse of *Ham*, whereas any child who can read can see that Noah's curse was on *Canaan*, Ham's son, not Ham, himself, at least directly. (But we all know that parents grieve over what happens to their children.)

Verse 25 says, "Cursed be Canaan: a servant of servants shall he be unto his brethren." Noah went on to repeat, for emphasis, that Canaan would be the servant of both Shem and Japheth, or by implication, their families or clans. How do we understand the reason for this? And why wasn't it Ham, personally, against whom Noah, his father, pronounced a curse?

The curse: when?

First, a word about when the curse may have been pronounced. We're given enough information in the text itself to ferret out what's going on. In verses 18-19 the text tells us that Noah's three sons left the ark, and then it says cryptically, "and Ham *is (or was)*

---

[22] John Bergsma and Scott Hahn, *Noah's Nakedness and Curse on Canaan*. Accessed March 10, 2022. https://www.godawa.com/chronicles_of_the_nephilim/ Articles_By_ Others/Bergsma-Noahs_Nakedness_And_Curse_On_ Canaan.pdf.

the father of Canaan." Depending on the translation you use, Ham either is or was the father of Canaan, with the King James using *italics* on the word *is,* meaning the word isn't there—which in fact it is, in most ancient text versions. The KJV is apparently expressing ambiguity. Three other, well respected translations render the Hebrew word "would become the father of" or "later had a son" or "later fathered" Canaan. The question is, when and how did that happen. Notice that v18 doesn't say anything about Shem or Japheth's children, just the one son of Ham's, and the very next thing the scripture records is this shameful story about Ham in the tent.

Well, first of all, the people in the ark were eight souls (2 Peter 3:20): Noah, his wife, his three sons, and all their wives. There were no children who went into the ark. When they emerged, no children had been born to them on the ark. When we come to this story about Ham and the tent, we either do or do not have any children yet in the picture. The note in v18 about Ham's being the father of Canaan doesn't mean he fathered him before the story that immediately follows. It just introduces the future fact because it's about to be significant for the upcoming tale of sordid behavior on the part of Ham.

Some sharp reader who is following this argument may interject, "Wait a minute: how did Noah know the name of Ham's son if he hadn't been born yet? Huh?!" Be patient.

It's easy for us to assume that when Noah "awoke from his wine and knew what his younger son had done to him," it all must have taken place in the space of a few hours or even less. It's also easy to assume that the curse of Canaan that followed took place immediately after Noah's night of drunkenness, requiring that Ham already have a son named Canaan, even though there's no evidence of that. As I say, it's easy to assume, but assumptions may also easily be mistaken.

I believe it's clear that when the incident with the first vineyard and Noah's wine and Ham's venture into the tent and having relations with his mother took place, Canaan was *not yet born*. I think what we're looking at here is one of many examples in the Old Testament, particularly in Genesis, of **narrative compression**. Some stories were compressed when first written down, but most were compressed in the telling of them over generations, even before they were written. The salient facts make it into the story, but by the time somebody writes it down, the chronology is condensed. To avoid wrongly interpreting this story, we have to use the context, along with the grammar of the writing and, frankly, some common sense, to unpack the facts and understand the timing.

In fact, there's a good example of compressed narrative in the first few verses of this account, which we have already read. In rapid-fire manner, the author tells us: "And Noah began to be an husbandman, and he planted a vineyard: And he drank of the wine, and was drunken; and he was uncovered within his tent." In less than ten seconds of reading we have Noah's decision to tend grape vines (and we don't know if the harvest upcoming were his first); his planting a vineyard (and, by implication, cultivating, and harvesting its grapes, and then pressing grapes, putting the juice in skins, and leaving them for who-knows-how-long to ferment); his drinking some of his product; his becoming drunk (and we don't know if this were the first time he imbibed his wine); and his being in his tent on some subsequent occasion naked. We could be dealing with a year's time or several year's time, in this compressed opening sentence. Moses wasn't writing a novel; he was telling theological stories for the instruction of his fellow Israelites.

Likewise, there appears to be a little bit of compression in the added remark about the disembarking of Noah's family from the ark and the footnote calling attention to Ham's progeny. In other words, we might paraphrase Genesis 9:18 by saying, 'Let me tell you a story about Noah after the ark, and about Shem, Ham and Japheth—and for later reference, you should know now that Ham later had a son named Canaan.'

The curse: why?

Now let's look at the reason for the specific curse Noah pronounced. We've already seen that he had great cause to be upset with Ham. Ham had violated the intimacy that belonged to Noah and his wife alone. Ham had sex with his mother—his "father's nakedness." We should have no doubt that Noah had some choice words for Ham at the point of the deed. But since, as I believe, Ham had no son yet, the curse came later, after the son was born and was named.

This brings up the vital question of whose child Canaan was. And there's little reason to go anywhere else for the answer but the dark implication of the scripture that Canaan was the son of Ham and his mother—his mother bore her son's child by incest.

This introduces us to the subject of familial sexual relations and what went on in clans, especially in royal dynasties, in the near east. In this day and time, people often don't know exactly how to deal with the widespread and accepted practice in ancient times of a man's having multiple wives and concubines. Today, it's controversial, and in most places having more than one spouse—for a man or a woman—is even against the law. But we read of men in the Bible who had more than one official wife, and had concubines as well. A concubine was a woman who had recognized social status in the household below that of a wife, and who usually had sexual privileges with the man of the house. It's outside our purpose here to discuss the phenomenon except to say that eventually the Jews realized—as God showed them—this was not God's ideal for marriage.

We introduce the subject only to call to your attention some biblical accounts about wives and concubines. Do you recall Reuben, one of the sons of Jacob? In Genesis 35:22, Reuben had sex with one of Jacob's concubines, Bilhah. Years went by after that incident, and Genesis 49:3-4 later records that Jacob's final "blessing" on Reuben was anything but. He began with what probably seemed to Reuben like a prologue to wonderful predictions: "Reuben, thou art my firstborn, my might, and the beginning of my strength, the excellency of dignity, and the excellency of power." Reuben probably had his thumbs under his suspenders, looking proud. But then Jacob recalled how Reuben"wentest up to thy father's bed; then defiledst thou it." A son who took his father's concubine or even one of his father's wives for himself, sexually, might be planning to supplant the other sons of his father with his own children by that woman. Jacob said Reuben would "not excel."

This intention of such sexual unions with one's father's wives or concubines to supplant—supersede someone else—is even clearer in 2 Samuel 12:8, where Nathan the prophet reminded King David that God had given to him everything that was Saul's, including his *wives and concubines*, and would have given him much more. But, not satisfied with that, David *stole* Bathsheba from Uriah the Hittite. Focus on the wives and concubines, here. It was general practice in near eastern culture that a conquering king could do anything he wanted with the conquered king's possessions and his household, *including his wives.* He could take them for his own, thus solidifying his power through what had been the other king's family.

Ironically, the same thing happened to David in 2 Samuel 16:20-23, where Absalom rebelled against his father, running David out of Jerusalem. Then he pitched a tent and "went into" —had sex with—all his father's concubines, *publicly,* which was a way of usurping his father's royal privilege and his very power. In 1 Kings 2, David has died and there is a serious contest for the crown between Adonijah, a son of David by Haggith, and Solomon, the son of Bathsheba. When Solomon prevails, Adonijah makes just one request of Bathsheba, the Queen Mother: he wants Solomon to give him Abishag, David's concubine, who had been brought on during David's last hours to try to "keep him warm" as he was dying. When the request was put to Solomon, he saw it for what it was, a move by Adonijah to establish himself as a permanent rival. Solomon says basically, 'Why doesn't he just ask for the entire kingdom?' (v22).

44

Adonijah's attempt to have Abishag for his own was a political move, not merely a romantic one.

So while we have the bare outlines of a story here in Genesis 9 about Ham's having illicit sex, we infer that there well may have been something other than what would later be called an Oedipal complex on the part of Ham. His action may have been an attempt to usurp superiority among the brothers, of which Ham was probably the youngest.

Some readers may accept the conclusion that the text is describing maternal incest, but they may insist that Ham wasn't thinking of taking the leading position among his brothers by appropriating his father's wife—his own mother. They may think it was simply an opportunistic act of sexual immorality. Even so, however, Noah's "curse" was fitting because it was directed at the *offspring* of this awful, illicit, grossly immoral sexual union.

The curse: what?

So now, if Ham was attempting to set himself up as the dominant brother—he had stolen the proprietary intimacy of his father—it would explain why Noah's curse on Canaan was that he would *by no means* have superiority over anyone. In fact, he and his descendants would be the servants of the bloodlines of the other two brothers.

Plenty of scholars have tried to trace the lines of Shem, Japheth and Ham to discover how this curse came into play.

- Many scholars agree that the descendants of Japheth spread to the north and east and that their descendants, the Persians, Macedonians and Romans became conquerors of others. Noah said they would be enlarged and would dwell in the tents of

Shem—their blessing would be derivative of the Shemites.[23]

- The descendants of Shem are known as the Shemites or Semites and include Hebrews, Arab tribes and Syrians. They were directly blessed by Noah's prophecy, and through Abraham the Hebrews became the Israelites and through Israel came Jesus Christ, who blesses all humanity.
- The descendants of Canaan spread out through the immediate region and into what later was referred to, not surprisingly, as Canaan, which was later in the crosshairs of Israel as it came out of Egypt to claim the Promised Land.

Some people who have tracked descendants of Ham have *assumed* that *all* of them—not just Canaan's descendants—shared in the curse on Canaan,[24] but this is irresponsible and impossible to defend. The maternal-incest view demonstrates that it was the fruit of *that illicit union* that garnered the curse, and therefore it would be the descendants of that one child, Canaan, who would be affected by Noah's prophecy.

Notwithstanding this logical conclusion, many 19th and some 20th century commentators have attempted to track the descendants of *Ham*, not merely *Canaan*, in search of justification for the institution of slavery. That anyone would do so today is not only an example of spiritual depravity on their part but also an example of the shoddiest sort of biblical exegesis and scholarship. The curse was on *one* son of Ham, Canaan. The Canaanites were the objects of

---

[23] As Donald Fleming put it, "This was fulfilled when the New Testament church spread through this region and multitudes of Gentiles believed." — Don Fleming, *Fleming's Bridgeway Bible Commentary* (Brisbane, Australia, Bridgeway Publications, 2005) 14.

[24] Multiple commentators of the past have held to this view, including Albert Barnes, author of *Barnes Notes on the Whole Bible*, a popular 19th century work, especially among preachers. Barnes acknowledged that "the other descendants of Ham are not otherwise mentioned in the prophecy," but he nevertheless said, "we may presume that they shared in the curse pronounced on Kenaan [Canaan]."

Israel's later conquest of the land of Canaan and were either wiped out by them or became the lowest of servants to the Israelites.

The curse of Canaan was a prophetic relegation of his descendants to servitude as a direct judgment on the attempt of their progenitor, Ham, to accomplish the opposite: superiority.

Noah's prophetic pronouncement was worked out in the centuries to follow. The history of the Bible shows how Canaanites were ultimately suppressed by the various descendants of Shem as well as being conquered by the family of Japheth.

Many views exist about the extent of Noah's prophetic curse—whether, for instance, it went past the next few centuries of history or continues today. We take the view that the most demonstrable and relevant fulfillment of the prophecy/curse pronounced by Noah was to be observed in the growth and movement of peoples through the history of Israel up until the time of Christ.

Learning the Lessons

Now that we have defined the terms, decoded the message, decompressed the account, and found out what was going on in this passage, our purpose should be to derive its lessons for us. What should we know that informs our belief? What should we believe that directs our lives? What should we do, or not do, in following the Lord?

There are some secondary lessons in this story about Noah and Ham—lessons that are valid irrespective of the primary point of the text. Among them are these:

1. Fixed right and wrong   A Truth to Believe ☑

Immoral sexual conduct is never justified by circumstances.

Ham's relationship with his brothers may have been full of

striving for position. Or, his raw ambition for dominance may have been mostly the expression of his own pride, irrespective of his brother's words or actions. But choosing to assert himself as he did was wrong, no matter what his situation or motivation may have been.

Likewise, modern sexual misbehavior is not justified by any set of circumstances in our lives: acceptance of "sexual liberation" by society; failure of parents to inculcate proper values in their children; the powerful passion of the moment; the assumption of future marriage; or any other circumstance making sex seem allowable when it isn't—not according to God's holy standard.

If something is wrong, it's wrong whether "we're consenting adults," "it feels so right," or "nobody cares" or anything else.

2. Consequences   A Truth to Believe ☑

Sexual sin always carries a penalty, sometimes far-reaching.

It isn't just the most forbidden kinds of sexual activity that carry with them a predictable penalty, but any immoral sexual union at all. In this day and time, many people of all ages assume that sex between consenting adults is okay. And because of the sexual revolution of the 1960s and 1970s, modern western culture has invisibly written into its code of conduct that marriage is no longer a qualifier for sex. On the basis of that widespread acceptance, young people and young adults in particular assume that sex is a normal part of regular dating, and they freely engage in it as if there were no consequences to pay.

They're wrong. For those who eventually marry, where there is no uniqueness of sexual unity between spouses—nobody else has ever shared it—every previous partner waters down the physical oneness of a husband and wife. The knowledge and memory of multiple sexual unions act as a pollutant to the potential of love between the couple. And the mystical union established by sex remains in the heart of the offending person(s) for life.

48

And those who don't eventually marry don't escape consequences. After a vague or even haunting sense of emptiness, or a futile search for fulfillment in prodigal living, comes the answer of eternity in the judgment of God.

3. Humility   An Attitude to Develop ☑

Those who humble themselves will be exalted, while those who exalt themselves will be humbled.

Ham's act was one of self-exaltation. Noah counteracted that act with a prophecy of Ham's subservience through his son, Canaan. This ancient story finds reverberations through the rest of scripture, with the most terse and memorable being uttered by Jesus: "For all those who exalt themselves will be humbled, and those who humble themselves will be exalted" (Luke 18:14).

If our strategy in life is to get ahead by any means, we will answer for it sooner or later. If we follow a course of being top dog and never the servant, we will be put in our place, sooner or later. Christ has called us to serve one another, with the promise that he will reward us for what we give up, forego, or forsake—sooner or later.

Even more important than the secondary lessons are the primary lessons of the story of Ham's sin and Noah's curse or prophecy. They're the most discernable lessons Moses meant to impart, the main theological points of the text. They are two grand principles for the Christian to believe:

4. Sovereignty   A Truth to Believe ☑

God controls history.

God's purpose is to bring the kingdom of God in the world, which involves the movements and character of men and nations. The blessings of the patriarchs spoken upon their children, usually near the point of those patriarchs' deaths, were utterances often pregnant with the prophetic inevitability of events. God's direction of the divine drama of history situates people and nations so as to position everything for the movement of his kingdom through a people, a Savior, and a church.

God's control of history is something to believe, a statement of faith that inspires the Christian to be at peace about what is going on in the world and to be confident about what is ultimately going on in his or her own life. The believer in Jesus Christ can look at early Bible stories like this one about Noah, and see how God fulfilled Noah's prophetic words. Then he can skip over to Revelation and see with glorious description how God is going to bring everything to perfect completion in the end of the age, at the return of Christ. The Christian is a part of the cast of thousands, but the director of this divine drama is the Sovereign of the universe, and his kingdom will come—fully, perfectly, and gloriously, just as he planned it.

5. Justice
A Truth to Believe ☑

In his sovereign direction over nations God does not unjustly condemn anyone.[25]

People who don't yet believe in Jesus Christ for salvation sometimes argue that the Bible's language of being "chosen by God" contradicts its message, "whosoever believes." That argument is as old as the gospel. Paul dealt with it in Romans 3. God's choice of a people to be his, which implies some are not chosen, is an expression of his sovereignty, but this fact doesn't conflict with his open-arms

---

[25] Bob Deffinbaugh remarks, "Noah foresaw that the moral flaws evidenced by Ham would be most fully manifested in Canaan and in his offspring …the Canaanites would be cursed because of their sin, not due to Ham's." — Bob Deffinbaugh, *Genesis: From Paradise to Patriarchs.* Accessed May 4, 2024. https://bible.org/seriespage/10-nakedness-noah- and-cursing- canaan-genesis-918-1032.

invitation to anyone who will repent and believe in the Savior God has sent. This is one of the mysteries of God we cannot fully fathom, at least here in this world. And it should never be an excuse for anyone to reject the gospel, as if he had caught God in a lie and invalidated God's word.

Every non-Christian should hear again the warning of the Bible that God's judgment will not rest on a prophetic casting of some people group in this or that role in history. Instead, every person who dies eternally will die for his own sins, including his failure to receive God's saving grace. As Barnes said, "[Canaan's] curse is not exclusion, either present or prospective, from the mercy of God. That is an evil he brings on himself by a voluntary departure from the living God."[26]

---

[26] Barnes, *Op. cit.*

LOT OFFERS HIS DAUGHTERS
Genesis 19:1-26 (4-8)

People who castigate the ancient culture of the Bible are right about some things: there was a lot of violence; there was a lot of sexual immorality; and there was a lot of inequity between the sexes. What critics of the Bible who don't believe the Bible anyway generally fail to recognize is that the Bible doesn't use these stories to teach us to imitate these behaviors.

Sometimes it teaches us *through* these stories to *reject* these behaviors. And sometimes, through stories of bizarre, ignorant, superstitious, or misguided actions, the Bible presents us with the intention of God—and his sovereign ability—to carry out a righteous master plan *in spite of* terrible human deeds. As one Bible teacher put it, "God hits some straight licks with crooked sticks."

In our chapter on Jephthah, one of the military leaders described in the book of Judges, we point out that the story of Judges teaches us to expect some of the most valuable lessons in our lives to come from the most abominable failures—some of them our own.

Another curious Bible story that exhibits a strange mix of morally reprehensible ideas and an honorable code of conduct is that of Lot, the nephew of Abraham, who was visited by angels on a mission to destroy the city of Sodom. The tale is in Genesis 19.

¹ The two angels arrived at Sodom in the evening, and Lot was sitting in the gateway of the city. When he saw them, he got up to meet them and bowed down with his face to the ground. ² "My lords," he said, "please turn aside to your servant's house. You can wash your feet and

52

spend the night and then go on your way early in the morning."

"No," they answered, "we will spend the night in the square."

³ But he insisted so strongly that they did go with him and entered his house. He prepared a meal for them, baking bread without yeast, and they ate. ⁴ Before they had gone to bed, all the men from every part of the city of Sodom—both young and old—surrounded the house. ⁵ They called to Lot, "Where are the men who came to you tonight? Bring them out to us so that we can have sex with them."

⁶ Lot went outside to meet them and shut the door behind him ⁷ and said, "No, my friends. Don't do this wicked thing. ⁸ Look, I have two daughters who have never slept with a man. Let me bring them out to you, and you can do what you like with them. But don't do anything to these men, for they have come under the protection of my roof" (Genesis 19:1-8 NIV).

Upon reading this encounter of Lot with the wicked and perverse men of the city of Sodom, modern readers are inclined to say, "Whoa!" We struggle to find an exact word to describe Lot's attitude toward his daughters. The entire story in its context is about three men (Genesis 18:2) who came to see Abraham and were headed toward Sodom in preparation for destroying it. Two of the men were revealed to be angels. The third was the Angel of the Lord (18:13, 17, 20, 22, etc.). While Abraham pled for the possible sparing of Sodom, the two angels left to go there.

The part of the story we're focusing on begins when the angels arrive at Sodom at an hour when anyone else traveling would be urgent to find a place to sleep. Verses 1-4 are fairly straightforward, and our particular concern is what happened just before everyone went to bed (v4).

Discovering the Text

Lust of the people

The unabashed perversity and lust of the people of Sodom is what smacks the reader in the face when taking in the utter depravity of this scene. "The repulsive incident recorded in this passage (vv 4-11) contrasts the hospitable conduct of Lot with the gross behaviour of the people of Sodom towards strangers, and has for all time associated the name of the city with shameless vice" (cf. Isa. iii. 9).[27] No one seriously attempts to justify or explain away the actions of the people who gathered around Lot's house that night.

According to the text, they weren't simply neighbors in the immediate vicinity. They came **"from every part of the city"** (v4), which most translators say is the sense of the Hebrew *miqqaseh*, literally, "every quarter." The Cambridge Bible says "the phrase means 'from all classes of the people' "[28]

The news of the arrival at Lot's house of these apparently wonderfully good looking men spread rapidly through the city (see the next chapter, where we describe more of Lot's extreme apprehension because of the experience described in this chapter's focus verses). When they surrounded Lot's house, they had one thing on their mind: "knowing" the visiting men. This is the classic "know in the biblical sense" that people sometimes joke about today. The root word in the Hebrew is *yāda*. The Bible uses this word as a euphemism repeatedly for sexual intercourse—having sex. The first usage is between the first couple, Adam and Eve. And it's something more than a euphemism. It's based in the concept that the sexual union of a man and woman results in a kind of knowledge that takes place on a fundamental level of body and

---

[27] Herbert E. Ryle, *Genesis*, The Cambridge Bible for Schools and Colleges (Cambridge, England, Cambridge University Press, 1929), 213.

[28] *Ibid, 213.*

spirit.

In the case of the men of Sodom, however, they were not seeking the holy union of one man and one woman in marriage. They were intent on having a mass, group experience of homosexual unions, possibly battering and abusing the visitors until they were dead. In addition, "both old and young" probably means that they were people routinely engaged in pederasty, "a crime very prevalent among the Canaanites (Lev. Xviii. 22 sqq., xx.23), and according to Rom. i. 27, a curse of heathenism generally."[29]

We are aware from our perspective that, even if they had succeeded in starting to lay their hands on the visitors, they would not have succeeded because of the angelic identity of the two young men. We have no way of knowing how sudden and destructive their exhibition of heavenly power would have been had they been assaulted, but we can be sure that it would have been dramatic and final.

Nor can we explain why, when Lot went out to confront them and shut the door behind him, they did not simply push him aside and force their way in. They didn't. Lot had a moment to reason with them and confront them, which he did. He was bold enough to challenge them not to "act so wickedly." But then he made them an offer that turns our stomachs. We're going to let the following chapter do more to suggest what might have been in his mind during these harrowing moments of threat at his front door. But briefly, what Lot did was to offer these male, *homosexual* predators the use of his daughters for sexual gratification. Further, they were *virgin* girls, which would have made such an offer even more attractive to *heterosexuals,* but possibly not to this crowd. We would be reading between the lines too much to insist that this was Lot's reasoning, but it's certainly possible.

---

[29] Carl Friedrich Keil and Franz Delitzsch, *Volume 1, Genesis - Judges 6:32,* Biblical Commentary on the Old Testament,(Lafayette, Indiana: Associated Publishers and Authors, 1960), 179.

However, it's more likely that Lot, figuring that something bad was going to happen that night, chose to try to deflect the crowd's intentions to something less awful—though still, by our standards, pretty awful. "Lot's proposal, so atrocious in our ears, may have been deemed meritorious in an Eastern country, where no sacrifice was considered too great to maintain inviolate the safety of a stranger who had been received in hospitality."[30]

The hospitality of the middle eastern world of that day—and indeed, today—is well known. In fact, it may put to shame the casual and scant neighborliness of people in western cultures today. Still, as Whitelaw notes, "[t]he usual apologies [including the ones we've outlined in this and the next chapter] …are insufficient to excuse the wickedness of one who in attempting to prevent one sin was himself guilty of another."[31] Whitelaw's characterization of Lot's "wickedness" is in stark contrast with the New Testament's summarization of Lot as "righteous," and we're left to figure out how the two are reconciled. Still, Whitelaw insists that Lot's offer was "an infamous proposal which nothing can extenuate and the utmost charity finds difficult to reconcile with any pretence of piety on the part of Lot."[32]

The New American Commentary observes, "Lot jeopardized the lives of his daughters, even any hope for a heritage—all for the sake of the strangers. By a bizarre twist, however, it is his daughters who finally take advantage of Lot, sexually abusing their father by which he gains male heirs after all (vv. 36-38)."[33]

Lot receives scathing rebuke from every worthy commentator,

---

[30] Ryle, 213.

[31] Thomas Whitelaw, *Genesis*, The Pulpit Commentary, edited by H.D.M. Spence and Joseph S. Exell, (Grand Rapids, Michigan, Wm. B. Eerdman's Publishing Company, 1950), 253.

[32] Whitelaw, 253.

[33] Kenneth A. Mathews, *Genesis 11:27-50:26*, The New American Commentary, edited by E. Ray Clendenen, (Nashville, Broadman & Holman Publishers, 2005), 236.

and, as we twenty-first century people think, he deserves it.

Punishment by angels

When Lot was rudely rebuffed by the threatening townsmen, the angels rescued him by pulling him back into the house, and then they used their heavenly powers to smite the men outside with blindness. The Hebrew is *bas-san-wê-rîm*, which as in 2 Kings 6:18 may mean a kind of mental blindness, "in which the eye sees, but does not see the right object."[34] Keil and Delitzsch argue that if it had been merely blindness, they could have felt their way around to some extent, but that as it was, they couldn't even find the door—which they were just in front of. Apparently it was a blindness with profound disorientation that left them helpless and exasperated with fright.

The rest of the story goes on to detail the flight of Lot and his nuclear family—sans the betrothed boys—out of Sodom to safety.

Learning the Lessons

The larger story about the destruction of Sodom would make—and has made—whole books and movies. The curious part of it is the moments at the door of Lot's house we briefly studied, where he almost inexplicably offered his virgin daughters to the abuse of a perverted mob in order to protect his guests. Why he thought protecting guests was more important than protecting his own daughters has continued to astound readers for several millennia. We understand that hospitality was a deeply rooted custom for the middle eastern culture, but we cannot help but conclude it was taken too far when it endangered sons *and* *daughters* of the householder.

As we said above, however, the lessons of this story are not to be

---

[34] Keil and Delitzsch, *op. cit, Vol 1*, 180.

found in an example to be followed—hardly! Any application we make will be found in something that transcends the immoral and horrible details of the behavior of most of the people in the tale.

1. The company you keep
A Teaching to Obey ☑

While avoiding contact with immoral people is hardly possible, choose to surround yourself with people who pursue discipleship to Jesus Christ.

When Abram and Lot parted ways for practical purposes, Lot's decision to take the "well watered plain" and live in Sodom was not coerced. He did it because of economic reasons, in spite of the growing reputation of the place. Nor did he continue to live there against his will. The immoral climate of the area (Sodom and Gomorrah) had a deleterious effect on his values, even though in the chief sins for which the place was known, he remained "righteous" (2 Peter 2:7).

Paul noted in one of his letters to the Corinthian church that if Christians tried not to keep company *at all* with immoral people of the world, they'd have to leave the world to do it! But he also told them that **"Bad company corrupts good morals"** (1 Corinthians 15:33 CSB). That means that except to continue to have a godly influence on the world and opportunity to witness to the gospel, the Christian should value most highly the company of other Christians. In a world where unbelievers and enemies of Christ are often aggressive in trying to bring down his followers, Christians need each other's continuing friendship and support.

2. No compromise
An Action to Take ☑

When confronted with evil, do not compromise: refuse to yield, purely and simply.

Just as the meaning of this curious story is not any mystery, so the lessons to be gained from it are straightforward. Lot faced an untenable, even an unthinkable, demand on his values of hospitality and his allowance of immorality. Instead of facing the men of the town bravely and simply refusing their demand, he tried to compromise with them. He should have told them No! and left it at that. No doubt, fear was part of his motivation, but where in scripture is the follower of God told to obey God and flee evil *unless* one is afraid?

At the point of his confrontation at the door, Lot didn't yet know the identity of his two guests, and he would therefore have been unaware that God's provision for his protection was right there with him. Modern followers of Christ may not be aware—indeed, probably almost never will be aware—of just how close God's protection, whether miraculous or otherwise, may be when they face evil demands or the most insidious and threatening of temptations. That's where faith comes in. Human beings have five physical senses. Where these are inadequate to detect God's present protection, faith knows he is there. In the power of God's Spirit, the Christian can simply do what is right—with *no compromise,* and God will provide for what comes next.

Some Christians will think of martyrs for Christ, who faced confrontation in the demand to deny him, simply said No, and were killed for it. True, if that is the inscrutable will of God, so it must be. But how many true Christians would say right now that if such a time ever came, they would recant just so they could live—if, in fact, their malevolent captors actually would let them? It's important to make firm decisions *long before confrontation* that we will hold fast to what is right and stand for Jesus Christ, no matter what kind of threat is at the door.

THE DESPERATE DAUGHTERS OF LOT
Genesis 19:30-38

Some stories get into the realm of community knowledge only because the principal people involved in them told someone what happened, even if it were not something they were particularly proud of. Most of us keep as secrets, all our lives, something we were involved in or did on our own. We don't want people to know about it because we're ashamed, even after many years have gone by. In some cases, the statute of limitations might not even have run out!

Such is one story in Genesis, about Abraham's nephew Lot, and his two daughters. The scene is right after the destruction of Sodom, when the two angels who brought that destruction led Lot and his family out toward Zoar. Lot had pleaded to be allowed to go only so far as Zoar instead of all the way up in the mountains, and the angels had consented to let him do that. You'll remember that Lot's wife looked back as they fled, and she became a pillar of salt.

When he got to Zoar, Lot was terribly apprehensive. That's where we look in on him and his two daughters, now the only three persons to escape the destruction of Sodom and Gomorrah.

> [30] And Lot went up out of Zoar, and dwelt in the mountain, and his two daughters with him; for he feared to dwell in Zoar: and he dwelt in a cave, he and his two daughters. [31] And the firstborn said unto the younger, Our father is old, and there is not a man in the earth to come in unto us after the manner of all the earth: [32] Come, let us make our father drink wine, and we will lie with him, that we may preserve seed of our father. [33] And they made

their father drink wine that night: and the firstborn went in, and lay with her father; and he perceived not when she lay down, nor when she arose. [34] And it came to pass on the morrow, that the firstborn said unto the younger, Behold, I lay yesternight with my father: let us make him drink wine this night also; and go thou in, and lie with him, that we may preserve seed of our father. [35] And they made their father drink wine that night also: and the younger arose, and lay with him; and he perceived not when she lay down, nor when she arose. [36] Thus were both the daughters of Lot with child by their father. [37] And the firstborn bare a son, and called his name Moab: the same is the father of the Moabites unto this day. [38] And the younger, she also bare a son, and called his name Benammi: the same is the father of the children of Ammon unto this day (Genesis 19:30-38 KJV).

Everyone who has ever read this story has flinched a little at the apparently unapologetic depravity of the actions of these two sisters, who had sex with their drunken father. In interpreting the story and applying its lessons, we certainly will make no excuse for their behavior, or for his, for that matter. We will, of course, try to understand their background, the context of their family, and the thinking that led to their actions.

Discovering the Text

Isolation in a cave

The text tells us that Lot and his two daughters, now without their mother, got to Zoar, but that Lot **"feared to dwell in Zoar"** (v30). We don't know why.

We could speculate that he was somewhat known regionally, as the one inhabitant of Sodom who bucked the trend—unsuccessful in any attempts he might have made to influence the behavior of the wicked population there. If that were so, perhaps the people of Zoar would have treated him with some contempt themselves. But we have no evidence of this.

Or, we might guess that the population of Zoar, seeing the smoke of Sodom in the distance (as Abraham did—Genesis 19:27), and learning what happened, might have been suspicious of Lot, and therefore at enmity with him. But if Lot were the only one to escape, how would they know what happened there, involving him, unless he told them? And for this conjecture, too, we have no evidence.

We might assign Lot's apprehension to the sheer enormity of what had just happened to him and the way that highly traumatic events have of igniting our fears and our imagining more adversity. He had been visited by angels—not an everyday event. Scores of sex-crazed perverts had stormed his house and demanded to have access to these angels, who appeared as, apparently, ideally attractive young men. A sudden event of miraculous proportions took place when the perverted men outside were struck blind. The angels escorted Lot, his daughters and his wife outside the city and told them to run and not look back. The angels then turned toward Sodom and fire rained from heaven and destroyed Sodom and Gomorrah, as Lot and the remnants of his family tried to resist doing anything more than listening to the devastation going on behind them. And then Lot's wife gave in to her curiosity—and probably regret—and turned around, which they all had been warned against doing, and she promptly turned into a pillar of salt, like a stalagmite, dead as stone, leaving her shocked family nothing to do but to keep going, their tears awaiting another hour or day to flow freely in grief.

Now Lot has come to Zoar, and though he asked to be allowed to stay there instead of going farther, perhaps Zoar was not a city of moral purity itself, and Lot was afraid to make his home there. For the time being, therefore, he found a cave in nearby hills and somehow managed to eke out a life there, possibly going into Zoar in disguise to get provisions, or having his daughters do so.

This cave living was distressing to the daughters. They became convinced that, living as virtual hermits, they would not be able to marry. The men associated with Lot's family (more on that shortly), who had declined to flee Sodom, had subsequently died in its destruction. In their culture, girls expected with the greatest certainty to marry and have children, and it was a terrible thing to be denied that opportunity. Lot's daughters saw their father's decision to live in a cave as a guarantee that they wouldn't have children, wouldn't carry on the family line, and would be lonely for the rest of their days.

But the decision Lot's daughters made to do what they did was not simply a rational conclusion from their living circumstances. It was certainly generated in part by what had preceded their flight to the hills outside Zoar. What took place in Sodom just before the fire fell influenced the way these daughters looked at their father.

Lot had persuaded the angels—whom he probably thought at first were simply two men passing through town—to stay at his home rather than bed down in the public square. But the social network of the perverted population had already broadcast the presence of these good looking men. And shortly a horde of them came to Lot's door and demanded he surrender the two men to them—they were fresh meat for the sex-craving residents of Sodom.

Do you remember Lot's response (re-read the relevant portions of the previous chapter)? He said, Oh, no, that wouldn't be right. Look, I've got two girls here. Why don't you take them and have sex with them. But leave these two men alone.

Do you imagine Lot's daughters were in the room and heard him offer them up? We may be relatively certain they were. The angels momentarily asked Lot if he had anybody else in the house, including more daughters, or sons, or a son-in-law—angels are not omniscient and apparently they didn't have an exact count of the house. At any rate, with all the commotion at the front door, we have little reason to doubt the daughters were at least within earshot and heard what their father said. In retrospect, by the time of our story, it is evident that they did hear their father, because if they hadn't, it is highly unlikely he would have revealed this shameful detail about his life later. It is even less likely than that his daughters would have later revealed what they did, because they had to have an explanation for their eventual pregnancy. Lot's immoral offer didn't bring about any questionable event that later needed explaining.

The incident doesn't necessarily suggest anything about Lot's general and normal attitude; people sometimes say or do things during moments of intense pressure or danger that they regret later. Most of us use self control to bury deeply some impulses that have tempted us but that we know are evil. Lot is called **righteous** in 2 Peter 2:7. Peter says Lot was continually distressed about the conduct of the people where he lived. His less-than-fatherly feelings about his daughters on this occasion in Sodom shouldn't be taken to imply that he was a vile and rank misogynist who didn't love them *at all*. But, at the very least, he crumpled under pressure.

It is also possible, of course, that he thought his offer would be routinely dismissed since the men who had gathered there were homosexuals—and in fact they did decidedly dismiss the idea of his giving them women instead of men. But still, the idea of his offering his daughters for sexual abuse is abhorrent. And besides, the men outside the door may have been bisexual degenerates, not exclusively homosexual. The point is, it was not Lot's finest hour.

Now here are Lot's daughters, living in a cave with him, wondering if they had a future, and no doubt still smarting from his degrading and repulsive behavior with respect to them not long ago. That bit of recent history had to have influenced the idea that formed in their minds as to how to carry on the family line.

A textual issue is interesting here in the references to these "sons-in-law." The word for "son-in-law" in v12 is *hātān* in the Masoretic Text and is singular, where the word for "sons-in-law" in v14 is *hătānāw*, the plural of the same word. Either the first word was a gloss (material inserted in the original text at some point as an explanation) which some scholars do think, or it is more evidence that the angels didn't know how many people were in the household. But another word in v14, *lōq^eḥē,* translated in the KJV as "who had married," seems unnecessary if the marriages had already been formalized (and consummated). Derek Kidner remarks that the RSV properly translated this word "who were to marry."[35] Indeed, the NIV, NLT, ESV, NASB, Amp, CSB and others also render the word with some expression meant to communicate that the men were *betrothed* to Lot's daughters but had not yet become their husbands formally. Hebrew marriage customs included a step in between an initial pledge and formal marriage that was more than our modern "engagement" but less than marriage with consummation. Thus, the daughters had not yet had sex with their intended husbands, which v8 specifically states. Their fears of being childless were a consequence of their being husband-less in the first place.

A desperate solution

Faced with the prospect of remaining single and childless, the daughters proposed an extreme solution. They would contrive some method of having sex with their father—the only man around. We hope that at least they came up with the idea with embarrassment, but the setting of this story suggests strongly that everyone in this nuclear family had been influenced for the worse by their residence in Sodom, where morality essentially did not exist.

We have already noted that Lot had offered these girls to the sex-hungry men at their family's door. The irony of what these daughters now propose to each other is glaring. "Earlier the father was willing to use his daughters for sexual purposes without their consent. Now they will use their father for sexual purposes without

---

[35] Derek Kidner, *Genesis*, The Tyndale Old Testament Commentaries, (Downers Grove, Illinois, Inter-Varsity Press, 1967), 135.

his consent."[36] There were differences, of course, but in both cases there was the idea that desperate circumstances justified otherwise immoral actions. They didn't, but such is the thinking of people who have stood long in the way of sinners[37] as Lot and his family had in Sodom.

The girls' plan was simple: to get their father drunk enough to keep him from objecting or doing anything to prevent their having sex with him, possibly even drunk enough that he wouldn't remember what had taken place after the fact. First one and then the other daughter proposed the plan (vv33-35), possibly the second, younger daughter reluctant at first until after her older sister had gone through with the act. But they both did so on successive nights, their father apparently willing in his depressed state to go on alcohol binges that rendered him both defenseless and mindless.

Not many commentators have mentioned an issue that arises at this point as the reader tries to make sense of what happened in the cave those two nights when Lot's daughters took advantage of him sexually. He was overwhelmingly drunk, and yet he had sex with his daughters, albeit as passively as one can imagine. Many men reading this account will wonder, How was that even possible?

It was Shakespeare who had one of his characters articulate the practical contradiction of drunkenness and sexual capability. The Porter in MacBeth, conversing with McDuff, says, "Drink sir, is a great provoker of three things...nose-painting, sleep, and urine. Lechery, sir, it provokes, and unprovokes; it provokes the desire but takes away the performance."[38]

A problem for Lot's daughters was the possibility that a severely

---

[36] Victor P. Hamilton, *The Book of Genesis, Chapters 18-50*, The New International Commentary on the Old Testament, (Grand Rapids, Michigan, William B. Eerdmans Publishing Company, 1995), 51.

[37] Psalm 1:1

[38] William Shakespeare, "Macbeth," Act 2, Scene 3. The author remembers vividly the portrayal of The Porter by a college classmate in 1970.

drunken Lot would be incapacitated and unable to have sex with them. As it happened, however, somehow he was able, and without our delving indelicately into what took place, the bottom line was that each had sex with him, and that afterwards, in each case **he perceived not when she lay down, nor when she arose** (vv33,35). Incidentally, as we said above, this story would not have been known had the girls not eventually owned up to what they did. Lot might have figured it out, but not with the details about their planning and execution.

Ultimate consequences

These two daughters of Lot were concerned each with their having children, but neither gives any evidence of having a sense of the ultimate, historical consequences of their actions. What the story tells us, however, is that they became pregnant and gave birth to two boys who would go on to become the progenitors of two ethnic groups: the Moabites and the Ammonites. The older daughter bore a son she named Moab, and her sister gave birth to a son she named Benammi. In both cases there is wordplay. Moab means "from the father." Benammi means "son of my kin."

Bible history does not at first negatively assess the subsequent emergence of the Moabites or Ammonites. But after Israel's sojourn in Egypt and their coming out to take the land of Canaan, both the Moabites and the Ammonites become a source of repeated danger and enmity to Abraham's descendants, and an eventual source of the worst influences of idolatry. So, Lot's "legacy, Moab and Ammon, was destined to provide the worst carnal seduction in the history of Israel (that of Baal-Peor, Nu.25), and the cruellest religious perversion (that of Molech, Lv.18:21)."[39] The actions of these two daughters of Lot therefore loom large in their historical consequences, but we are entirely justified in laying the ultimate

---

[39] Kidner, *op. cit.*, 136.

blame for their lack of moral fiber on their father.

Despite Lot's being "righteous" (2 Peter 2:7), relative to the Sodomites at any rate, he had a history of incomplete faithfulness to the God of his uncle Abraham. In the terminology of drama, he had a tragic flaw, a defect in his character that ultimately led to his downfall in life. His inability to separate his strong urging to prosper from the necessities of doing God's will put him in Sodom in the first place. His unwillingness to leave a place that daily and yearly brought him down spiritually resulted in his development of compromised morality. And his daughters, not only the fruit of his loins but also the product of his ineffectual character training, became the instruments of his undoing. God saved Lot through human agency (Genesis 14) and by angelic intervention (Genesis 19), because of the promise made to Abraham. But Lot, who just couldn't manage to let go of the world enough to find the fullest life in fellowship with God, finally made a mark on history full of sadness and regret.

Learning the Lessons

The historical lessons for the Jews have already been described above. In looking at this story in the 21st century, what else may readers take away? The Apostle Paul taught us, "All Scripture is inspired by God and is profitable for teaching, for rebuking, for correcting, for training in righteousness" (2 Timothy 3:16 CSB).

1. Alcohol   An Attitude to Develop ☑
Drunkenness never led to anything good, and frequently leads to something bad.

When this story occurs in Genesis 19, the book has already provided us with the example of Noah, captain of the ark of humanity's salvation, who got drunk and became defenseless against the perverted impulses of his son, Ham. Our previous chapter on that curious story and this chapter on the tale of Lot and his daughters demonstrate the principle that being drunk is a virtual invitation to misbehavior—our own or someone else's. We can apply this lesson about alcohol quite literally to the issue of sexual sins, with many a rape involving a man's plying a woman with drink, if not overcoming her with more potent drugs. And many a couple who perhaps would not have engaged in illicit sex did so under the mutual influence of alcoholic beverages.

2. Corruption   A Truth to Believe ☑

Ineffectual faith frequently leads to failure of obedience and corruption of principle.

No hard and fast rule can be made that people in the top 10% (or whatever) of Christian commitment *will not fall into great sin,* while people in the bottom 90% *always will.* It doesn't work that way. But it can be said definitively that those who surrender themselves daily and continually to the Lordship of Christ are *not as likely* to compromise biblical principles of living as those who, subsequent to their conversion to Christ, fall into a *pattern* of uncommitted living.

This likelihood is so strong that the Apostle John wrote, "No one who lives in him keeps on sinning. No one who continues to sin has either seen him or known him" (1 John 3:6). This slight hyperbole is illustrative of the principle that following Christ faithfully and with determination, letting the Holy Spirit fill and guide, is a believer's best defense against temptation and the terrible sins of life—and even the small ones. And being a Christian, but being entirely lax about commitment, spiritual growth and coming to know the Lord, is a prelude to a fall—perhaps a great one.

SACRIFICING THE FUTURE
Genesis 22:1-2

In planning this book, this author looked carefully at possible chapters, including this one about Abraham taking his son Isaac into a mountain to sacrifice him to the Lord. The details of the story are not obscure, not packed with hidden meaning that requires a lot of textual study—in short, not curious in some ways. Why include it in the book?

Other opinions were consulted and confirmed this author's instincts. This story is curious for one central fact: that God instructed Abraham to sacrifice the as yet unmarried son he had promised him, the one who was supposed to be the father of a nation and untold descendants after him.

Here's the core text from Genesis:

[1] **After these things God tested Abraham and said to him, "Abraham!"**

"Here I am," he answered.

[2] **"Take your son," He said, "your only son Isaac, whom you love, go to the land of Moriah, and offer him there as a burnt offering on one of the mountains I will tell you about." (Genesis 22:1-2 CSB).**

We've quoted only the first two verses of the story, which continues through v19, because apparently that part of the account is the only one that most casual critics of the Bible focus on. Persons who are neither Jews nor Christians whose purpose in reading the Bible is to gather ammunition so as to find fault with it, tend to cherry pick the strange elements of Bible stories and to launch their attacks against what they think are glaring mistakes, obvious inconsistencies or insoluble contradictions. The common complaint about this story is that God was contradicting his own previous promises about Isaac, or else deliberately trying to confuse Abraham about his plans.

One particularly skeptical author, Lippman Bodoff, wrote that even though the text says God commanded him to go sacrifice his son, Abraham didn't plan to actually do it. Bodoff opines that Abraham believed God didn't intend for him to.[40]

Other critics, published and not, find fault with God for ordering Abraham to do something he prohibited: child sacrifice. Several scriptures have God saying through his prophets to Judah later on that he was bringing judgment on them because they had offered their children in sacrifice to Molech, **"though I never commanded —nor did it enter my mind—that they should do such a detestable thing and so make Judah sin"** (Jeremiah 32:25 NIV). This is the most serious criticism of this story, and we will address it first.

Discovering the Text

Commanding the forbidden

Even before considering the apparent contradiction of God's having earlier promised Abraham his offspring would be traced through Isaac (Genesis 21:12), we must deal with God's commanding Abraham to do something unthinkable in itself: make a burnt offering of his son (v2).

Everyone in the middle and near east would have been familiar with the fact that some cultures practiced child sacrifice. Delitzsch

---

[40] Lippman Bodoff, *The Binding of Isaac, Religious Murders & Kabbalah: Seeds of Jewish Extremism and Alienation?*, (Devora Publishing / Urim Press).

notes that Abraham "saw how the heathen surrendered their dearest to appease the deity and render him propitious."[41] When God told him to go through with such an act, it would have brought up any feelings and convictions he had about the matter.

Although prohibition of child sacrifice was not codified for the Jews until later, such a law of God was understood. Later in the account of Isaac the LORD appeared to him and said, **"Abraham obeyed my voice, and kept my charge, my commandments, my statutes, and my laws"** (Genesis 26:5). What laws? The Ten Commandments were yet a few hundred years in the future. But there were worshipers of the true God in various communities in the region, and God had made known many principles for living to the consciences of those who would seek him. Among these was the prohibition of offering one's own children in human sacrifice.

So when God said, **"...offer him there as a burnt offering"** (v2) it should have seemed to Abraham as something unthinkable. **Why would God issue such a command?** This is where the skeptics and unbelievers stop reading and launch salvos of judgment against God.

But the answer to the question is found: in the immediate Old Testament text; later Old Testament laws; and even later in the New Testament. And the answer to "why" also reveals the ultimate purpose of God for more than just the life of Abraham.

First, the remainder of the story makes crystal clear that God was testing Abraham's willingness to obey *every* command of the Lord, no matter what it was. Verse 12 says, **"I know that you fear God, since you have not withheld your only son from me."** God interrupted Abraham at the very point of his slaying his son with a knife, before burning him—which Abraham would have done, had not the Angel of the Lord called to him and stopped him. While some critics think the entire matter was some kind of drama that Abraham carried out with a wink and a nod, the Bible presents it as

---

[41] Franz Delitzsch, *A New Commentary on Genesis,* (Edinburgh, Scotland, T. & T. Clark, 1889), 97.

a genuine test of faith in which Abraham was challenged to go through the unthinkable because of his conviction of the authenticity of God's command. He passed the test because he didn't hesitate and question God.

Second, God's laws regarding sacrifice were later given specifically in Exodus 34. There, God told the Israelites that the firstborn male from *every womb* belonged to him (i.e. was to be sacrificed) including all their livestock and their sheep. But he added, **"You must redeem all the firstborn of your sons"** (Exodus 34:20). In other words, they *would* have been required to sacrifice their firstborn sons, but for the exception made for *human children,* that they could **redeem** them—through the sacrifice of other animals as offerings to God symbolic of their sons.

This understanding of the death of one being—an animal being —in the place of a *human* being goes all the way back to Genesis 4:4, where Cain brought beautiful fruit from his groves as an offering to God but Abel brought a slaughtered firstborn of his flock. He knew that what he offered God could not be acceptable on the basis of its being the best he could do—like Cain offered—but instead because it was something he treasured but that had to die.

In fact, the understanding of this rudimentary fact about approaching God to worship him goes even further back, to Adam and Eve in Eden. When they sinned, they immediately felt shame and covered themselves with leaves. Then, when God sent them out of the garden, **"The LORD God made garments from skin for Adam and his wife, and clothed them"** (Genesis 3:21 NET). Animals died to cover the first couple's shame. They understood the message in this act. Clearly, they passed down that understanding, which explains the cultural retention of some of God's fundamental laws in the conscience—expectations that were laws long before the time of Moses.

Later, the prophet Micah expressed powerfully the heart of this law concerning sacrifice:

Will the LORD accept a thousand rams, or ten thousand
streams of olive oil?

Should I give him my firstborn child as payment for my
rebellion, my offspring—my own flesh and blood—for my
sin?

He has told you, O man, what is good, and what the LORD
really wants from you:

He wants you to promote justice, to be faithful, and to live
obediently before your God (Micah 6:7-8 NET).

The heart of God's commanding Abraham to do the unthinkable
was to push him to the limits and bring out his faith that no matter
what other notions Abraham might have had, he knew that God
would not violate his own holy nature. After all, it was Abraham
who had said to the Angel of the Lord earlier, when pleading for
him to spare any righteous people of Sodom, **"Shall not the Judge
of all the earth do right?"** (Genesis 18:25).

And so he did.

Finally, the answer to the question of why God would issue such
a command to Abraham is found also in the interpretation of the
New Testament writer of Hebrews. In that masterful chapter
describing the faith of various Old Testament saints, the author says
of Abraham's preparing to offer Isaac: **"he reasoned that God could
even raise him from the dead, and in a sense he received him
back from there"** (Hebrews 11:19 NET). The author of Hebrews
believed that Abraham thought through the matter carefully and
arrived at a position of faith that even if he carried through with the
sacrifice all the way, God could *and would* raise Isaac from the dead.

There are indications of Abraham's confidence even in the Old
Testament story itself. Before they left home, Abraham told his
servants, **"The boy and I will go over there to worship; then we'll
come back to you"** (v5). "We." And when Isaac became curious as
they went to the place of sacrifice about the lack of a lamb,
Abraham said, **"God himself will provide the lamb"** (v8).

Abraham's language was deliberately cryptic to avoid explaining what terrible, awful thing he was about to do, but it contained the undeniable revelation of his faith that God was in charge and would redeem the act in his own—even if necessarily miraculous—way.

The ultimate purpose

Testing Abraham's faith was the more immediate reason for God's command—a lesson that his family including Isaac could clearly appreciate. But the ultimate purpose of God in sending Abraham to Mount Moriah was the creation of a theological type, a symbol, a foreshadowing of the sacrifice of the Only Son of God the Father: God the Son, Jesus Christ.

The image of Christ in the event at Moriah is strengthened by its likely location. "The prevalent Jewish and Christian tradition puts the scene on the Temple mount at Jerusalem."[42]

Jews (other than "messianic Jews") do not accept the identity of Jesus as their Messiah. But the message of Abraham's virtual sacrifice of Isaac is one of many, many images and prophecies in the Old Testament that point powerfully, convincingly, and overwhelmingly to Jesus as the Incarnate Son. Abraham, though unknowingly, was imitating God himself who, two millennia later, in the person of God the Son, would give his life on the cross as a sacrifice for the sin of the human race (Romans 3:25, Hebrews 2:7, Hebrews 10:12, 1 John 2:2, 4:10, etc.).

Learning the Lessons

As with many of the stories in this book, the lessons of this curious account of God's seemingly countermanding himself are wonderfully obvious.

---

[42] John Skinner, *A Critical and Exegetical Commentary on Genesis*, (New York, Scribner, 1910), 328.

1. God's provision for sin
A Truth to Believe ✔
While only man deserves to die for his sin, God himself has provided someone to die for him: Jesus Christ.

Abraham was unaware of how God would ultimately resolve the continuing situation of man's need of redemption, just as he was unaware of how God would work down through the generations of his son Isaac, his sons, and their sons and beyond, to be a blessing to all the world (Genesis 12:3). Hebrews 11:40 explains that this was in fact part of God's plan: that through the faith of many who lived and died and never saw (on earth, at least) what ultimate blessing God was planning, in his perfect timing it would be revealed eventually: **"For God had provided something better for us, so that they would be made perfect together with us"** (NET). **"But when the appropriate time had come, God sent out his Son, born of a woman, born under the law, to redeem those who were under the law, so that we may be adopted as sons with full rights"** (Galatians 4:4 NET).

The Christian can read about Abraham and Isaac on Mount Moriah and see the death and resurrection of Jesus Christ encapsulated in a powerful metaphor.

2. Have faith in God
A Teaching to Obey ✔
Always, but especially when you can't see how he is going to work out his purposes, *have faith in God.* He always does right.

Our concept of our future is often the product of worldly expectations, the natural desires of humanity, or the hope of human emotions. Even when we express our desires for future outcomes in biblical terms like "for God's will to be done," or "for God's blessing," sometimes we're really saying we desperately hope we will not eventually suffer any loss, will not feel any pain, but will see our fondest *earthly* dreams fulfilled. However, our *human hopes* may not be the template God will follow.

The lesson of Abraham's faith is that what God has *already promised,* he will do, no matter how inconsistent with that promise our present circumstances seem to be. If we have truly apprehended God's promise and understand it, we can be certain that he will not break that promise, and we can continue to live obediently and even sacrificially, knowing that the Judge of all the earth will do right.

Jacob's Theory of Animal Husbandry
Genesis 30:37-39

Long before man discovered that he was made up of cells that contained DNA, he had discovered a lot of other things about life, including the breeding of animals—we call it animal husbandry, today. Not all of his ideas, however, were accurate. We run into one of those misguided ideas in the book of Genesis, as part of the story of Jacob and his interaction with Laban, his father-in-law.

Laban was a scheming and deceitful man who attempted to cast his behavior as reasonable and justified. He protested that he was cheated when he was the one cheating. He gladly profited from the labor of others and boasted that his stinginess was really generosity.

Early in Jacob's relationship with him, Laban supposedly gave his daughter Rachel to Jacob in marriage. But in the dark of the marriage night, Laban sent his elder daughter Leah into the consummation tent, providing a surprise in the morning. While Rachel was given to Jacob in another week, Jacob had to work another seven years to earn her after the fact, and he didn't forget the lesson to beware the wiles of his new father-in-law.

Our story begins after a number of years in which Jacob's two wives as well as Leah's servant Zilpah bore him a number of sons. Eventually, Jacob was ready to go back to his homeland. He told Laban of his intentions and Laban first attempted to bargain with him to stay. But Jacob was firm, and what's more, he wanted something for all the time he had spent with Laban's clan. Laban had gotten wealthy with Jacob's help. Laban agreed, and would have given him money, but Jacob didn't want it. Instead, he proposed that Laban let him take all the speckled and spotted sheep—which would have been a very small number of the total. Laban probably thought he was getting off cheap with this proposal, and he agreed.

Here's the heart of Jacob's strategy:

> [37] Jacob then took branches of fresh poplar, almond, and plane wood, and peeled the bark, exposing white stripes on the branches. [38] He set the peeled branches in the troughs in front of the sheep—in the water channels where the sheep came to drink. And the sheep bred when they came to drink. [39] The flocks bred in front of the branches and bore streaked, speckled, and spotted young. [40] Jacob separated the lambs and made the flocks face the streaked sheep and the completely dark sheep in Laban's flocks. Then he set his own stock apart and didn't put them with Laban's sheep. [41] Whenever the stronger of the flock were breeding, Jacob placed the branches in the troughs, in full view of the flocks, and they would breed in front of the branches. [42] As for the weaklings of the flocks, he did not put out the branches. So it turned out that the weak sheep belonged to Laban and the stronger ones to Jacob. [43] And the man became very rich. He had many flocks, female and male slaves, and camels and donkeys (Genesis 30:37-43 CSB).

This story has been lampooned by critics of the Bible for being an example of superstition that those critics think the Bible teaches. Under-informed Bible believers may find themselves embarrassed when they read the story, thinking the critics are right, and having an insufficient, or having *no*, defense ready.

In fact, this curious story is one of a number of Bible accounts that *reflect* mistaken ideas of their time but that *do not teach* those ideas. But in this particular case, we have enough additional information in the larger account that actually explains that Jacob was acting superstitiously.

Discovering the Text

Jacob's choice

According to the previous verses, 30:25-30, Jacob politely rebuffed Laban's plea for him to stay (and keep making Laban wealthier), and said that he wanted to take his wives and children and go back home. Laban proceeded to open negotiations. He knew that Jacob had been his main source of enrichment and he told him so (v27)—a concession intended to compliment Jacob and make him more receptive to an offer—and then he offered him some sort of wages, or increase in such, to stay on (v28). Jacob echoed Laban's admission of how his work contribution had enriched Laban (vv29-30), but he insisted it was time for him to go and make something for himself (v30). Laban countered with a re-offer of wages (v31)—"name your price."

At this point, Jacob partly relented—which he may have intended all along to do at least for a time (several years). It appears that he had thought through what he would ask to keep tending Laban's flocks for a while, perhaps as a time of transition.

Jacob didn't want money. He wanted the speckled and spotted sheep and goats; 30:32 tells us this, but we learn later, in 31:10ff, where Jacob got the idea. He told Rachel and Leah that God had given him a vision in a dream. In that dream he saw male goats mating with the flock, and they were streaked, speckled or spotted. In the dream or vision, God said, **"Look up and see that all the male goats mating with the flock are streaked, speckled or spotted, for I have seen all that Laban has been doing to you"** (Genesis 31:12 NIV).

There is gentle disagreement among scholars as to when Jacob had this dream. The New International Commentary says, "The dream is apparently subsequent to or near the end of the events in ch. 30, not previous to them, or even concurrent with them, since ch. 30 said nothing about a dream."[43] Derek Kidner in The Tyndale OT Commentaries agrees. But Wenham, in his comprehensive and voluminous work as part of the Word Biblical Commentary, says that the description of the dream in 31:10-13 contains differing suggestions as to its time. V10 says, **"In breeding season I once had a dream in which I looked up and saw that the male goats mating with the flock were streaked, speckled or spotted"** (NIV). That, says Wenham, suggests the dream was some years previous. But at the end of that dream "the angel of God" said Jacob was to go back to his native land, which might suggest he was to leave immediately. Deciding how to interpret the timing of the dream is not all-important, but it isn't insignificant.

We think the dream came before Jacob's breeding venture.

- The appearance of the spotted herds was not merely a memory that God brought to Jacob's mind; it identified the resource Jacob should focus his attention upon, because God intended to bless that resource.
- Jacob devised his plan from his anticipation of seeing the speckled and spotted animals increase and of his owning them.
- Jacob's agreement to work on for Laban for a while was a transition time between his sojourn in Laban's country and his return to his own—a temporary measure to allow him to increase his "wages," which God allowed.

Jacob's strategy

The most curious part of this story, of course, is *how* Jacob went about trying to increase his herd of speckled, spotted and streaked sheep and goats.

Taking the dream he later reported to his wives as something

---

[43] Victor P. Hamilton, *The Book of Genesis: Chapters 18-50*, The New International Commentary on the Old Testament, (Grand Rapids, Michigan, Wm. B. Eerdmans Publishing Company, 1995), 289.

that occurred *before* Jacob decided to leave, we note two important things about his strategy.

First, he employed what was believed by some sheep herders in those days, namely the idea that what breeding animals saw or experienced around the time of estrus and copulation affected what their progeny would look like. That belief explains Jacob's using sticks with some of the bark peeled off to influence the sheep and goats to bear spotted young.

In this part of his strategy Jacob was **entirely mistaken!**

Note that in Jacob's dream or vision God *did not* say anything to him about stripping branches of bark here and there and putting the speckled results in the watering troughs (30:38). *The entire idea of trying to influence what color the lambs and kids would be by making them see speckled branches was Jacob's alone.*

A few older commentaries miss this point and assume that God laid out the plan of de-barking tree branches. He *did not.*

Some of the older Bible commentaries acknowledge that it was commonly *believed* in the ancient world that what breeding animals saw constantly would affect what their offspring would look like or be like. Our usually reliable Keil and Delitzsch remark that such a method was "a fact frequently noticed."[44] K&D first published their Old Testament commentary in 1864, long before the discovery of DNA and the modern knowledge of what controls reproduction and breeding.

Benson Bible Commentary was written in the early 1800s—also well before the knowledge of modern genetics—but Benson says on this passage, "it cannot be proved that the method which Jacob used is a natural and effectual way to produce variegated cattle," and then he says that "the ancient naturalists...carried their thoughts upon these

---

[44] Karl Fredrich Keil and Franz Delitzsch, *Volume 1, Genesis to Judges 6:32, Biblical Commentary on the Old Testament*, (Lafayette, Indiana, Associated Publishers and Authors, 1960), 225.

subjects much further than they will bear."[45] In other words, long before our understanding of genetics, Benson was arguing that what Jacob did was mere superstition. At the most, while Benson opines that such methods of affecting reproduction "might" work, he insists the results must be attributed to God.

Although nucleic acid was discovered by Friedrich Miescher in 1869, it was well into the 1900s before DNA (deoxyribonucleic acid) was discovered. It was Oswald Avery who proposed that "hereditary units, or genes, are composed of DNA"[46] and the double helix form of DNA wasn't decided until the 1950s. Today, of course, we have mapped DNA extensively. We know where a plethora of bodily characteristics—human and non-human—come from, and it's not from spotted sticks.

We'll excuse Messrs. Keil and Delitzsch and other Bible commentators for not knowing the future. In this book we have readily referenced older commentators for their knowledge of writings predating them, but we haven't used them for a resource on modern science. (Nor, we believe, has it been an issue so far.)

But we return to our previous assertion about what God showed Jacob in his dream: God *did not* tell Jacob to use spotted sticks to influence breeding results. Critics of the Bible have no basis for finding fault with God in this story.

Jacob, on the other hand, is another matter. First, there's the matter of what he thought his vision meant. His first step, requesting that Laban give him the spotted and speckled sheep and goats, seemed an obvious move, and Laban went for it undoubtedly because it wouldn't cost him much. He said, *kidbārekā!* (Heb. כִּדְבָרֶךָ), "according to your word!" Or, "*You* said it!" In the middle east sheep are regularly white and goats black, with spotted examples consisting of no more than 20% of either—usually many

---

45 Joseph Benson, *Benson's Commentary*, (New York, Carton & Porter, 1825), 104.

[46] Pray, L. (2008) Discovery of DNA structure and function: Watson and Crick. Nature Education 1(1):100.

fewer than that. Laban's "loss" would be minimal. The text tells us that Laban himself took the spotted ones out and gave his sons the care of them (30:35). Then he put a distance of three days between himself and Jacob, to prevent any subsequent mingling of flocks.

The explanation of this separation in 30:36 is confusing, and there are textual issues that have led interpreters to differing conclusions over the years.

- Some think that Jacob immediately took ownership of the separated animals, though for some reason Laban's sons were put in charge of them. After all, when he proposed the separation, Jacob said, **"Such shall be my wages"** (Genesis 30:32 CSB).
- Others think the separated animals were still Laban's, and that Jacob had only a few solid colored animals to tend before eventually leaving with the separated ones.[47] This view doesn't explain how Jacob was better off to begin with, his having no spotted animals.

We think Jacob took ownership of the spotted animals right away, and that the sons of Laban tended them at a distance of three days away in order to keep them from being mixed with the solid colored animals Jacob continued to tend nearby. Laban's thinking was probably that when Jacob had made all his preparations to leave and finally set a date, the few animals the sons had tended would be transferred to Jacob and he would be on his way.

This was fine with Jacob, because he intended to go further than just culling the spotted sheep. He was going to attempt to increase his speckled and spotted herd even without mingling the ones Laban's sons were guarding carefully.

Jacob apparently thought his technique of spotted sticks was

---

[47] Clyde Francisco writes, "To Laban's surprise his nephew wanted nothing at present, but only the off-color animals born in the future." (Clyde T. Francisco, *Genesis*, The Broadman Bible Commentary, (Nashville, Broadman Press, 1973), 217.)

working, because he did get some speckled and spotted lambs and kids over the next months. But Jacob didn't know what we now know about DNA.

Even the perfectly white sheep and black goats were not without recessive genes that would now and then produce spotted progeny —that's where Jacob's separated flock had come from. Here's a brief—very brief!—summary of how things worked:

> The flock tended by Jacob had only monochrome animals in respect of phenotype. As regards genotype, however, a third were pure monochromes (homozygotes) and two-thirds were heterozygotes (who contained the gene of spottedness). By crossing the heterozygotes among themselves, Jacob would produce, according to the laws of heredity, twenty-five percent spotted sheep. Thus he multiplies his flock.[48]

Further, Jacob didn't breed the animals indiscriminately.

> ...Jacob applied the breeding method of vv. 37-39 selectively. The stronger animals are the heterozygotes. The feebler animals are the homozygotes. Jacob crossbred only the former. How he could distinguish one from the other is made clear in 31:12—the heterozygotes are excessively potent and conceive earlier than homozygotes. Jacob's knowledge of zoology is far from primitive."[49]

What this means is that Jacob identified the animals that had the potential to breed spotted young, by picking out the ones that gave birth earliest in the season, which were also the stronger animals.

---

[48] Hamilton, *op. cit.*, 284. Hamilton footnotes the text: "See J. Feliks, "Biology," *EncJud*, 4:1024-10278.

[49] Hamilton, *op. cit.*, 284.

If any unusually elevated numbers of speckled and spotted lambs and kids were added to Jacob's number beyond those predicted by statistics, we may attribute the blessing to God's providence. As he had told Jacob in the dream, **"[f]or I have seen all that Laban has been doing to you"** (Genesis 31:12 CSB). As Wenham says, "[t]he obscure vision shows that God is behind Jacob's selective breeding techniques."[50] Wenham means those methods Jacob employed *other* than spotted sticks.

Commentators on this strange Bible story still struggle to explain why God blessed Jacob's strategies, even when Jacob followed naturalistic—but mistaken—ideas of his day, involving sticks in the water trough. Most scholars who remark on this curiosity say that "the effect must still be ascribed immediately to God himself,"[51] or that "God...caused the right rams...to mate."[52]

Told briefly, this curious story is about a trickster, Jacob, who for the price of a wife goes to work for his new father-in-law, Laban, a trickster himself, and makes the elder man rich over a period of some years. To get away from him, Jacob makes a deal for a transition period in which he will acquire spotted and speckled sheep and goats, which Laban agrees to because he believes it won't affect him much. But Jacob employs every trick he knows to increase his multi-colored animals—some methods well ahead of his time and some superstitious—all of them blessed by the hand of God irrespectively.

Learning the Lessons

As always, the reader of even the most strange tale in the Bible

---

[50] Gordon J. Wenham, *Genesis 16-5*, Word Biblical Commentary, (Dallas, Texas, Word Books, 1994), 272.

[51] Benson, *op. cit.,* 104.

[52] Francisco, *op. cit.*, 218.

is confronted with the challenge of deriving what lessons may be there. What can we learn from this story?

1. *Wise foresight*   A Teaching to Obey ☑

A Christian should employ all possible wisdom with foresight in providing for himself and family.

As a very general lesson, the story of Jacob's management of sheep and goats illustrates for us the wisdom of making use of every legitimate resource to secure our financial futures. There is plenty of material in both the Old and New Testaments about financial responsibility and planning for days ahead. There is no conflict between this duty and Jesus' parable about the man who built more and more barns to store his goods and told himself, "Eat, drink and be merry!" The point of that story was that the man provided for *this* life but not at all for *eternal life*.

But Jesus told another interesting parable in Luke 16:1-9 about a shrewd steward who, facing dismissal for squandering money, took steps to provide for his own future, using his employer's money. On some level the employer commended him because in order to ingratiate people to him, the steward had collected portions of large debts to his employer that might never have been collected at all, thus resulting in a large cash flow. Jesus applied the parable by observing that God's people are often not as smart in using their resources for godliness as worldly people are in using theirs for purely worldly goals. The lesson was for God's people to stop being careless or simpletons in their use of money, and to learn how to make the most of what they have for their futures *in God's will*.

2. *Trust God for your future*   A Teaching to Obey ☑

Sometimes, *getting out* of a stressful situation isn't as important as detecting God's will to *get through* that situation.

Most people will discover only through hindsight what God was "up to" at difficult times in their lives. But it's important *at the time* of those difficult experiences to resist taking the fastest route out of them no matter what the loss. Through reflection, patience, study of the word of God, the counsel of others, and much prayer, one may discover that God is *up to something* important that shouldn't be short-cut. Like Jacob, who got into the entire sojourn with Laban in the first place because of his need to escape the brother he had cheated, we might find that our predicaments lead to personal growth, circumstantial blessing, the emergence of a promise for our future, and unexpected improvement in our lot all around. God's "plan B" might surprise us if we just trust him to work it out while we wait on him.

Jacob Wrestles with God

Genesis 32:24-30

An even more fitting description of this chapter's subject as "curious" would be "remarkable," or "amazing," instead. It is the account of a wrestling match between a man and God.

[22-23] Jacob got up in the middle of the night and took his wives, his eleven children, and everything he owned across to the other side of the Jabbok River for safety. [24] Afterwards, Jacob went back and spent the rest of the night alone.

A man came and fought with Jacob until just before daybreak. [25] When the man saw that he could not win, he struck Jacob on the hip and threw it out of joint. [26] They kept on wrestling until the man said, "Let go of me! It's almost daylight."

"You can't go until you bless me," Jacob replied.

[27] Then the man asked, "What is your name?"

"Jacob," he answered.

[28] The man said, "From now on, your name will no longer be Jacob. You will be called Israel, because you have wrestled with God and with men, and you have won."

[29] Jacob said, "Now tell me your name."

"Don't you know who I am?" he asked. And he blessed Jacob.

[30] Jacob said, "I have seen God face to face, and I am still alive." So he named the place Peniel (Genesis 32:24-

30 NIV).

On the heels of the previous curious story—where Jacob used "every trick in the book" to increase his flocks before leaving Laban for home—comes this story of an encounter Jacob had on the way back to his home country, an encounter that left him wounded but blessed and inspired for life.

Every worthy interpreter who comes to this text has to stand in awe of what it says. It is no mere idiom for something else, no symbol only with nothing literal at its heart, no legend without factual basis: it is an account of a human being wrestling with a human form of God.

Discovering the Text

A quest for God

The story begins with Jacob's setting up camp for the night on one side of the Jabbok River while the rest of his entourage was on the other side "for safety." Scholars have tried to locate this place with exactitude. The river Jabbok, more a wadi, ran east toward the Jordan river, and formed "the boundary between the kingdoms of Sihon at Heshbon and Og of Bashan."[53] Jacob took his family and others from one side of this wadi to the other, returned, and the wadi separated them for the night.[54]

The geography isn't necessarily significant for the purpose of the

---

[53] Keil and Delitzsch, *Genesis*, 233. This political identification seems odd at the time of Jacob, since it was some 400 years later, *after* the sojourn in Egypt and during the conquering of the Promised Land, that we learn what we know—at least Biblically—about Og and Sihon. If they had been rulers of these lands to the east of the Jordan during the time of Jacob, they would have been beings of quite extended lifetimes. Indeed, the Talmud says that they were giants, who did have long lives.

[54] Ellicott was convinced that Jacob remained on the south side, but Barnes was certain he was on the north, each for their own reasons.

story. If "for safety" he sent his wives, children or belongings into a more friendly region than where he had been during the day, we might have gained a possible spiritual lesson. But the kingdoms of Sihon and Og were equally dangerous. We can't be certain why sending his family across (whichever direction that was) provided them with more safety. It simply did.

What is more worth considering is why Jacob needed the time alone.

The answer to this question is easily derived from looking back at all that had happened to Jacob, beginning with the trickery of Esau in his youth. The brothers had been at odds with each other all their young lives, having not only very different interests but also having separate champions in their parents. Jacob's taking Esau's birthright created a division that virtually forced Jacob to flee, though he did so with his father's blessing to go find a wife from among distant family. But for all the years after his leaving home until now at Jabbok's ford, Jacob assumed that Esau's wound had festered and that his brother was his avowed enemy. He had no information to the contrary. Returning home, therefore, was going into hostile territory.

Nor was Jacob's life in another country without its tensions. He had fallen in love with a young woman named Rachel and worked for seven years to earn her father's consent for their marriage, only to be tricked—ironically enough for Jacob the trickster—into marrying Rachel's sister, Leah. In another week he also married Rachel but had to work another seven years to earn her after the fact. The experience told him that Laban, the women's father, was not to be trusted.

Over the next few years he had children by these two women as well as by a servant of Leah's, Zilpah. As he built his family, Jacob continued to work for Laban, who through his relationship with Jacob kept him essentially an employee. Yet Jacob had invested his life in his new, larger family's enterprises. At some point, he realized he had to stand on his own, which meant extracting himself from

Laban, possibly incurring enmity with the man.

Jacob's decision to leave and go home was partly to make something for himself (Genesis 30:30), but also partly to repair his relationship with his brother Esau. Clearly he had matured a good bit during his years in Paddam Aram and he longed for the family he had left. Jewish tradition is that his mother, Rebekah, may have died sometime during Jacob's return from Paddam Aram to Succoth near home. He must have anticipated that she was dead by the time he had spent years in the far north country. Now with no parents left, Jacob felt the need of repairing things between himself and his only brother.

And he didn't know how things were going to go. A report from messengers sent ahead to gather intelligence said that Esau was headed to meet him, and he had 400 men with him. That sounded like trouble.

Jacob had had dreams from God. He was convinced that the God of Abraham his grandfather and Isaac his father was working in his life as well. Both his dreams at Bethel (Genesis 28:10ff) and Paddan Aram (Genesis 31:10ff) and his very experience of life convinced him of God's providence and his intent to reveal his leading to Jacob and to use him for some important purpose—indeed, to bless "all peoples of the earth" through his offspring (Genesis 28:14). While Jacob didn't understand entirely how this purpose would be worked out, he was convinced it involved his returning to his familial home, which meant reuniting with Esau somehow. The journey from Paddan Aram was stressful from the start because it was fraught with uncertainties and possibly great danger.

When Jacob arrived from the north at the Jabbok River, he was not far from home. Something about those last few miles brought him to the conviction that he was not finally prepared for the encounters that lay ahead. Jacob sent everyone else ahead of him where they themselves would encamp for the night, and he remained alone, because he felt the overwhelming need to seek the presence of God and sense what the Almighty wanted him to do. God had met him in dreams before. Perhaps he would grant him such an experience now that would give him direction and understanding.

A nameless man

Once Jacob was alone, a man began wrestling with him. Most scholars read the Hebrew verb as indicating wrestling though it may mean simply "struggle." Outside of some kind of boxing, however, it is difficult to imagine what the struggle might have been unless it were some kind of wrestling, even if not formal, as developed later by the Greeks. Clearly it involved constant entanglement.

But "[t]he brevity of the account leaves it unexplained, who the man is, how he appeared, and how the contest began."[55] We are simply clueless about how the encounter took place. The modern mind, accustomed to cinematic depiction, wants its imagination to have the void filled by an envisionment of the scene:

> In the gloom of a nearly dark night, Jacob comes back into the place he had planned to sleep. There he sees the outline of a dark figure awaiting him. Without any introduction or prelude to what was about to take place, the man approaches him and takes him in a wrestling grip. The two struggle, first one gaining the advantage and then the other. An inexplicable understanding of the rules of the engagement and the essentially matched skills and strength of the opponents comes over Jacob, and he realizes it isn't an attack by an enemy but something more transcendent. They engage and disengage, first one the aggressor and then the other. It isn't a playful struggle; it is serious, but respectful.

---

[55] Ryle, 324.

—We get none of this from the biblical text, though we would love to. (We will bring up this modern desire for cinematic envisionment again in the upcoming chapter on Balaam's Talking Donkey.)

Instead, what we have is the introduction of "a man." Period. If, as we think is probable, Jacob had no source of light, the man may have been indistinguishable in the desert gloom, just a figure barely outlined against the background of sand and shrub, looming in the darkness, waiting for Jacob as he came to the place he planned to bed down. And then, as the wrestling match began and continued, perhaps for hours, several details appear that lead to our certain understanding of who the man is. In fact, he left Jacob with no doubt as to his identity, even though he declined to tell him his name when Jacob asked for it. When the man was gone, Jacob said, **" I saw God face to face, and yet my life was spared"** (Genesis 32:30 NIV).

The first, curious clue of this man's identity was actually in something that seems counterintuitive. At some point near daybreak, the unidentified man **"saw that he could not overpower him."** (Heb. *lo yākol* - "did not prevail"). Translators variously render this verb as "could not prevail," "would not prevail," or simply "did not prevail," but solid thinking will yield the conclusion that if he *did* not, it was because, for whatever reason, he *could* not.

One would think that if "the man" were God in human form, he would have been able to prevail against Jacob with essentially no effort at all. But here is where the concept of a theophany comes into play.

We referred briefly to the concept previously in this book. A theophany is a physical appearance of God. Specifically, in the Old Testament God appeared numerous times to ancient figures, patriarchs and a few others, in human form for a brief encounter, usually to deliver very specific instructions, challenges or promises. And by the time of the New Testament events, it had become clear that God was triune—one God in three persons—and that the person of God who had walked with Adam and Eve in the garden, appeared to Abraham, spoken to Moses, shown himself as a warrior to Joshua, and wrestled with Jacob, was God the Son, many years prior to his incarnation as Jesus Christ.[56] In the centuries before there was anything constituting a written word of God, the Lord provided definitive elements of his revelation and leading through appearances of angels and sometimes of the Angel of the Lord— God the Son himself.

Some commentators define "theophany" differently; Henton Davies says "the story is not…a theophany." But elsewhere he writes plainly that this "man" who wrestled with Jacob was "God disguised as a man," and "Jacob has wrestled with God, seen his face, and still lives."[57] Davies' concept of theophany is apparently not the prevalent one as other scholars use it.

But there is a long history of denial that this unnamed man was God the Son. Targums (pre-New Testament Rabbinic commentary on scripture) repeatedly made word changes in this passage to downplay the actual divine identity of "the man." In v31, Targums read "an angel of the Lord" instead of God.[58] Such denials, involving a deliberate change in the original text, actually reinforce the obvious fact that the man was deity.

The head-scratching part of this story about the man wrestling with Jacob, a man unable to best him—who wouldn't or couldn't prevail against Jacob—is explained easily in understanding that the man was God the Son. He had taken a form commensurate with his purpose that evening, to wrestle one-on-one with Jacob. He had limited himself to human form in the first place—astounding in a

---

[56] The upcoming book, *Theophanies*, by the author, and many other books on the subject, go into great detail to elucidate the identity of God the Son in the theophanies of the Old Testament. Many prefer to call these "Christophanies."

[57] G. Henton Davies, *Genesis*, The Broadman Bible Commentary, Edited by Clifton J. Allen, (Nashville, Broadman Press, 1969), 235.

[58] Hamilton, 328.

way but quite simple for an omnipotent God, really. And so, in limiting himself to appearing and acting as one of his own creations, a human being, he also became the kind of man who had skills and strength very much like Jacob's. If he had not limited himself in that way, it would have been no match at all. Jacob would not have struggled; he would have been defeated in an instant. The ability of "the man" to prevail or not was the result of God the Son's having gotten down on Jacob's level in every way relevant to the night's event.

A draw

The wrestling match came to a remarkable conclusion. The text says that the unnamed man **"saw that he could not win"** (v25). As we pointed out above, translations of the tense and mood of this Hebrew verb, *yākōl,* vary widely. But the most important thing about the phrase is that this man, who turns out to have been God himself, is described as "realizing" at some point what, by implication, he didn't know before. This would be an argument against the divine identity of the man it if weren't for the fact that this is simply a prime example of anthropomorphism, widely occurring in the Old Testament. A similar statement casting God in the likeness of human beings is found in Jonah 3:10: **"When God saw what they did and how they turned from their evil ways, he relented and did not bring on them the destruction he had threatened"** (NIV). An omniscient God knew they would repent before they did. But rather than go into a parenthetical explanation of God's omniscience every time it figured into some event, biblical writers, who knew quite well that God wasn't limited in knowledge like man, often simply described his actions in human terms. In the case of Jacob's wrestling match, the man came to a point at which it was evident that with the limitations he had imposed upon himself in taking on flesh for that night's event, the match was a draw.

So, what did he do? **"He touched the socket of Jacob's hip"** (v25). The Hebrew root is *naga,* which can mean to touch or to strike, depending on context. Here, in the midst of physical struggle, one inclines to think it was more of a strike or hit. Davies says, "The 'unknown' unable to vanquish Jacob appears to foul him, for he touches, i.e., hits on, the socket of his thigh bone, so that Jacob's thigh is dislocated."[59] The characterization of the "touch" as a "foul" is consistent with formal wrestling, where a hold or contact disallowed by the rules is called a foul.

For God, of course, his actions were nothing unfair. The match was a draw. It would have gone on and on, since Jacob was clearly a man who did not, would not, give up—one of his admirable and useful characteristics. And even when his hip was put out of joint, he clung to the unnamed man the best he could. But the disjointed thigh would have quickly put an end to Jacob's struggling, and the conversation that brought things to a conclusion ensued.

The man wanted to be let go, **"for it is daybreak."** Scholars have debated why he gave this as a reason for the end of the match. Some commentators, not devoted to seeing "the man" as deity, suggest that folklore of the time about desert demons held that they had to perform their deeds in the dark of night and cease during the day. But nothing about this entire encounter suggests that Jacob was wrestling with a demonic being or a desert spirit. Everything says it was God. Why, then, an end to the match because it was about to dawn? Wenham says "it indicates a desire to continue to hide his identity. It may also hint at the idea that no man can see God and live."[60] We think it wasn't quite either of those reasons, for the simple fact that his identity *wasn't* obscured by leaving before the sun was up, and also that Jacob proclaimed he had, in fact, seen God and lived. The wrestling match was simply planned by God to be a nighttime event, akin to a restless night of fitful sleep, bothered

---

[59] Davies, 235.

[60] Wenham, 296.

by worries and uncertainty about decisions to be made or directions to be taken. God had taken a form appropriate for the most basic kind of contention, designed to reveal his identity not by some glorious visage, but by gradual recognition as Jacob both fought and thought. When the man's purpose was accomplished, Jacob's dark night—physical and spiritual—was over. But Jacob had a condition for letting the man go:

Request for a blessing

Jacob knew by now who the man was. He was the only one who could pronounce a blessing on him. Mere angels—God's messengers—never pronounced blessings. People could "bless" their children through some prophetic prediction, and fathers often did. But as for other-worldly beings, only God could bless. Jacob asked this God-man to bless him, before he would release his hold on him.

There was no hesitation on the man's part. As a preliminary to his blessing, he asked Jacob's name, not because he didn't know it, of course, but to emphasize the point he was about to make. Nor did Jacob hesitate to give it, though by now he knew that the man well knew who he was. And then the man said this:

"Your name will no longer be Jacob, but Israel, because you have struggled with God and with humans and have overcome" (v28). (Nearly every other translation unabashedly says "men" except the NRSV, and it as well as the later revisions of the NIV unnecessarily say "humans." The word in Hebrew is "men.") The blessing is the new name.

Ryle says, "The blessing is the sign of God's Presence and the pledge of man's salvation."[61] Ryle also points out that the name Israel can mean either "he who strives with God" or "God strives" —polar opposites. The Word Biblical Commentary notes that "Jacob recalled his past underhanded dealings; his new name, Israel,

---

[61] Ryle, 325.

recalled this incident in which he wrestled with God and prevailed."[62] We think the mere definition of the word does too little to give substance to the blessing, and that simply recalling one's history is not in itself blessing. The blessing is found in the implied prediction given by the man in the explanation of the new name: **"You will be called Israel, because you have wrestled with God and with men, and you have won"** (v28). The name set a precedent that would prove to be prescient for future centuries. Despite the opposition of enemies and even their taking Israel captive, the nation that came from Jacob would come back and prevail. And although with the destruction of the Temple and the further dispersion of Jews following the events of A.D. 70, and almost two millennia of their having no homeland, Israel's re-emergence as a nation in 1948 probably set in motion events that will culminate in what Paul described in Romans 11:26: **"All Israel will be saved."**

It should be added that as a prediction of his prevailing, Jacob was to understand that the one he had struggled with that night, who was God, would be the power by which Jacob would prevail in his future struggles with men.

The rest of the conversation was brief. Jacob asked for a fair exchange of names, which the man denied, but only because he implied that Jacob already knew it. And then before he left, he blessed Jacob. In spite of the fact that this blessing is spoken of explicitly in v29, the substance of the blessing is explained in v28, in the giving of the new name.

Jacob himself participated in a little naming, calling the place of his encounter "Peniel." Penuel, which occurs in v32, is the same word with a different grammatical case in old Hebrew.[63] Peniel means "the face of God."

---

[62] Wenham, 297.

[63] See Davies, 235.

Learning the Lessons

Jacob certainly learned some lessons from his experience that night at Jabbok's ford. In looking at the passage, what can we take away to our benefit?

Certainly, there are lessons, but we must do two things in deriving them: (1) avoid the kind of lightweight spiritualization that simply equates Jacob's night of physical struggling to a modern time of intense prayer; and (2) allow the wrestling of Jacob to inspire us to engage with God energetically in both prayer and life until we have felt his presence and received his blessing.

If these two things seem somewhat contradictory, that's because they are: the lessons of Jacob's wrestling with God are to be found in a dynamic tension between our puny powers and God's complete mastery over us.

1. *Life is not a breeze* An Attitude to Develop ☑
Authentic Christian living is not simple, not without adversaries, and not without struggle. If yours is, it's not authentic.

Some people find out immediately upon becoming Christians that theirs will not be an easy road. They may be surrounded by vehement or even violent opposition to Jesus Christ, or they may have to contend with the most Christ-less of atmospheres, going it alone for the Lord.

Other people realize with growing distress that their lives are increasingly defined by continual trials, personal failures, and directional uncertainty that have filled their pilgrimages. They may compare themselves with some others who seem to have had none of their troubles, and wonder if they have been on the wrong road all along.

The truth is that the typical Christian will eventually recognize that struggle has marked his life and some kind of persecution is *normal.* Realizing this and being at peace with it is important. As Paul wrote to Timothy, **"In fact, everyone who wants to live a godly life in Christ Jesus will be persecuted"** (2 Timothy 3:12 NIV).

2. Engage with God in prayer   A Teaching to Obey ☑

The Christian's prayer life should be a struggle against banal platitudes, an unburdening of a troubled heart, and a continual plea for guidance and blessing.

In some Christian traditions personal prayer is largely the repetition of the Lord's Prayer or liturgical prayers. The authentic Christian cannot even get by on such prayers much less grow deeper in his relationship with God. A serious Christian's prayer should engage him with God in the kind of spiritual conversation that allows him to be both honest and forthright with God (!) as well as humble and confessional.

David wrote in Psalm 142:2, **"I pour out before him my complaint; before him I tell my trouble"** (NIV). Every major translation employs the word "complaint" for David's Hebrew word *siach* in that verse. We should not apologize for unburdening ourselves to God. We have troubles and don't understand them. While we want to avoid grumbling and accusations that God is unfair or uncaring, telling him what we're going through and how we hurt or get angry or feel bewildered is not forbidden conversation on our part. Yes, God knows what we need before we ever speak, but we are human beings: we need to express ourselves, and prayer is how we do it.

Some Christians have discovered that the purpose of the Lord's Prayer in the individual's life is better served by using it as a skeleton to hang the rest of one's prayer life on. A serious and reflective believer will not be able to say, "Hallowed by thy name," many times by rote before he becomes aware that he may not be hallowing God's name, then and there or during the rest of his or her day. He may pause to fill in the blanks, think of other things he needs to say to God in the way of acknowledging his holiness. He or she may recall or realize other things that should be said or offered up in trembling silence as praise to the Almighty, the King of Creation.

By the time such prayer has worked through half the framework of the Lord's Prayer, it may have consumed more time than you think. Take time to pray. And engage with God. It's more important than you may have thought.

3. Don't give up
A Teaching to Obey ☑

Don't stop praying and don't stop struggling—against what holds you back and for what God wants you to be.

One of the greatest temptations of the Christian is to stop moving forward with God, stop struggling to understand, stop resisting the forces arraigned against him. While probably every Christian has wished for a sudden and miraculous solution to what fights against him, for most of us the answer is more *keeping on* than anything else:

- Mark 13:33   "Keep on the alert for you do not know when the appointed time will come" (NASB).
- Matthew 7:7 "Keep asking and it will be given to you; keep searching and you will find; keep knocking and the door will be opened to you" (HCSB).
- 1 Peter 4:19   "Keep on doing what is right and trust your lives to the God who created you, for he will never fail you" (NLT).
- 1 Peter 4:13   "Keep on rejoicing so that also at the revelation of his glory you may also rejoice and be overjoyed" (NASB).

Coitus Interruptus
Genesis 38:8-10

From the very first chapter of this little volume the reader has been reminded that the Bible can be a very "earthy" book. While some stories are couched in highly figurative language, others lay it all out in unapologetic detail—forget delicacy.

This little tale from the life of Judah and his sons Er and Onan deals with a subject that would be embarrassing for most contemporary people to talk about in anything less than a single-sex group, and probably only in clinical settings even then. It's just not table talk.

But it's a story with a biblical purpose, and it certainly fits our theme: it's downright curious!

> [6] Judah got a wife for Er, his firstborn, and her name was Tamar. [7] But Er, Judah's firstborn, was wicked in the LORD's sight; so the LORD put him to death.
>
> [8] Then Judah said to Onan, "Sleep with your brother's wife and fulfill your duty to her as a brother-in-law to raise up offspring for your brother." [9] But Onan knew that the child would not be his; so whenever he slept with his brother's wife, he spilled his semen on the ground to keep from providing offspring for his brother. [10] What he did was wicked in the LORD's sight; so the LORD put him to death also (Genesis 38:6-10 NIV).

This story is strange from stem to stern—from Er's death by the divine hand to Judah's shame in the latter part of the chapter.

103

We're going to focus on the part historically subject to the widest disagreement as to interpretation—v9. All the same, we have to set the scene by looking at what led to Onan's actions.

Discovering the Text

Levirate duty

Our story opens as Judah, one of the sons of Jacob, sets up a marriage for his son Er. Some modern people are routinely put off by this ancient custom. But in fact, what most people today in western cultures take for granted—that teens fall in love, get engaged, then tell their parents, then get married (in that order, at least in the *moral* tradition)—is a *very* late development in recorded history.

The young woman's name was Tamar, which means "date palm." Bible readers familiar with the history of King David will remember a couple of Tamars in his life (2 Samuel 13:1 and 14:27). Traditionally, many scholars have accepted the view that this Tamar that became Er's young widow was a Canaanite woman, possibly a Philistine, though there is no direct evidence for this belief.

She was a hapless woman from the start, however, as Er incurred the wrath of God for an entirely unexplained evil (v7), and God took his life. Much speculation has been done about this detail of the larger story, with at least one Targum holding that Er did the same thing his younger brother Onan did when having sex with Tamar.[64] Most scholars, if they comment at all on the scriptural assessment that Er **"was wicked in the LORD's sight,"** just think it was general depravity. It is interesting to note, however, that it is the first record in the Bible of God's putting someone to death—there had been some really evil characters described in the first thirty-seven chapters of Genesis, so this may be significant. But it

---

[64] Targum Pseudo-Jonathan Bereshit 38:7.

really isn't necessary to know. The implication is further that his death took place very early in the marriage, perhaps within days, and that poor Tamar was a widow before she had gotten used to being a bride.

Er's death invoked another practice that seems strange to the modern mind: the next oldest brother would have sex with the widow until she conceived and bore a boy. The child would be officially considered the child and heir of the deceased older brother—not the actual brother who fathered him. The next oldest brother was Onan.

Though it was later called the Law of Levirate Duty by the Hebrew people, it was a custom in the near east, middle and far east, and in some portions of Africa before the time of Abraham. Moses encoded some restrictions on it in what became Deuteronomy 25:5-10.[65] Some difference of opinion exists among scholars as to whether the widow became the next son's wife. We agree with the preponderance of them, who hold that she remained a sister-in-law.[66]

Onan objected to following through with this practice. The Scripture explains, **"Onan knew that the child would not be his."** It would not be *considered* his, even though it was.

Why was this a problem for him?

Evading responsibility

One of Onan's objections was the obvious element of greed. When the practice of the Levirate Duty was codified for Israel, Numbers 27:8-11 stated that "if a man dies without a son, then his inheritance is to pass to his daughter; if he has no daughter, then the inheritance is to pass to his brothers. Onan apparently [did] not want to father a son who [would] prevent him from receiving his

---

[65] Keil & Delitzsch, *op. cit. Vol 1,* 261.

[66] Hamilton, *Genesis,* 435, *et al.*

deceased brother's inheritance."[67] Keil and Delitzsch note that Onan apparently displayed "a despicable covetousness for his possession and inheritance."[68] Some commentators work out the fractions, which are not "all or nothing," but which would redound to Onan's benefit if he simply did not impregnate Tamar.

Onan and Er also may not have been on wonderful terms with one another. That may explain the fact that Onan, though he went through with taking Tamar to bed, made certain that she wouldn't have his child. Maybe he intended that to be his last slap in the face to his brother.

We might infer that another reason Onan took this tack was because he didn't want to experience the shame of not complying with the ancient custom. When Moses later wrote Deuteronomy and articulated what should happen to a man who wouldn't do his deceased brother the honor of raising up children to his name, he said the man should be publicly shamed. In a public ceremony the widow would spit in his face, take off one of his sandals—surely the man would have to be restrained for this to happen—and he and his whole other family would get the name, "The Family of the Unsandaled."

The method he used

Not wanting to be shamed, Onan probably thought he would get away with sabotaging the reproductive process by engaging in *coitus interruptus*—withdrawal before ejaculation, perhaps the first method of birth control ever devised. Since it's unlikely that he himself then told anyone what he was doing, it's almost certain that Tamar did, and that's how it became known.

The biblical account simply says, **"But Onan knew that the**

---

[67] Hamilton, 436.

[68] Carl Friedrich Keil and Franz Delitzsch, *Volume 1, Genesis - Judges 6:32*, Biblical Commentary on the Old Testament, (Lafayette, Indiana, Associated Publishers and Authors, 1960), 261.

offspring would not be his, so whenever he slept with his brother's wife, he released his semen on the ground so that he would not produce offspring for his brother" (Genesis 38:9 CSB). Nor was this a one-time thing. Commentators note that "[t]he tenses of the Hebrew verbs in verse 9 are frequentative,"[69] meaning that "whenever he had sex with her"[70] he practiced *coitus interruptus*. Virtually all translations now reflect this fact. Commentator Hamilton adds, "what makes Onan's sin so offensive is that he appears to undertake his responsibility, but he fakes it."[71]

Why he was put to death

The story, at least as far as Onan is concerned, concludes with the summary statement that **"What he did was wicked in the LORD's sight; so the LORD put him to death also"** (v10).

The major question for interpreting this curious story centers around **"What he did."** Why, specifically, was God angry?

The instruction to "raise up offspring for your brother" did not come directly from God; it came from Judah. But it was the instruction of a father in the line of Abraham, Isaac and Jacob, and surely carried the imprimatur of the Lord for carrying on the family line. God certainly wanted the instruction to be carried out. It wasn't, and the question is what was **"wicked in the LORD's sight"**?

The answer to this question places the interpreter in one of two major camps throughout history. One consists of those who believe that Onan's refusal to obey the instruction to produce children for his brother was an act of contempt for his brother and unconcern for his brother's legacy, disrespect for his father, and disregard for Er's widow, who would likely be childless. Further, it was disrespect for the long-term plan of God. As Wenham say, it was Onan's

---

[69] Davies, 257.

[70] Hamilton, 436.

[71] Hamilton, 436.

"disregard for the patriarchal promises."[72] Combined with the evident covetousness involved, these things made Onan's determined plan to evade responsibility a cause for divine displeasure. When **"the LORD put him to death"** he did so for these reasons.

The other interpretive camp sees the act of *coitus interruptus* itself as sinful, and identifies it as the focus of God's anger—though numerous sources combine this reason with Onan's contempt for family and tradition. Lengthy explanations of this view go back at least as far as St. Augustine, who helped originate and articulate the position of the Roman Catholic Church that sex for pleasure alone and not for procreation is sinful. Other Catholic notables chimed in over the centuries doubling down on this position. It explains why Catholics oppose birth control except for the "rhythm method." This interpretation gave rise to the term "onanism" for both *coitus interruptus* and masturbation.

The interpretation that sex is sinful unless it can—unimpeded—result in pregnancy, and that even ejaculation by any other means is equally wrong, is not supported by the broad spectrum of scripture. In fact, only this story supports it, and only by taking God's anger to refer to Onan's bedroom act, not his disobedience to his father and his contempt for his brother and for sacred tradition. While it is true that God's initial command to Adam and Eve (and then again to Noah) was to be fruitful and multiply, it is not true that the sexual knowledge of a husband and wife cannot be had for pleasure alone.

If anything, in fact, once you get to the New Testament, specific teachings by the Apostle Paul on the subject say nothing about procreation and everything about the appropriateness of marital intimacy for its own sake:

---

[72] Wenham, 365.

A husband should fulfill his marital responsibility to his wife, and likewise a wife to her husband. A wife does not have the right over her own body, but her husband does. In the same way, a husband does not have the right over his own body, but his wife does. Do not deprive one another sexually—except when you agree for a time, to devote yourselves to prayer. Then come together again; otherwise, Satan may tempt you because of your lack of self-control (1 Corinthians 7:3-5 HCSB).

Paul was quite clearly talking about sex for its own sake, irrespective of procreation. Not only is no hint of procreation found in these verses, but Paul taught that not only does a husband owe his wife the privilege and pleasure of sexual union, but also she owes him the same. This is manifest proof that the Scriptures teach that married couples should enjoy sex whether or not it even *can* lead to pregnancy.

While most modern commentators focus only on evasion of sacred responsibility as the reason for God's anger, some (Derek Kidner, for one) play both ends against the middle. Kidner writes, "The enormity of Onan's sin is in its studied outrage against the family, against his brother's widow and against his own body."[73] We have the impression that Kidner and others who include a sort of left-handed reference to *coitus interruptus* as part of the reason for God's anger do it as a nod to the Catholic view, which they go no further to defend. We think the rejection of this view is demanded not only because of the purely sexually repressive nature of the idea but also mostly because of the lack of biblical evidence that in itself it was offensive to God.

While the pursuit of this issue has taken us just slightly off course with the interpretation of this curious story, it has helped us

---

[73] Kidner, 188.

deal with a gross distortion of the story's meaning as proposed by some interpreters in history. The notion that Onan's act should militate against birth control *per se* or even masturbation is simply not a legitimate part of this scriptural account. To make it so is to de-emphasize the seriousness of the customs by which the patriarchs lived and the expectations of their conduct in all kinds of situations. The Levirate Duty was a vital part of family progeniture and the societal structure. It was not to be taken lightly or thwarted for covetous reasons.

Learning the Lessons

The Levirate Duty in our day is certainly not part of western culture in general, though it is subject to varying traditions among orthodox Jews. The State of Israel outlawed it. It has seen spotty incidence in other middle eastern cultures.

But we needn't concern ourselves with what is basically proprietary to Judaism, not Christianity. Our concern is what lessons we can derive from this ancient tale for modern living as followers of Jesus Christ?

1. Respect for family
An Attitude to Develop ☑

Growing up and becoming adults, all of us should develop and demonstrate a deep respect for family and for parental guidance.

Whatever the sin of Er was, we can easily deduce that Judah had lost any authority over his first son. One cannot imagine that Judah didn't try to teach Er how to live, but Er obviously rebelled thoroughly and became so wicked that the biblical writer recorded the first divine execution—God put him to death.

Onan may not have gone as far as his elder brother by the time Er dropped dead, but in doing what he did he showed exceeding disrespect for his father and for what he no doubt knew about the divine promises to great, great, grandfather Abraham, great grandfather Isaac, and grandfather Jacob. Onan was out for himself, exclusively.

There has always been a thing we now call a "generation gap." In some eras it seems more pronounced because of dramatic cultural changes. A popular song in 1988 (and since) begins, "Every generation blames the one before." It goes on to say: "So we open up a quarrel / Between the present and the past / We only sacrifice the future / It's the bitterness that lasts."[74] No one expects the younger generation to mirror the lives of their parents or grandparents. But what *should be* expected of every generation is a mature attempt to understand the good things that formed their parents lives, and theirs before them, and to respect and reflect those values in their own lives. Apart from entirely superficial artifacts of culture that change, the lingering values of family and the wisdom achieved by forebears should not be dismissed by the young.

It helps for parents to be convincing rather than coercive, and to demonstrate their wisdom rather than simply demagogue it. But however good or not-so-good parents are at doing their job, children —and we're all children of someone—should do their best to respect what their forebears brought to their lives in the way of tradition and wisdom.

2. Greed and generosity
A Teaching to Obey ☑

Everyone makes a choice in life whether to be greedy or generous. Make the right one.

Wall Street's Ivan Boesky famously said, "Greed is all right, by the way. I want you to know that. I think greed is healthy. You can be greedy and still feel good about yourself." Fictional character

---

[74] Brian David Robertson, "The Living Years," 1988, Atlantic, Track 2 on "Living Years," 1988, LP.

Gordon Gekko in the film "Wall Street" later shortened that to simply, "Greed is good."[75] Despite attempts to defend it, however, greed is not good. In seeking one's own benefit only, one usually ignores or deliberately excludes the benefit of others, and that produces hurt, loss, and bitterness.

Greed isn't the same as "enlightened self-interest," which is basically doing things that bring good to a wide range of people, that avoid hurting people as much as possible, and that benefit the doer as well. An example would be a business that provides a needed service at a fair price that, while not taking advantage or price-gouging, still earns the businessperson a good living.

Some careers are ready-made invitations to developing greedy living, and avoiding falling into the greed-trap becomes a lifetime challenge. And what people do with their money reflects whether they are basically out for number one or actively responsive to the needs and the good of other people. Remember, in the end you can't take it with you. No one ever saw a Brinks armored car following a hearse.

---

[75] "Wall Street," directed by Oliver Stone, (American Entertainment Partners, 1987).

GOD FIXIN' TO KILL MOSES
Exodus 4:24-26

Some of the most unusual and widely misunderstood stories in the Bible are undoubtedly very ancient tales. They are often both arcane and archaic, and contain terse language and a lack of linguistic transitions that fuller, more contemporaneous stories would have. And sometimes, they're situated in larger accounts as if they had been cut and pasted from their external sources.

Such is a brief travel story about Moses and his wife, after Moses had been commissioned to lead Israel out of Egypt, and his little family left Midian to go there. The last word Yahweh gave Moses about his upcoming mission was that after many wonders from God's hand, Pharaoh would still, and finally, refuse to let the Israelites go, and Moses would tell him that God would take the life of his—Pharaoh's—son.

With that ominous message, Moses got the family together and headed for Egypt. Here's where the odd travel story appears in the account:

> [24] At a lodging place on the way, the LORD met Moses and was about to kill him. [25] But Zipporah took a flint knife, cut off her son's foreskin and touched Moses' feet with it. "Surely you are a bridegroom of blood to me," she said. [26] So the LORD let him alone. (At that time she said "bridegroom of blood," referring to circumcision.) (Exodus 4:24-26 NIV).

We've chosen the New International Version for our beginning text for the overall quality of its rendering. But it should be noted right away that there are some words the NIV has used that vary from the original text.

First, in v24 the Hebrew has the Lord meeting "him," and the NIV has supplied "Moses" as interpretive clarification. There can be no serious doubt that Moses was meant, but the reader should know when the translators are dipping into the realm of interpretation. The original Hebrew has only "him."

Second, the NIV renders the Hebrew word for "sharp stone" as "flint knife," which no doubt it was, but not so specific. However, it was a flint knife that had been used from ancient times in the circumcision ritual—many other rituals in not only Hebrew but other cultures employed the flint knife—and though by Moses' time various metals were in common use, the flint knife was kept around for traditional uses.

When Zipporah was finished with the circumcision she either "touched" Moses' feet with it[76] or she "threw" it at his feet, depending on the translation. Many of the older or "mainstream" translations —KJV, NKJV, NASB, AMP, CSB, JPS, WBT, and WEB, for instance —have some version of "cast" or "threw" for the Hebrew verb. Others—NIV, NLT, ESV, BSB, LSB, CEV, DRB, GWT, ISV, LSV, NET, NRSV, and YLT (whew!)—have "touch." The difference is dramatic. In English, "threw" or "cast" implies some level of irritation, complaint, or even animosity in Zipporah. "Touched" communicates perhaps only some kind of ritual motion. Whether Zipporah was angry is left for her subsequent words to suggest.

Further, the Hebrew reads literally "at his feet" (*l*e*raglaw*), and the NIV translators chose to tell us that "his" means "Moses' feet." There is not unanimity on this interpretation, however. Some older and respected commentators think it was the visible Yahweh's feet

---

[76] More on "feet" when we reach that word specifically.

114

that was meant, and a few (Jewish interpreters among them) think it was at the feet of Moses' son Eliezer. But among all the translations we've already mentioned, none gives a name other than Moses, and the rest render the word literally as "his," and leave the interpretation to us.

The NIV goes on to say, "the LORD let him alone" when the Hebrew says only that "he" let him alone. There is virtually no disagreement with this interpretation, but again, the reader is advised that the original text doesn't have "the LORD."

Comparisons of various translations in the case of these words have already given us some insight into the way the story has been understood by theologians. Let's dig a little deeper to discover what this story is about.

Discovering the Text

"a lodging place"

The mysterious nature of this tale begins right away in v24, which tells us that, obeying the command of the Lord, Moses and his family left for Egypt, and that on the way they stopped at **"a lodging place"** (Hebrew *bammalow^{e}n*) which some translators render as "an inn" and others, such as CSB, have "campsite." The difference is not significant.

"the LORD met"

The reason they stopped and perhaps the length of stop they made, however, may have been affected by what is said next. **"The LORD met Moses and was about to kill him."** Depending on the translation of two words in the original, several quite different views have been proposed for what the verse means.

First, the word the NIV renders as **"met"** seems straightforward, but "met" in the Hebrew often carries with it an implication of something more than just one's happening to see someone in passing. It is that sense that the CSB tries to get at when it translates the word as "confronted." And the Legacy Standard Bible translates it "encountered." This was a meeting called by God. It was an intervention.

If, as we think, "met" means something more significant here than a happenstance meeting, it is possible that the confrontation was more than Moses' just "feeling like God was present." John Gill and others think the Lord may have met Moses in the way that the Lord met Balaam (Numbers 22:20-24) and under interestingly similar circumstances. God told Balaam to go with Balak's men if they asked him to; yet when he did just that, "the angel of the LORD" confronted him with "drawn sword in his hand" (v23, NIV). Here in Exodus, Moses is told to go to Egypt and begin to deliver the Israelites, and when he starts out to do that very thing, the Lord meets him and is about to kill him. Might God have done so through a theophany—the angel of the LORD—as with Balaam?

The Pulpit Commentary is indecisive and therefore inclusive on the matter: "A sudden seizure, followed by a dangerous illness, is generally thought to be intended ...but the words seem more appropriate to a miraculous appearance, like that of the angel to Balaam (Numbers 22:31). Still, it is quite possible that nothing more than an illness is meant."[77]

So far, there isn't enough evidence merely in the possible implication of the verb "met" for us to decide whether or not a theophany was being described.

However, the sense of "met" is tied intimately to what God intended to do to Moses, and how:

"was about to kill him"

What is meant by "kill?" If it were a theophany Moses

---

[77] George Rawlinson, *Exodus*, The Pulpit Commentary, (New York, Funk and Wagnalls, 1897), 161.

encountered, one could easily envision a divine sword doing the job, but the weight of interpretation is on the side of God's striking Moses with a physical malady.

Alan McNeile described the whole phrase as a "primitive anthropomorphic way of saying that Moses had fallen dangerously ill."[78] Gispen calls it an "acute illness" and Gill says, "a disease that threatened him with death."[79] If either of the two generally mentioned possibilities of what "was about to kill him" is more likely than the other, it would seem to be this (probably) sudden onset of some illness that, if not forestalled, would lead to Moses' death in short order.

More evidence that this may be true might be found in the implication that Zipporah, not Moses, conducted the circumcision —assuming for the moment that it was one of the sons, not Moses, who was circumcised. Moses may have been suddenly bedridden and seriously out of commission due to incapacitating illness, and therefore unable to perform the circumcision himself.

Of course, if God's whole intent were to kill Moses with illness, a heart attack or stroke would have been quicker than whatever it was. Instead, we are told that the Lord **"was *about* to kill him"** (emphasis ours) as in the NIV, NLT, CEV, *et al.* Other versions even more strangely say, "tried to kill him" (GNT, RSV), or "sought to kill him" (KJV, NKJV, NASB, HCSB). Oddly enough, the HCSB, which is the parent translation to the later CSB (the name "Holman" simply removed) changed "sought" to "intended" in the latter. Several commentators remark, perhaps wryly, that if God were merely "trying" to kill Moses, he certainly would have succeeded.

Perhaps an even more casual modern translation with a Southern American flair might say, "God was fixin' to kill him!"

---

[78] Alan H. McNeile, *The Book of Exodus*, (London, Methuen Publishers, 1908), 27.

[79] John Gill, *An Exposition of the Old Testament*, (In the public domain).

For "tried" (or "was about") the Hebrew text has the word *baqash*, which can be rendered as "seek, desire, try, attempt, require, asked, look for, intend to, etc,"[80] depending on context. We think the context here requires something less "anthropomorphic" than "tried" or even "sought," and the translators of the NIV, NLT, and the CSB agreed. The Lord was in no way thwarted in his "attempt" to kill Moses. Instead, the verb communicates the idea that in God's providential timing and sovereign control of events, he was confronting Moses with what Bruckner labels *"the sine qua non. Moses cannot lead the people without a circumcised family."*[81]

Before we leave this phrase, however, we still have to decide who is meant by "him." Kill *him.* Who is *him?*

It seems obvious, but historically, is hasn't been. Adam Clarke thought "him" meant one of Moses' sons, either Eliezer or Gershom. John Gill and most others since have concluded that "him" means Moses. John Durham, in his major work on Exodus, says that "it is hardly reasonable to claim that anyone except Moses is the object of Yahweh's encountering action."[82] We agree.

Now, oddly enough there is no explanation after the words of v24 as to why Zipporah went into action performing a circumcision. We can only conclude that Moses knew instinctively, or that God, who had struck him with his sudden illness, revealed it clearly to his heart and mind. Zipporah may have said, 'Why would God be doing this to you?!' And Moses probably told his wife, 'I know why, and so do you. One of our sons has not been circumcised.' This would have prompted her to act quickly:

---

[80] Stackexchange, Accessed May 2, 2024. https://hermeneutics.stackexchange.com/questions/68942/what-is-the-meaning-of-sought-to-in-exodus-424.

[81] James K. Bruckner, *Exodus*, (Peobody, MA, Hendrickson Publishers, 2008) 54.

[82] J. I. Durham, *Exodus*, Word Biblical Commentary, (Dallas, Texas, Word, Inc., 1987) 59.

"Zipporah took a flint knife"

We have already looked at the fact that the Hebrew in this phrase is literally "sharp stone" and that without any debate it meant a flint knife. Commentator Jack Sasson says it was the mandatory implement for circumcision.[83] Many sources tell us that flint knives were used for ceremonial cutting of flesh, such as embalming, and that the reason is that "stone was regarded as a purer and more sacred material than metal."[84]

Readers familiar with the original science fiction television series "Star Trek" may remember an episode in which Captain Kirk and Spock time travel and get stuck in 1930s America. Spock is trying desperately to construct a sophisticated computer circuit they have in their future. Frustrated, he says to Kirk, "Captain, you're asking me to work with equipment which is hardly very far ahead of stone knives and bearskins."[85] Spock was disappointingly aware of the antiquated equipment he was forced to use. But in our tale, Zipporah did not simply "make do" with her stone knife. She used the time-honored implement that carried the significance of tradition going back to Abraham.

However, we might well be curious as to why Moses and Zipporah had a ceremonial flint knife with them in the first place. Did people regularly carry them around? Perhaps the chances of there being a flint knife increase if the traveling group was not just Moses, Zipporah and their two sons, but a larger entourage managing tents and other packs. We have no clue about these things. But it is possible that, considering that only one son was circumcised during this "lodging place" incident, the other son had

---

[83] Jack M. Sasson, *Journal of Biblical Literature*, 85.4 (1966), (Society of Biblical Literature, 1966), 474.

[84] Albert Barnes, *Notes on the Bible*, (Grand Rapids, Michigan, Baker Books, 2001), 16.

[85] Star Trek, Season 1, Episode 28, "The City on the Edge of Forever," April 6, 1967.

already been circumcised, meaning that Moses and Zipporah probably did possess the ceremonial instruments for accomplishing the rite.

"cut off her son's foreskin"

After acquiring, or simply finding, a flint knife, Zipporah then "cut off her son's foreskin" (the Hebrew does not have the specific word "circumcise" here). Several questions arise at this point, including why Zipporah and not Moses performed the act and how she knew what to do. If, as we have suggested already, Moses was too desperately ill to do it himself, that may answer one question. And if one of their sons had already been circumcised, that may imply that Zipporah had been involved and knew how from that experience.

Older sources suggest: "How Zipporah knew what to do is unclear, but it may be that as Moses held his sons down, she wielded the knife."[86]

The remaining question is which son Zipporah circumcised. Most commentators agree that it would have been Eliezer, the younger of the two if, as it appears, the firstborn, Gershom, had already been circumcised. There being absolutely no clue in the text why Eliezer would not have been circumcised when he came along, suggestions have been made by many commentators going way back. Keil and Delitzsch decline to say specifically which son, but imply Eliezer when they say, "Moses had probably omitted circumcision simply from regard to his Midianitish wife, who disliked this operation."[87] Apparently, she had seen it done once, to Gershom, and decided enough was enough. Jamieson-Fausset-Brown Bible

---

[86] Connectusfund, May 17, 2024, https://connectusfund.org/exodus-4-24-meaning-of-the-lord-met-moses-and-was-about-to-kill-him. Numerous websites quote this same material, whose original source is not known to the author and may well be in the general domain.

[87] Keil and Delitzsch, *op. cit. Vol 1*, 352.

Commentary says of Moses that "he was deeply pained and grieved at the thought of having, to please his wife, postponed or neglected the circumcision of one of his sons, probably the younger."[88]

So it was Eliezer who was circumcised on this occasion. Undoubtedly, however, what comes next raises the most widely debated subject in this story.

"and touched Moses' feet with it"

As we noted previously, the name "Moses" is not in this phrase, which in the Hebrew is simply, "at his feet." But undoubtedly Moses is the target. John Gill was aware in the mid 1700s that there were those who thought it was Eliezer's feet that were meant, and he argued against that idea, mostly because of what Zipporah subsequently said. The Cambridge Bible, taking the position that it was Moses who was uncircumcised, says that Zipporah "made [the foreskin of her son] touch his feet," meaning Moses', "to make her son's circumcision count as her husband's."[89] Is it possible that Moses himself was uncircumcised—perhaps in addition to his younger son?

The question is important, because it would affect our understanding of why God "was about to kill him." Not only would it have been inappropriate for the man who was about to deliver the Israelites from Egypt to have an uncircumcised son, but more seriously it would have been a major violation of the pre-existing covenant of God with Abraham for Moses himself to be uncircumcised.

Sources such as H. L. Ellison say, "Clearly Moses was circumcised,

---

[88] Robert Jamieson, A. R. Fausset and David Brown, *A Commentary, Critical, Practical, and Explanatory on the Old and New Testaments*, (Hartford, Connecticut, S. S. Scranton and Company, 1878), 50.

[89] S. R. Driver, *The Book of Exodus*, Cambridge Bible for Schools and Colleges, (Cambridge, England, Cambridge University Press, 1929), 32.

for this was the case with probably all upper-class Egyptians."[90]

John Cragan isn't so sure: "The Egyptians did not practice circumcision, whereas the Hebrews [in Egypt] apparently did."[91]

John Durham, in his tome of research, speaks of the compiler of Exodus who included this story, and says, "he [the compiler] clearly believed that Moses was uncircumcised and that Yahweh determined to stop him en route to Egypt for that reason."[92]

"However," says another writer, "in ancient Egypt and elsewhere in Africa, only part of the foreskin was removed."[93] An incomplete circumcision would have been objectionable to the Israelites.

But the Egypt Museum states categorically, "Circumcision was practiced in ancient Egypt. It was a common cultural and religious practice that dates back to at least the Old Kingdom period (2686-2181 BC)."[94] Clearly the experts do not agree.

Perhaps a better way to arrive at a probable answer is to consult Exodus, which says, "Now a man from the house of Levi went and took as his wife a Levite woman. The woman conceived and bore a son, and when she saw that he was a fine child, she hid him three months" (Exodus 2:1-2). The child was Moses, subsequently "discovered" by the daughter of Pharaoh floating in a basket in the Nile, and adopted by her as her son. But for his first three months he was with his faithful Israelite parents, descendants of Levi. Is there really any possibility that Moses wasn't circumcised, given these facts?

---

[90] Henry L. Ellison, *Exodus*, (Philadelphia, Westminster Press, 1903), 28.

[91] John F. Craghan, *Exodus*, (Collegeville, Minnesota, Liturgical Press, 1985), 20.

[92] J. I. Durham, *Exodus*, Word Biblical Commentary, (Dallas, Texas, Word, Inc., 1987), 58.

[93] Wikipedia, "History of Circumcision," Accessed May 17, 2024. https://en.wikipedia.org/wiki/History_of_circumcision) The article cites as its source Doyle, D. (October 2005). "Ritual male circumcision: a brief history" (PDF). The Journal of the Royal College of Physicians of Edinburgh. 35 (3): 279–285.

[94] Egypt Museum, "Circumcision in Ancient Egypt," Accessed May 17, 2024. https://egypt-museum.com/ circumcision-in-ancient-egypt/.

We don't think so. Whether or not the Egyptians circumcised, or how, Moses wasn't in Pharaoh's household until after three months. We think it not defensible to claim that Moses was uncircumcised. The encounter at a "campsite" on the way to Egypt was about one of his sons, probably Eliezer, being uncircumcised.

Part of the reason some interpreters think it was Moses who was uncircumcised is the assumption that God's confrontation with Moses, with its attendant threat of death (by whatever means), was inexplicable as to its seriousness unless it were Moses who didn't conform to the covenant condition. Their conclusion that Moses himself must have been the cause of the threat led some theologians to say that Zipporah's act of throwing the circumcised flesh at Moses' feet (or touching them with it) was a means of ritually and symbolically transferring the benefits of circumcision to Moses, when—in these interpreters' view—Moses would have been unable to sustain the rite himself and continue promptly on his journey. Those "facts" all fit together, but if even one of them is disproved, the notion falls apart. And, we argue, a "symbolic" circumcision would seem to have been entirely insufficient to satisfy God's demand. If it were vital enough for God to interrupt Moses' journey and set about killing him, nothing but the real thing would satisfy his purpose.

Bottom line, we think it's Moses' son Eliezer who was uncircumcised.

But now, what was it that Zipporah did when she had finished circumcising her younger son? She **"touched Moses' feet with it"** (v25).

Let's list a few of the comments made by scholars on this phrase:

- "Zipporah touched Moses' feet with the proof of circumcision."[95] (*Why proof was needed, or why touching Moses' in any way was*

[95] GotQuestions, Accessed May 10, 2024, https://www.gotquestions.org/kill-Moses.html.

necessary, rather than simply showing him, we're not sure.)

- "The touching of Moses' feet with the foreskin of her son was symbolic of the sacrifice…that her marriage to Moses had required of her."[96]
- "…the literal rendering is 'his feet', which in reality refers to the private parts (cp. Isa. 6: 2)."[97]
- " To transfer the effect of the rite, Zipporah touched the severed foreskin of her son to the genitals of Moses."[98]
- "Zipporah touched the foreskin of Gershom to Gershom's genitals from which it had been removed. 'Feet' is one of the Hebrew euphemisms for genitals. She thus had physically circumcised Gershom, then immediately she symbolically used the removed foreskin to touch Gershom's genitals and said the 'right words.'"[99] *(As Keil and Delitzsch said, such an allusion would give no reasonable sense.[100])*
- "'Feet' *(regel)* here is likely a euphemism for male genitalia, as in Isaiah 7:20 (with reference to pubic hair) and in Judges 3:24 and 1 Samuel 24:3 (with reference to relieving oneself)."[101]
- "Moses' feet, undoubtedly. The action was petulant and reproachful. Zipporah regarded the bloody rites of her husband's religion as cruel and barbarous, and cast the foreskin of her son at his feet, as though he were a Moloch requiring a bloody

[96] W. H. Gispen, *Exodus*, (Grand Rapids, Michigan, Zondervan, 1982), 63.

[97] Ronald E. Clements, *Exodus*, (Cambridge, England, Cambridge University Press, 1972), 31.

[98] Durham, *op. cit.*, 59.

[99] Douglas K. Stuart, *Exodus*, The New American Commentary, (Nashville, Holman Reference, 2006), 155.

[100] Keil and Delitzsch, *op. cit. Vol. 1*, 352.

[101] Ralph F. Wilson, JesusWalk Bible Study Series, Accessed June 6, 2024. https://www.jesuswalk.com/moses/appendix_4.htm.

offering."[102]

Interestingly, but perhaps not surprisingly, commentators from the 1700s and 1800s are not inclined to say that "feet" might have meant "genitals." It isn't that they were unaware of the probably euphemistic usage of "feet" in other Bible texts. It may have been the inward pressure of modesty or delicacy that kept them from consciously even considering the word to be a circumlocution. But it's entirely possible that, believing that it was *not* Moses who was uncircumcised but rather his son, they reasoned that touching Moses' privates with Eliezer's foreskin wouldn't have made any sense. A rendering of "feet" as "feet" and nothing more would therefore be called for.[103]

As Freud famously said, "Sometimes a cigar is just a cigar."

Finally, we come to the words Zipporah spoke when the circumcision was completed, as she then interacted with Moses:

"'Surely you are a bridegroom of blood to me,' she said."

This phrase, which seems to be an incantation or a formal pronouncement, occurs nowhere else in scripture, where in this verse it is repeated by way of explanation, that it referred to the circumcision. The modern reader generally isn't acquainted with this saying. Again, we gather from commentators:

- "This ancient phrase, as Mitchell [VT 19 [1969] 94–105, 111–12) has demonstrated, is a phrase of marital relationship

---

[102] George Rawlinson, *Genesis-Numbers*, A Bible Commentary for English Readers, (London, Cassell and Company, LTD, n.d.), 204.

[103] Even Durham, who thinks that Moses was uncircumcised, called this symbolic event "a temporary remedy," in his cited work, p59. Moses would have had to be actually circumcised eventually. We have no record of that, which may or may not help prove that he was circumcised to begin with.

…Perhaps there was a similar ritual statement in the wedding ceremony."[104]

- "…the fact that she called Moses 'bridegroom of blood' shows that she felt that circumcision was cruel to her child, and yet this was the only way for her to keep Moses as her husband. …Moses was her bridegroom through the circumcision of her sons and had become her bridegroom once again since his life was spared, but not without the shedding of blood."[105]

- "A bloody husband. Literally, 'a bridegroom of blood.' The words are clearly a reproach; and the gist of the reproach seems to be that Moses was a husband who cost her dear, causing the blood of her sons to be shed in order to keep up a national usage which she regarded as barbarous."[106]

- "Zipporah calls Moses a blood-bridegroom, 'because she had been compelled, as it were, to acquire and purchase him anew as a husband by shedding the blood of her son' "[107]

- "The meaning is: The marriage bond between us is now sealed by blood."[108]

- "…having brought the bloody evidence, exclaimed in the painful excitement of her feelings that from love to him she had risked the life of her child."[109]

- "…not in an angry upbraiding way, as if he was a bloody cruel man to oblige her to do such an action, but rather in a congratulatory way, as being thankful and rejoicing, that by this means, through the blood of the circumcision, she had saved her husband's life; and as it were in that way had bought him, and

---

[104] Durham, *op. cit.*, 59.

[105] Gispen, 64.

[106] Rawlinson, 161.

[107] Keil and Delitzsch, *op. cit.*, Vol.1, 352.

[108] Barnes, *op. cit.*, 16.

[109] Robert Jamieson, A. R. Fausset and David Brown, *op. cit.*, 50.

afresh espoused him to herself as her husband."[110]

- "She was not an Israelite and may have thought it a barbaric custom."[111]

What we learn from these commentators is that Zipporah was bitter, or she wasn't. She was thankful, or not. And she knew Israelite marriage customs, or maybe she didn't. In English, her words seem a bit short or angry.

While there is no hard evidence of Zipporah's attitude in this incident, we think George Rawlinson was onto something in his remarks quoted above from Ellicott's *Bible Commentary for English Readers.* We think Zipporah was being reproachful, and that throwing the bloody skin at Moses' feet was not particularly symbolic, just an obvious place to toss it, as if to say, "There! I hope it makes you happy!" And if Durham is right as he suggests above, that the words were part of an ancient wedding ceremony, Zipporah simply chose them to express sarcasm, lacing them with her disgust. We don't think she was being deeply spiritual about anything at this point, although it would seem from later passages about her and the children (Exodus 18:2-7) that she got over the incident. It simply took a while for her to come to accept and value the customs of the Jews.

With the circumcision and the ritual completed, v26 says **"the LORD let him alone."** The Hebrew word is *wayyirep*, which often carries the idea of loosening one's grip. The Lord relented.

Looking at the entire story, perhaps it's best to observe that many scholars believe that the version of Exodus we have in the Bible is the result of not only Moses' basic writing, but also a few rabbinical edits in the early years as the Pentateuch was kept. We know of some of those edits or additions because they're so obvious:

---

[110] John Gill, *op. cit.* 52.

[111] EnduringWord, Accessed April 25, 2024, https://enduringword.com/bible-commentary/exodus-4/.

the statement in Exodus 12:3 that Moses was the most humble man on earth—hardly the sort of thing a humble man himself would write; and the concluding verses of Deuteronomy about Moses' burial and how great a man he was—again, an obvious addition by subsequent writers, probably rabbis.

This story about Zipporah and the circumcision bears evidence of that very kind of rabbinical editing in the last phrase of v26, where the explanation is given that Zipporah said, "bridegroom of blood," in reference to circumcision—as if the reader might not know. Moses would have known, for certain, so the explanation doesn't seem to come from his hand. But in a generation or two, when perhaps the words used in what was then possibly an ancient marriage ceremony might have been lost, maybe his readers wouldn't know them anymore. So a redactor, whoever he may have been, added the explanation. Clearly the Holy Spirit deigned to approve of the amendment.

This entire story appears to have been dropped into the overall Exodus account. Perhaps, even though the tale was well known, Moses left it out for reasons of his vaunted humility. In its present, awkwardly brief and somewhat confusing form, it seems difficult to interpret. But as Ellison wrote, "It is just an incident like this, as mysterious to the early rabbis as it is to us, which shows how carefully old material was preserved, even if it was no longer understood."[112]

After all this discovery, we can posit an expanded translation of our own, incorporating what we've learned:

[24] At a stopping place on the way, the LORD confronted Moses, striking him with a sudden and serious illness, and he would have taken his life in that way. [25] But Zipporah, learning Moses was at the point of death because of an

---

[112] Ellison, *op. cit.*, 28.

uncircumcised son, took a flint knife, circumcised Eliezer, and took the foreskin and threw it at Moses' feet, saying, "Surely you are a bloody bridegroom to me." [26] (The words were part of an ancient ritual referring to circumcision.) And when she had done that, the Lord relented: Moses quickly recovered (Exodus 4:24-26 RFS).

As obscure as this story seems to be, it opens up like a desert flower when subjected to intense scrutiny. And as we get the flavor of its factual matter and its principles, we can gather some theological and practical lessons for Christian living.

Learning the Lessons

1. Hypocrisy   An Action to Take ☑

God expects those who *preach* obedience to him to *be* obedient to him.

While in no way minimizing the obligation *every* follower of Jesus Christ has to be an obedient disciple, we recognize there is a heightened expectation of those called to particular and public ministry to be in conformity to the spiritual, moral and ethical standards God has revealed in his word. A preacher of the gospel or other minister in the church is under special scrutiny. More than most other Christians, leaders are the standards by which non-Christians judge the truth of the Bible and the validity of the gospel. Paul listed for Timothy numerous things that an overseer (pastor, elder, etc.) in the church should conform to in a special way—faithfulness to his wife, self-control, temperance, peacefulness, etc. He must also manage his own household well and see to it that his children are obedient. Then Paul adds parenthetically, "If anyone does not know how to manage his own household, how will he take care of God's church?" (1 Timothy 3:5, CSB). Hypocrisy in leaders is particularly inappropriate.

Again, exemplary discipleship should characterize all Christians, but God holds leaders to an even higher standard (see James 3:1).

2. *Effectiveness* A Teaching to Obey ☑

Effectiveness in every area of Christian living is dependant on personal surrender to the mastery of Christ over your life.

Christians often wonder why they aren't "going great guns" in their Christian living, and it may just be that upon inspection their lives would be found to be not fully surrendered to Jesus' lordship in perhaps many areas. But often it's just one area, something they've denied was wrong, something they've ignored with the hope it would go away, or something they needed to do and haven't done yet. And that something, though it may be private, might also be quite glaring.

Sometimes, as with Moses, God reveals the un-surrendered area of life, the critical disobedience, the flawed faithfulness, before the believer launches into his special calling. Other times, a Christian may forge ahead into an area of service before preparing sufficiently. He may be destined to sputter and backfire because of some crucial weakness in his commitment.

God doesn't forget what he tells us to do or not do. When he breaks through our willful distraction and makes us see where we're not surrendered to him, we have the opportunity to yield, be restored, and go on to effective spiritual living in the fellowship of Christ.

NEVER HEARD OF A TALKING DONKEY?
Numbers 22:20-35

Long before the early 1960s television show about a talking horse, "Mr. Ed," there was a story in the Bible about another talking equine, a donkey, belonging to the infamous Balaam, a diviner.

The whole Bible story about Balaam takes up three chapters in Numbers and then is discontinued, meaning that several other Bible writers mention Balaam but the tale is mostly told when Numbers 22-24 have wrapped it up.

What makes the story curious is, of course, the aforementioned talking donkey, an account that takes up just thirteen verses in Numbers 22. The short title given to the story is usually "Balaam's ass," which comes from the King James and older translations, where most new ones render the Hebrew word (אתון - *athon*) as "[female] donkey," for obvious and unfortunate, modern linguistic reasons. This little beast of burden garners our sympathy for being the object of Balaam's temper, when all she did was stop when confronted with her maker.

²⁰ God came to Balaam at night and said to him, "Since these men have come to summon you, get up and go with them, but you must only do what I tell you." ²¹ When he got up in the morning, Balaam saddled his donkey and went with the officials of Moab.

²² But God was incensed that Balaam was going, and the Angel of the LORD took His stand on the path to oppose him. Balaam was riding his donkey, and his two servants were with him. ²³ When the donkey saw the

Angel of the LORD standing on the path with a drawn sword in His hand, she turned off the path and went into the field. So Balaam hit her to return her to the path. ²⁴ Then the Angel of the LORD stood in a narrow passage between the vineyards, with a stone wall on either side. ²⁵ The donkey saw the Angel of the LORD and pressed herself against the wall, squeezing Balaam's foot against it. So he hit her once again. ²⁶ The Angel of the LORD went ahead and stood in a narrow place where there was no room to turn to the right or the left. ²⁷ When the donkey saw the Angel of the LORD, she crouched down under Balaam. So he became furious and beat the donkey with his stick.

²⁸ Then the LORD opened the donkey's mouth, and she asked Balaam, "What have I done to you that you have beaten me these three times?"

²⁹ Balaam answered the donkey, "You made me look like a fool. If I had a sword in my hand, I'd kill you now!"

³⁰ But the donkey said, "Am I not the donkey you've ridden all your life until today? Have I ever treated you this way before?"

"No," he replied.

³¹ Then the LORD opened Balaam's eyes, and he saw the Angel of the LORD standing in the path with a drawn sword in His hand. Balaam knelt and bowed with his face to the ground. ³² The Angel of the LORD asked him, "Why have you beaten your donkey these three times? Look, I came out to oppose you, because what you are doing is evil in My sight. ³³ The donkey saw Me and turned away from Me these three times. If she had not turned away from Me, I would have killed you by now and let her live" (Numbers 22:20-33 HCSB).

It's generally important to know what surrounds this part of the story featuring the donkey. Balaam was a diviner paid by the Moabites to curse the Israelites for them. Balak, king of Moab, felt immensely threatened by the Israelites, now a great nation and moving like a swarm through the region. Balaam apparently accepted fees for divination and got a quick answer from the Lord, who told him not to go and not even to think about cursing Israel, because they were blessed. Balaam sent the messengers from Moab back to Balak with this message, but they returned insistent that he go with them, and they promised him more, and significant, payment. Balaam asked God what he should do, and God said Go, but say only what I tell you. This is where our curious story begins.

Unlike some other strange tales in the Old Testament, this one is told in relatively great detail, such as the description of Balaam's passage on the donkey's back through a narrow and then narrower path in a vineyard with walls on either side. It isn't an obscure narrative but a fairly picturesque one. The striking elements are only two: first, the appearance of the Angel of the Lord, and second, a donkey who holds a short conversation with her rider.

Let's see if we can uncover anything more about the story than the obvious facts.

Discovering the Text

Divining

An underlying question that needs to be answered is how Balaam was communicating with God in the first place.

We can pick up useful information first from other scripture references about Balaam. In 22:7 the elders of Moab headed off to see Balaam with the "fee for divination" in hand. The root word for "divination" there is the same as in Joshua 13:22, where Balaam is called a "diviner" (NASB, Amp, Young's *et al.*). The Hebrew there is *qosem*, also translated "soothsayer" and "fortuneteller."

Moses told the Israelites in Deuteronomy 18:10 that they were not to have diviners in their midst. The list there means to reject an entire class of spiritualism:

> [10] No one among you is to make his son or daughter pass through the fire, practice divination, tell fortunes, interpret omens, practice sorcery, [11] cast spells, consult a medium or a familiar spirit, or inquire of the dead. [12] Everyone who does these things is detestable to the LORD and the LORD your God is driving out the nations before you because of these detestable things (Deuteronomy 18:10-12 HCSB).

What diviners or anyone engaged in any of these other spiritualist arts or activities did in order to contact spiritual entities is not completely known. Some diviners gazed into pools of water, or into crystals, while attempting to open themselves spiritually to communications from other worldly beings. Astrologers, of course, studied the formations of stars and attempted interpretations from a growing history of previous students of the art/science. Some sorcerers, diviners or mediums used primitive drugs to produce a psychic state, expecting their thoughts to be inhabited by spiritual beings. Others shuffled or tossed items such as bones or specially carved sticks and read the patterns produced, according to symbolic arrangements that had been acquired through generations of their art.

It was certainly possible for people to fake powers of divination, and no doubt many did. But divination and the like were professions that often arose within a class of people who were variously respected for their undertaking. In some societies certain forms of divination had risen to a priestly height, such as in whatever foreign country the Magi of Luke 2 came from, who of course were astrologers/astronomers.

The key element by which diviners were capable of making any sort of pronouncements at all by means of the techniques they used was their willingness to make their minds and spirits open and vulnerable to the intrusion of spiritual entities who might have the information, often prophecy, they needed. This was what made spiritualism, including all the above forms mentioned in Deuteronomy, detestable to the Lord. His people were to commune with him, not other spiritual beings, for guidance and help.

Nowhere do we read anything that casts any doubt about whom Balaam was talking to, or who was talking to him, on this occasion. Balaam, whatever kind of diviner he was, was talking with the LORD God and clearly he knew it. The repeated messages to the elders and the king came from the God of gods and the Lord of lords.

Furthermore, it appears very possible that Balaam sought to divine answers to the questions asked of him exclusively from Yahweh, on this occasion anyway, and not other divine beings.[113] If this is so, it is probable that Balaam had experienced encounters with Yahweh previously. Possibly he had done so over the years, but had gradually succumbed to the lure of inappropriately profiting from his gift to discern the voice of God.

On the other hand, Balaam may be a special case. It is possible that he aspired to prophetic heights but had not acquired them. An interesting contrast is drawn in the larger account of Balaam between how he addresses God as opposed to how God is referred to by the writer of Numbers. Balaam told the Moabite and Midianite elders he was going to speak to the LORD (22:8,18&19, 23:3,12&15). He used the personal name for the Lord that had been given to Moses: יהוה (Yahweh). But in these encounters Numbers says God (elohim) spoke to him: 22:9-11 says "God" (אלהים - elohim) spoke to him, but when Balaam reported the words to the elders, he said "the LORD" (Yahweh) said. Verse 9 says "God" (elohim) came to

---

[113] We use "divine beings" here to represent the Hebrew word elohim as used in the scriptures without the definite article. When elohim appears in the Bible without the definite article, it is often translated "gods," or sometimes, following the Septuagint, "angels."

Balaam and spoke to him, and v12 again says "God" (*elohim*) gave Balaam that first, undebatable answer, "Don't go!" When the elders went back, then returned to Balaam, he continued to say he would find out what "the LORD" would say, but the text continues that "God" came to him and gave him further instructions. This contrast continues throughout the account. Possibly the writer intended to communicate the fact that Balaam's self-vaunted association with "the LORD" was one sided: God spoke to him when it suited his divine purposes, not Balaam's.

The venerable Matthew Henry says, "It is not known whether the Lord had ever spoken to Balaam, or by him, before this; though it is probable he had, and it is certain he did afterwards."[114]

Scholars Keil and Delitzsch say that very likely "Balaam belonged to a family in which the mantic character, or magical art, was hereditary…" though "he is never called a prophet," but that he "was not without a certain measure of the true knowledge of God, and not without susceptibility for such revelations of the true God as he actually received; so that, without actually being a prophet, he was able to give utterance to true prophecies from Jehovah."[115]

Balaam's answers to the elders of Moab and Midian throughout the entire account show that he had a fundamental and sober respect for the person of the LORD. That attitude was likely derived from reportage of the goings on within Israel over time, including the dramatic accounts of their deliverance from Egypt. But what happens in the larger account of Numbers 22-24 and the smaller story of Balaam and his donkey illustrates the important truth that Balaam was not making use of his interactions with God so much as that God was using Balaam to accomplish his purposes, in spite of Balaam's pecuniary interests.

Now that we've somewhat established what Balaam was, we

---

[114] Matthew Henry, *Concise Commentary on the Whole Bible*, Accessed May 15, 2024, https://www.studylight.org/commentaries/eng/mhn/numbers-22.html.

[115] Keil and Delitzsch, *op. cit., Vol. 1,* 876.

should look at the divine messages that resulted in his mounting his donkey to trek to Moab.

The officials pleaded with him to come with them and curse Israel (22:11). The account implies in 22:13 that accordingly Balaam attempted to communicate with the Lord during the night. But God's answer is actually recorded in the previous verse, 22:12, rather suddenly after the elders' articulation of their request. In other words, God's answer was immediate and categorical.

What part of No...

God said to Balaam, **"You are not to go with them. You are not to curse this people, for they are blessed"** (22:12 HCSB). Since the detail we might have expected about Balaam's secluding himself that night to divine an answer is entirely skipped over, it's almost as if the writer is saying God spoke the instant the subject came out of the visiting elders' mouths. Certainly the impression v12 leaves is that there were no ifs, ands or buts about the matter. Balaam not only was not in any way to curse Israel; he wasn't even to go to Moab in the first place. What would be the point, if there was nothing to decide when he got there?

So what part of "No" didn't Balaam understand? Granted, v13 says that he told the officials, "God said No." But when they went home and then came back, why didn't he tell them, "God's answer hasn't changed"? But in fact, he didn't say that, exactly.

King Balak's second urging included what might seem threatening words—**"Let nothing keep you from coming to me."** Of stick and carrot, this might have been the stick. But the carrot was the promise of even more handsome reward. Faced with that kind of enticement, Balaam gave lip service to the authority of God's first word: **"If Balak were to give me his house full of silver and gold, I could not go against the command of the LORD my God to do anything small or great"** (22:18 HCSB). But then he "knocked the edge off" that answer by telling the contingent from Balak to stay the night to see if the Lord had anything else to say.

Evidently he was hoping for a change of mind on God's part.

Here's where the account becomes odd, setting up Balaam for the even stranger encounter on the road to Moab. **"God came to Balaam at night and said to him, 'Since these men have come to summon you, get up and go with them, but you must only do what I tell you'"** (22:20 HCSB).

Go, don't go

At the very least, God's instruction in 22:20 is *seemingly* at odds with what he first commanded Balaam: Don't go. Right away the question arises as to what God is up to, and even more significantly, whether this is God's contradicting himself. As we read on, shortly in 22:22 we see that **"God was incensed that Balaam was going."** Why, when it was God who told him to go?

Readers who have already read the previous chapter about Moses' trip with his family from Midian to Egypt will remember that we pointed out that God had told Moses to go to Egypt and tell Pharaoh to let Israel go, but that when Moses got on his way, God confronted him and was about to kill him. In that account, we were dealing with a godly man who had not taken care of necessary duties to prepare himself for service. God's almost deadly interruption was a lesson about holiness and obedience.

By contrast, in this story about Balaam, we are dealing with someone who was certainly less than godly, who was inclined to succumb to the inducement of wealth, even as he tried to follow a course of spiritual communication with the God he knew to be supreme. God's different second answer to the question of going with the Moabite elders was not a contradiction of himself, but rather a change of strategy on a *subsequent occasion,* as we might call it. God's answer to Balaam's first inquiry was appropriate for his plan on that occasion. But this was a different day, and God's plan was addressing the situation as it took place.

As an illustration, think of Jesus' answer to his brothers who told him he should go up to Jerusalem for the Feast of the Tabernacles.

Jesus said, "I'm not going" (John 7:8). But then, after v9 says he stayed in Galilee, v10 says, "He also went up, not openly but secretly." So, did he lie in v8? A few translators over the years (embarrassed?) have supplied the word "yet" in v8 (KJV, HCSB, ERV *et al.*) though that word isn't in the Greek. The Greek has *ego ouk anabaino* (εγο ουκ αναβαινω), which is simply "I am not going up." Most versions leave us to figure out what Jesus meant.

It isn't difficult to realize that Jesus was responding negatively to his yet unbelieving brothers and declining to make a show of "going up" to Jerusalem, which was often done in groups with a public demonstration of celebration. When Jesus "went up," he did so basically *incognito*. The fact is that a different, later day made all the difference in the world as to his going or not going. He didn't contradict himself. He wasn't going the first day, but he was going on a later day, and on his own terms, not others.

Here in Numbers we have a meeting of God with Balaam on what we could call day one of the encounters with the elders of Moab. When they got that simple answer that Balaam could not go with them, they turned and left. We don't know how long it took them to get back to Moab. We don't know how long the king mulled over the answer and gave them new marching orders. We don't know how long it took the elders to get back to Balaam. It could have been a matter of weeks. When they came back for a second try, it was a different day. The ante had been upped, the situation had become more critical for king Balak, and the first phase of God's plan may have been accomplished in the blanket refusal to allow Balaam to go and consider some kind of pronouncement. If God gave some limited kind of permission on this second encounter, it was because this was a different occasion with different conditions.

One of those different conditions was Balaam's avarice. It had always been one of his character traits, but it intensified when the potential profits increased dramatically. On this second occasion Balak offered him a handsome reward, which probably meant much more than he usually got for divination.

At this point, the reader should recall the cultural inclination of middle eastern peoples, from the most ancient of times, to haggle. Many if not most deals people reached were the result of an expected process of: bid and denial; offer and limited rejection; re-offer and demurral; elevated tender and acceptance. In other words, two parties entered into a process of bargaining that both expected to succeed at some level after obligatory positioning designed to show respect of each other and reach a reasonable agreement. Abraham had such an encounter with the Hittites in Genesis 23:3ff about a burial place for Sarah. It makes interesting reading.

Here, the bargainers were Balaam on the one side and the king of Moab on the other. God knew, as God always knows, what mettle Balaam was made of and what he was eventually going to do. But God dealt with Balaam in such a way as to make the divine blessing on Israel extraordinarily evident, by repeated blessings that, if anything, increased in their unambiguousness.

God's fundamental answer to cursing Israel didn't change one iota. But as Balaam and Balak haggled over the possibility of an exchange of wealth for a curse, God let Balaam try every possible angle, expressly because he wanted there to be no doubt about his answer. There isn't anything unusual about the Hebrew word *lek* (go) that God spoke to Balaam in v20. But the force of what he said was "go ahead." It wouldn't make any difference to what answer God gave when Balaam got there.

Furious...

So Balaam saddled his donkey—we wish we had a name for her, don't we!—and he started out, apparently with the elders from Moab, to go to their country. They may have been strung out in a long line, not grouped tightly together, because nothing in the story of the talking donkey suggests they witnessed what Balaam and the donkey experienced. The setting, on a narrow pathway through what may have been hundreds of yards of hilly vineyards, suggests a significant separation between each rider and the others. On the other hand, *somebody* who witnessed the event told the story, and we don't know who. Balaam himself, however, is a good candidate for recounting the tale. (There were also two servants with him, perhaps behind him some yards away.)

Soon after they got on their way, 22:22 says, **"But God was incensed that Balaam was going, and the Angel of the LORD took His stand on the path to oppose him."** For "incensed," the Hebrew has the word *ap*, meaning "anger," and a verb meaning "arouse." Most older translations render the phrase, "anger was kindled." The Aramaic Bible in Plain English says, "the wrath of God was provoked."

We've already introduced the matter of how it seems contradictory that God should tell Balaam to go, and then become furious with him when he did. This *apparent* contradiction is one of many examples of the *seeming* dichotomy between the freedom all human beings have to choose and to act on their own, on the one hand, and the sovereignty of God in directing the course of human events, on the other. It is simply one of the fundamental truths of scripture that nothing thwarts the purposes of God, that people do what they want to but ultimately it becomes evident that God's will was done.

As a prime example, theologians have always pointed out that Pharaoh "hardened his heart" against the Israelites, but then that God hardened his heart. Both are true. Not only is it true in the ultimate sense that God sovereignly controls history and each part of it, but in the immediate sense, as well, we often see God hardening hearts that are predisposed to rebel and disobey anyway. In other words, God will hold people responsible for hardening their hearts against him, even though ultimately he is sovereignly in control of them.

In the New Testament, Paul describes this dynamic in Romans: **"They exchanged the truth of God for a lie, and worshiped and served the creature rather than the Creator...For this reason God** gave them over to dishonorable passions" (Romans 1:25-26 HCSB). God's withdrawal of himself from influencing them toward right worship and living resulted in their becoming damningly evil, but God held them responsible for it, because it was their predilection in the first place.

Here in the story of Balaam, God sends him on his way, then displays to him what he should have known would be the divine response, because of what God told him to begin with, which had not changed: Israel was blessed.

What is striking about God's method of opposing Balaam is that he did more than arrange circumstantial obstacles, more than produce bad weather that might suggest Balaam shouldn't go. God **"took His stand on the path"** in the form of **"the Angel of the LORD."**

The HCSB, NKJV, Amplified, and some others *rightly* capitalize Angel because this is undoubtedly an appearance of the second person of the trinity, God the Word or God the Son, and this is often his title when he so appears. That others, including the translators of the NIV, do not capitalize Angel is probably not their denial of the identity of this person, but simply a reflection of the fact that there are no capitals in Hebrew, and our use of them in English is governed by accepted standards—for instance, the beginnings of sentences and proper names.[116] Whenever we come to "Angel of the LORD" in the Bible, we are faced with deciding whether it is one of the many messengers God employs to tell human beings things they need to know, or instead an appearance of God himself, and thus a proper name.

---

[116] The author has vigorously argued elsewhere against the capitalization of pronouns for God, such as HCSB and some other modern translations employ. Not only was it not the practice of the KJV and other classic translations, but it unnecessarily causes a halting effect in reading the text, where a capital letter on a word usually not capitalized elsewhere causes the reader to employ emphasis and a rise in tone. Capitals on pronouns for God are reproduced in this book only when used in quoted material.

In an upcoming book, this author will deal with the subject of how the many appearances of "the Angel of the Lord" in the Old Testament demonstrate and prove the trinity—one God in three persons. For our purposes here, the reader is invited to look at other encounters with this Angel, such as Genesis 16:11ff, Judges 16:12ff, and other stories where God "appeared" to patriarchs, etc. This Angel is not a lesser heavenly being but the person of God who represents God while being very God: God the Son. This was whom the donkey saw.

What do animals see?

From Balaam's perspective, what took place started with his donkey's veering off to one side and going into a field. Balaam had no idea why, because he didn't see anything that was blocking them or that might have frightened the donkey.

But the donkey did.

We're always interested in discoveries about what animals can see. Studying the eyes of various kinds of animals, scientists tell us that bees see ultraviolet, blue and yellow. Reptiles see some color and infrared. Birds see five to seven colors. Cats and dogs see two colors, weakly. Equines, including horses and donkeys, tend to see the world in two colors, blue and yellow, with just a little red, which looks more like shades of gray to them. Otherwise, their vision is a lot like a human being's, except that in addition to being able to see binocularly to the front, they can see monocularly to each side.

But none of this accounts for what happened to the donkey that day. It had nothing to do with what colors she could see. She simply saw what neither Balaam nor any of the servants (if they were close enough) could see at all, and it was because God wanted her to see him, to see the glory of his Angel standing there in the way blocking them. What she saw made her veer off the path. And for this, Balaam, who didn't see anything up ahead, beat her.

It's not stated, but apparently the donkey got back on the path in response to the beating, and then **"the Angel of the Lord stood** in a narrow passage between the vineyards, with a stone wall on either side" (v24). There is nothing obscure about the original language here. Our only challenge is to visualize what is being described in fairly picturesque terms. The donkey again saw the Angel of the LORD, and the only way she could signal her angered rider was to sidle off into one of the stone walls, which she did, crushing his foot and resulting in another beating. The Angel moved ahead a bit, to a place where the path was so narrow that there was nowhere to go but through it, and he was still blocking the path. And so, peering at the visage in front of her, the donkey did the only thing she had left to do. She sat down under her rider. She wasn't going anywhere.

Of course, this prompted yet another beating. The text doesn't say whether Balaam did it while still on her back or whether, his feet probably already on the ground straddling her, he stepped off to the side. We like the image of the latter, because it would have allowed him to face her for what happened next.

Then the LORD opened the donkey's mouth, and she asked Balaam, "What have I done to you that you have beaten me these three times?" (Number 22:28 HCSB).

Apparently, she assumed Balaam could see what she did. Since he didn't, however, Balaam thought she had earned the beatings, because she was being inexcusably stubborn. He saw no reason she was stopping or straying off to the side. But she did, and she confronted him with his indefensible cruelty to her.

But to do this, she had to have something more in the way of mentality than a donkey ordinarily has, as well as a way to express herself to Balaam. And this is where the heart of the story takes place. The Lord gave the donkey what she needed to register her justified complaint. He **opened the donkey's mouth**. That's just shorthand for giving her the ability to speak in human language.

In addition to the donkey's acquisition of human-like mentality, the miraculous nature of this event is evident in several other things, including first the fact that donkeys don't have the precise physiological equipment—vocal chords, tongue facility, lips, etc.—to effect human speech. A great deal had to be done by the divine hand in order to give this hapless donkey the ability to converse with Balaam. But then, that's nothing for the God who created the universe, and it's one of the points of this account.

Undoubtedly most people think this is a fanciful story, that *if* there were a person named Balaam in the first place and *if* the story is generally true, then the donkey didn't *really* speak to him. She just brayed in complaint, and Balaam, like most people who tend animals with a personal touch, or who have pets, "put words in her mouth"—he interpreted what she said as he told the story later, or as someone else did.

We don't take the scripture that way. The entire account makes it perfectly clear that unusual, dramatic, supernatural things were going on here, in an encounter that would play a critical part of the larger story of Israel and its conquest of the Promised Land. Further pointing to the actual occurrence of a talking donkey is the fact that it happened for only a moment, and then happened no more. It stood apart as an event that amazed Balaam (and perhaps his servants) and was to be memorialized in the Bible for its historical and spiritual lessons.

Once having been provided with the necessary mental and physical ability to converse with her rider, the donkey said, **"What have I done to you that you have beaten me these three times?"** (v28). And the story moves directly between this question and Balaam's answer to it, when probably what took place immediately upon the donkey's verbalization was a long moment of shock and amazement, as Balaam tried to take in what was happening.

In this modern day of highly developed cinematic storytelling, we are used to seeing how writers and directors carry moviegoers through moments of revelation. Cuts of the film back and forth between characters may reveal progressive emotional and mental processes, even without a word being spoken. So, the modern reader of the Bible may approach a story like Balaam and his talking donkey as if the dialogue took place just as written, and that if the writer didn't put anything in the account that took place between one character's speech and the other one's, it didn't take place.

But we're sure it did. Without suggesting that the writer of Numbers left anything out that God wanted in, let us suggest what a motion picture scriptwriter might have written for this scene:

1.   EXTERIOR. VINEYARD ROAD – MIDMORNING

A narrow dirt road. DONKEY is sitting in the road. BALAAM stands beside her, a stick in his hand. He has just beaten DONKEY. Totally unexpectedly, DONKEY speaks.

> DONKEY
> What have I done to you that you've beaten me these three times?

BALAAM freezes, unbelieving. Cut to BALAAM's face, which displays a startled, almost horrified look. Cut to DONKEY's face, which looks quizzical and hurt.

> BALAAM
> I—I—you—

> DONKEY
> (Brays in a sound exactly like, "huh?")

BALAAM speaks haltingly and with continuing unbelief.

> BALAAM
> You—you made me—you made me look like a fool!

BALAAM can't believe he's talking with a donkey. His complaint sounds weak and his threat, spoken next, sounds hollow.

> BALAAM
> If I had a sword in my hand,
> I'd kill you now.

> DONKEY
> Am I not the donkey you've
> ridden all your life until
> today? Have I ever treated you
> this way before?

BALAAM's voice is almost childish, as he is caught up in this surreal scene.

> BALAAM
> N-n-no.

Our point is, Balaam did not fall immediately into easy conversation with the donkey. We believe a considerable interchange of looks of disbelief and shock took place.

What happened after Balaam admitted that DONKEY's behavior was out of character for her was that he suddenly became able to see what she had been balking at. But before we go on to take in that part of the story, let's consider what was happening from the donkey's perspective. The scripture has described what she *did*. Let's look at what she might have *thought*.

Here was a beast of burden, graced by creation with what the Bible calls "the spirit of the beast,"[118] a soulish element sufficient to animate her, to give her the instinct of relationship to her mother, and to give her the natural sense of her kind. The spirit of this beast was sentient enough to know that its surroundings

---

[117] Film scripts have a certain format accepted in the industry. This was an approximation of that format.

[118] Ecc. 3:21 KJV.

were benevolent or not, aware enough to detect friend or foe, and inclined toward obedience to the human beings who had broken her. She had no language, and her soul required none. She had no sense of morals, no conversation with God, indeed no capacity to know God. Her natural capacity for thought was no greater than she needed for the mundane challenge of her kind of existence, and her level of intelligence was not high enough to make her resent her lot in life or thirst to be more than she was. She was a donkey, and no more.

But on the day she saw the Angel, something happened. I believe it happened when the Angel took his stance in the roadway. For a brief moment, the Lord by his power lifted the spirit of this beast, her soul, to a level of consciousness, awareness, and sentience she had never experienced. Suddenly, she not only saw the road before her, but she also peered into the spiritual realm and saw a being unlike any who had ever held her reins or bound packs on her back. And she had the good sense to stop dead in her tracks.

Can we imagine what her thoughts must have been like in those moments? And when Balaam began to beat her, she was still dealing with this strange experience of transcendence and awareness, as she held her ground and even sidled into the wall nearby to crush Balaam's foot as he prodded her violently.

But after the third thrashing, she felt something welling up inside her, a brighter thought than had ever occurred to her, vivid thoughts taking on some sort of new impulse that rose in her throat and came out as *words*—what were words?! But they seemed natural to her in the brilliance and stirring of all this new awareness. She had heard men speak before, and though their words were merely sounds, what she sensed was sometimes anger, other times affection. But now she was making the sounds they made, and they not only made sense, they also came out of her own mind, which was suddenly filled with images and thoughts that welled up in her emotions (what were *emotions?!*) and expressed her indignance at her treatment.

The context and the tone of the passage in Numbers leads us

to realize that God did not merely use Balaam's ass as a puppet, moving her mouth and making sounds for her. The ass was fully aware of what she was saying. She had a conversation with her master, the only one she would ever have, and she had a full appreciation of what she was doing, and why.

Their exchange lasted only a few moments. Shortly, Balaam turned and began speaking to the Angel. We don't know if his faithful donkey understood what was said, and we have no scripture suggesting that she remained capable of conversation after that incident on the road. We are safe in assuming that whatever happened when the Lord opened her mouth, whatever combination of unprecedented enlightenment of soul and refinement of body for the miracle of that moment, it was over in a few heartbeats.

The brightness of the donkey's thoughts faded. The words that sprang into her new and fascinating consciousness dropped away, and the consciousness itself faded as a dream upon waking. Not only did her words disappear, but the sounds were just sounds again, the feeling of insult and exasperation quieted and became a dull displeasure with no further intention to express itself. The chaotic excitement of reasoning quieted to a murmur, and the clear arguments that had momentarily formed in her brain became instead fuzzy feelings little different from hunger, thirst, and sleepiness. She was just a donkey again, with nothing more about her than any other donkey, and the thing was, she probably didn't think about it at all subsequently. What had happened stuck in Balaam's mind, and was found on the pen of Moses before long, but probably no remembrance remained on the simple mind of the little donkey that warned Balaam that day. For a moment, the "spirit of the beast" took on the consciousness and reasoning of the soul of a man, and felt and thought like God's highest creation does. Then it was gone.[119]

---

[119] Robert Simms, *Where Did I Come From?*, (Greer, SC, Robert F. Simms, 2011), 150.

When the surreal moment was over, an even more startling and glorious moment took place. The Angel of the Lord opened Balaam's eyes so he could see his divine person, and he asked Balaam why he had beaten the donkey.

This question was much like the first question we know of from the mouth of God, namely the Lord's query, "Adam, where are you?" God knew very well where Adam was, and there was no mystery why Balaam had beaten his donkey, either. It was a chiding remark, not a question that needed answering. The Angel of the Lord continued, surely after a short beat during which Balaam gulped. **"I came out to oppose you because what you are doing is evil in my sight"** (v32).

We return to our previous thoughts about the appearance of conflict between what God told Balaam to do and his subsequent anger at Balaam for doing it. Our bottom line previously was that both human choice and divine sovereignty are at work. God has a right to judge human behavior he permits.

But what also may be going on in this passage is that while God permitted Balaam to go to Balak and even said, 'Go ahead,' Balaam did not go with pure motives. His previous actions in going back to inquire of God a second time (v19) indicated that he was trying to get a variance on God's original pronouncement. As he went with the officials to get the lay of the land, so to speak, he did not go with rock solid resolution to say, "No curse. Blessing!" In fact, as he went he was looking for a way to earn his next rich, diviner's fee from Balak. The only way he could do that was to issue some sort of curse, if only implied. Could he put together something ambiguous that could be taken as a curse but wouldn't actually be? And once he had humbly and graciously accepted the rich reward promised, how would he spend it?

It was that furious mental activity that Balaam was probably engaged in as he rode along toward Moab. And it was his strategizing, his scheming, with which God was angry. God told him so, in no uncertain terms, and then added, **"The donkey saw Me** and turned away from Me these three times. If she had not turned away from Me, I would have killed you by now and let her live" (v33). What a dressing down this was, and how humbling it should have been! God would have spared the donkey but slain Balaam. It turns out the dumb animal wasn't so dumb.

Balaam answers the Angel of the Lord by saying he'll go back home, but the Lord says, 'Go on, but *again, say **only** what I tell you.*' God knew that Balaam was still trying to think of any possible way he could earn his fee.

From this point in Numbers 22 the account goes on to deal with Balaam's multiple blessings on Israel, some of which must have come out of clenched teeth. The scene with the donkey is over. She goes backstage to observe her master. He had accused her of making a fool of him; shortly he was playing the fool all on his own.

Learning the Lessons

What this curious Bible story has to teach us is fairly obvious.

1. Stubbornness   A Truth to Believe ☑

God will sometimes give free reign to us in our stubborn pursual of sin, and then judge us for it.

Every once in a while, God prevents us from doing things that would ruin us. Especially if we're otherwise on a good and faithful track with him, he may providentially keep us from making a mistake that would be fatal to our future service in his kingdom.

At first glance, it looks like God was preventing Balaam from doing something disastrous to his life, by literally blocking his road. But then, God let him go on, with the repeated and strong warning to do and say *only* what he tells him. God was giving Balaam the freedom to do what he insisted on doing, because Balaam was unwilling to take God's first word as final. As a result, Balaam struggled against what he knew was God's will until finally he figured out a way to avoid God's providential hindrances and earn his reward for divining: he went to Moab and advised them to infiltrate Israel with idolatry and to send all their seductive women there and lead them into sexual sin (Numbers 25:1,6; 31:16), knowing that God would punish the Israelites for unfaithfulness.

The result was that Balaam was ultimately killed (Numbers 31:8) and his name became a byword for influential evil. Peter later wrote that "Balaam …loved the wages of unrighteousness"(2 Peter 2:15). Jude wrote, "…these people …have abandoned themselves to the error of Balaam for profit" (Jude 1:11). And the Apostle John said that Jesus told him about the church at Pergamum, "You have some there who hold to the teaching of Balaam, who taught Balak to place a stumbling block in front of the Israelites: to eat meat sacrificed to idols and to commit sexual immorality" (Revelation 2:14 HCSB).

In our own lives there may be strong urges to do things that we know well the Bible says are sinful. They may be desires of great longstanding, temptations we have fought with for years, or they may be the product of recent events that have ignited some ambition. If we are followers of Christ and determined to be faithful to our commitment, God in his providence may put up road signs and light better paths for us every time our strong temptations lure us onto the wrong route. But if we feed our sinful passions and try to rationalize compromising our principles, God may eventually let us pursue them. Doing so will show us what God was trying to spare us. And it will expose us to the discipline he may justly impose because of our actions.

2. God's wisdom

A Truth to Believe ☑

God may use unlikely sources to communicate his wisdom or guidance to us.

"In the Western world, the donkey is a slow, dull, and foolish animal. But in ancient times they were honored for their strength and loyalty to their master, particularly in ancient Israel."[120] This story about Balaam shows that for a long time his donkey had served him well, but it also shows us that human beings can develop contempt for "dumb animals" just as they can for other, disliked human beings. It didn't occur to Balaam that his donkey might have had a very, very good reason for not going forward. And had Balaam been going east with the elders from Moab for the best of reasons instead of the worst, or had he been ruminating on holy thoughts while traveling instead of how to enable his greed, he might also have seen the Angel of the Lord—if the Angel would have made an appearance in the first place. Instead, God used the donkey to introduce a divine directive.

In the New Testament, when the rulers, elders and scribes were squared off with Peter and John, Peter preached a short sermon to them about how "you crucified him." And the Bible says, "When they saw the courage of Peter and John and realized that they were *unschooled, ordinary men,* they were astonished and they took note that these men had been with Jesus" (Acts 4:13, emphasis ours). The rulers were inclined to think that if God was going to speak to them it would be through people who were educated and extraordinary. But God chose to send his most important message through some of the commonest of messengers.

What that means for the Christian is to resist judging the validity of the message by *his prejudice against* the messenger. If there is a just and holy reason to disbelieve the messenger, that's one thing. If there is only prejudice or a personal reason to reject the message, that's another. It may be God, using an unlikely voice to call a disobedient person to repent.

---

[120] Biblical Hebrew Studies, Accessed June 5, 2024, https://www.chaimbentorah. com/2020/07/ hebrew- word-study-donkey/.

COOKING GOAT
Exodus 23:19, 34:26, & Deuteronomy 14:21

This chapter doesn't concern a story *per se*, but rather a curious phrase—an unusual dictum. And because it is such a short dictum— only five words in Hebrew—this little chapter may be something of a breather!

Here's the saying from the pen of Moses:

> ¹⁹ …**You shall not boil a young goat in its mother's milk** (Exodus 23:19b NKJV).

Let's wade into the matter of this verse's context.

Discovering the Text

Context of the phrase

This directive about cooking a young goat appears in Exodus 23:19 and 34:26 in virtually the same surrounding material. In both, the context is about Jewish feasts, specifically about not offering the blood of sacrifices along with leavened bread, and in both cases the saying about a goat is tagged directly onto the end of these words: **"The first of the firstfruits of your land you shall bring to the house of the LORD your God."** The previous few verses in each place are nearly identical. Moses repeated himself—or God did—for emphasis.

A third place our curious phrase appears is Deuteronomy 14:21. There the discussion is about things that Israelites were to consider clean or unclean for purposes of being a holy people and worshiping in a holy manner. After telling his readers that they aren't to eat animals that die on their own, Moses again immediately tacks on this curious phrase: **"You shall not boil a young goat in its mother's milk."**

The purpose of the instruction

Some scholars tell us that this terse little prohibition "was pointed against an annual pagan ceremony" (Jamieson-Fausset-Brown Bible Commentary). And the Cambridge Bible makes this comment about boiling a goat in its mother's milk:

> That it occurs among laws on ritual implies that the practice it vetoes had a sacramental meaning …that both in E and J[121] it immediately follows the offering of first-fruits suggests that this meaning was connected with the security of the harvest or of the fertility of the soil: 'a superstitious usage of some of the Gentiles, who, *'tis said,* at the end of their harvest seethed a kid in its dam's milk, and sprinkled that milk pottage in a magical way upon their gardens and fields to make them the more fruitful the next year[122] *(emphasis ours)*.

Naturally, the Israelites were not to observe some familiar regional— *but not divinely directed*—ceremony that had any tinge of paganism about it. One of the most important areas of God's commands to the Israelites as they prepared to go into the promised land and conquer its people was that they were not to do what the peoples of those lands had been doing in the way of worship. That

---

[121] For non-scholars, E and J are two of four theorized sources for the books of the Pentateuch, these two representing the Elohistic and Jahwist (Yahwist) sources. A full discussion of the four-document hypothesis is not practical in this book.

[122] Driver, *The Book of Exodus,* 135.

was the reason for the prohibition of intermarriage with those peoples: putting two religions together *always* introduces compromise and adulteration.

However, while *some* scholars think this is the reason for the prohibition of cooking a young goat in its own mother's milk, others are either uncertain, or are quite definite, in their opposition to this explanation. Notice the italics we used for *"'tis said"* in the quotation from the Cambridge Bible: the sources for this interpretation are not exact.

The respected Keil and Delitzsch say that the proposition that cooking a young goat in its mother's milk was a religious rite of pagans is "without any definite historical proofs, and for the most part on the strength of far-fetched analogies."[123] And Matthew Poole wrote that even if the mostly baseless supposition that it was an idolatrous custom were true, it would *not* "seem to be a rite of that importance or probability to entice the Israelites to imitate it, [or] that there needed a particular law against this, more than against a hundred such ridiculous usages which were among the heathen, and are not taken notice of in the book of God's laws."[124]

The Pulpit Commentary acknowledges that the practice of cooking a kid goat in milk existed, saying further, "Kids were thought to be most palatable when boiled in milk."[125] The Cambridge Bible also admits it was an Arab custom and cites some ancient sources for the fact. Neither of these more contemporary sources has any information about the cooking being done "in its mother's milk." That detail carries the practice into an area that seems relevant to the scriptural context.

Most commentators who think the prohibition wasn't

---

[123] Keil and Delitzsch, *op. cit.*, Vol. 1, 494.

[124] Matthew Poole, *A Commentary on the Whole Bible*, "BibleHub," July 15, 2024, https://biblehub.com/commentaries/exodus/23-19.htm.

[125] George Rawlinson, *Exodus, Vol. 2*, The Pulpit Commentary, (New York, Funk & Wagnall's, 1897), 203.

particularly (if at all) aimed at pagan practices say that the saying was included to teach the Israelites to avoid actions that displayed a lack of respect for natural sensibilities. The Pulpit Commentary says that by cooking a kid in its mother's milk, "the mother was made a sort of accomplice in the death of her child, which men were induced to kill on account of the flavour that her milk gave it. Reason has nothing to say against such a mode of preparing food, but feeling revolts from it."[126]

That's well said. And Barnes Notes on the Bible says the prohibition was "a protest against cruelty and outraging the order of nature."

Our conclusion is that this curious phrase was a Hebrew saying, possibly of some greater antiquity than Moses' day. In fact, it may have been a saying in the general area, not proprietary to the Hebrews. Most significant about the saying is the fact that it's the *mother's milk* that isn't to be used to cook the young goat. It's not a prohibition of cooking a kid in milk in general. The focus is on the relationship between the young goat, which was being taken for food, and the mother's milk, which might have continued to nourish the kid had the little one been left with her until weaning. Clearly, the saying has in mind the prohibition of something that *in itself* was singularly inappropriate.

That self-evident inappropriateness may have been the connection between the prohibition and the material preceding it in both Exodus and Deuteronomy. The Israelites were not to accompany blood offerings with leavened breads (Exodus 23:19 and 34:26) because it was *self-evident* that this was inappropriate, just like boiling a young goat in its own mother's milk. These were simply things *you just don't do.*

As for the appearance of the prohibition again in Deuteronomy 14:21, the context is different—a command against eating an

---

[126] Rawlinson, *Exodus, Vol 2*, 203.

animal found already dead. But the connection with the prohibition about cooking young goats is the same: this is something *you just don't do*. In Moses' day, there were no automobiles hitting deer, which some people today (especially if they were the unlucky drivers) harvest on the road and donate to food banks. In Moses' day, it might be presumed in most cases that an animal found dead had died from disease, and even if that wasn't certain, that very uncertainty made the idea of taking that carcass for food a potentially foolish act. So, as a pervasive general rule, people weren't to eat animals they found dead, anymore than they would boil a young goat in its mother's milk. This saying was an illustration of the principle involved in the law about eating dead animals.

A *dual purpose?*

It's possible, of course, that there was an element of both these interpretations in the use of the goat saying. The forcefulness of some scholars' positions on interpretation suggests that what had arisen in mid-eastern cultures as a sensible saying might also have taken on further significance. Pagan worship is often known to pervert the divine order of things. And though the saying immediately and obviously seems to frown on a lack of sensitivity for the natural order, one could argue that the context of these *three* instances of the saying strongly implies that it had some connection with rules for worship and sacrifice.

Perhaps we could say that just as some things were glaringly inappropriate, the Israelites should come to regard the revealed mode of their worship as being divinely approved, with anything borrowed from surrounding cultures being obviously inappropriate for them to do. Thus, the saying about cooking a young goat in its mother's milk *punctuated* the previous directives about worship or ceremonial cleanliness.

Learning the Lessons

Is there anything we can carry away about this prohibition by way of application to modern Christian living? Two applications correspond directly to the two, related interpretations above.

1. Self-evident truths   A Truth to Believe ☑

Some behavior is so obviously inappropriate that it is inexcusable for us to engage in it.

What we call "a conscience" can be described at least one way as a sense that all of us have that some things are just wrong. There are seriously abnormal persons whom psychologists calls sociopaths, who have little to no sense of right and wrong and no remorse for hurtful actions. That's why sociopaths, or psychopaths, are classified as abnormal: normal people have a conscience.

This sense of right and wrong tells us, deep inside, that some things we are tempted to do we *shouldn't* do, and that we do them to our peril or the peril of others. Moreover, there are things we know are wrong in the sight of God and that even if we get away with them as far as their impact on others or on our immediate, daily living, they will catch up with us eventually. **"Be sure your sin will find you out"** (Numbers 32:23). Even worse, if we continue to ignore and suppress our consciences, the consequences will be damning in an eternal way. Paul wrote in Romans, **"The wrath of God is being revealed from heaven against all the godlessness and wickedness of people, who suppress the truth by their wickedness"** (Romans 1:18). He went on to talk about how people knew very well there is a God because creation makes it quite plain, but they deliberately *dis*-believed in him and carried on lives that were full of immorality and perversion—things they *knew very well were wrong*. For that reason God "gave them over" (v26) to their cravings and let them bury themselves in wrongdoing. Essentially they had their consciences **"seared with a hot iron"** (1 Timothy 4:2).

People who ignore the natural sense of what is wrong eventually don't feel their consciences tugging them away from wrong and toward the right direction, and they may finally feel they are "free." But in fact, they're actually thoroughly enslaved. They just don't know it.

When something deep inside you tells you that what you're thinking or what you're about to do is wrong, *listen to it!*

2. Adulterated worship

A Teaching to Obey ☑

A Christian must purify his life and worship of any worldly practice or activity that is clearly inconsistent with godliness.

The church in the Middle Ages had what turned out to be a destructive habit, that of going into new areas and combining church holy days with the festivals of the local populations, hoping thereby to make the teachings of the church more readily accepted. What resulted from that practice, however, was corrupted church holidays. Christmas, for example, which early on was not a complex holiday celebration, was simply the Christ-mass celebrated in worship. But when it got mixed with the features of Saturnalia and other pagan celebrations, the burgeoning Christmas celebration took on many traditions that have nothing to do with the birth of Christ.

Easter, too, suffered from the accretion of customs not related to the Bible—starting with the name "Easter," which is an Anglicized form of Oestre, the name of a west Germanic spring goddess. Easter eggs, bunnies and other things came from pagan religions. These traditions, associated with the celebration of the resurrection of Christ, have long since left the back seat and taken a front seat in the public mind, leaving the church—mostly Protestant churches —to grapple with the mythical distractions and try to focus their members' minds on the "real meaning of Easter."

160

Another church holiday, All Saints Day, began in the 9th century in the Catholic Church, fixed on November 1. It started with a vigil on the night before, called All Hallows Eve, or Halloween, which at first included such things as children going door to door asking for "soul cakes" to eat as representatives of the dead saints, known or unknown. Sometimes they carried hollowed out gourd lamps to ward off evil spirits. From there, all manner of celebration of the supernatural, the macabre, and devilry has become part of the celebration. Today's Halloween is a glorification of the very opposite of what All Saints Day was supposedly about.

But it isn't just church holidays that need to be stripped of pagan traditions or thoroughly worldly practices. The adulterated holidays of the church are a powerful illustration of how individual Christians mingle worldly personal habits with their daily living. Some habits may have started early. Others were adopted perhaps during a time of being backslidden spiritually, and were never abandoned. Sometimes Christians become chronically backslidden *precisely because* they don't—they *won't*—removed these ungodly habits or behaviors from their lives. But confronted with the truth of God's word, they know, *they just know*—that these things need to go. Now!

THE SUN STANDS STILL
Joshua 10:12-14

Among the curious stories in the Bible perhaps no miracle story has attracted more interest than the one about Joshua, when "the sun stood still." Certainly, judged by the attention given it by authors of scholarly papers and commentaries, the account of Joshua's victory over the Amorites, with its centerpiece of what certainly sounds like a miracle without parallel, has fascinated, perturbed, excited, and confounded scholars for generations.

The larger passage is more generally about troop movements, strategies, and battle details, but the curious miracle story proper begins in Joshua 10:12:

> ¹² On the day the LORD gave the Amorites over to the Israelites, Joshua spoke to the LORD in the presence of Israel:
> "Sun, stand still over Gibeon,
>> and moon, over the Valley of Aijalon."
> ¹³ And the sun stood still
>> and the moon stopped
>> until the nation took vengeance on its enemies.
> Isn't this written in the Book of Jashar?
> So the sun stopped
>> in the middle of the sky
>> and delayed its setting
>> almost a full day.
> ¹⁴ There has been no day like it before or since, when the LORD listened to the voice of a man, because the LORD

fought for Israel (Joshua 10:12-14 HCSB).

If read in the English, and without any knowledge of the underlying linguistic issues, the story sounds for all the world like Joshua prayed the day would be longer and it turned into practically forty-eight hours instead of twenty-four.[127] But is that what the text means?

Someone once said the Bible doesn't always say what it means, but it always means what it says. That depends on what you mean by "says" and "means." One thing is for sure: God always means to say what he said, and he always means what he meant when he said it.

Confused yet? What we're trying to say is that the Bible is chock full of metaphor, symbolism, and hyperbole, and lots of other linguistic features that writers used then and still use to say things indirectly, beautifully, poetically, controversially, or interestingly. Sometimes such language was meant by the biblical speakers to intentionally obscure meaning. For instance, Jesus often spoke in parables for the very purpose of communicating with willing disciples while confusing obstinate opponents. He explained to them: **"Unto you it is given to know the mysteries of the kingdom of God: but to others in parables; that seeing they might not see, and hearing they might not understand"** (Luke 8:10 KJV).

And when was the last time you thought about Mark 1:5, **"All Jerusalem and Judea were going out to him [John the Baptist] and were all baptized by him"**? Really? No, not really. The writer of Mark used hyperbole, same as we do (like the teen who defends her request of parents by saying, "Everybody's doing it!"). Jerusalem and Judea were not emptied of their populations.

What is sometimes difficult about interpreting the Bible is

---

[127] We could actually say twelve hours longer rather than twenty-four, since twelve would be more nearly the amount of daylight.

getting acquainted with the often very significant differences between the nature of writing two and three thousand years ago as compared to today. Anybody who has ever tried to read those "classic books" of, say, two or three hundred years ago knows that the style, vocabulary, verbiage, euphemisms, and dozens of other elements of writing can render older writing difficult if not utterly painful to read. How much more can we expect to find writing ten times that old—and from a very different part of the world with a vastly different culture—sometimes precarious to interpret?

If it sounds like we're trying to prepare the reader for an interpretation of Joshua 10:12-14 that eliminates his having to believe in miracles, *we're not*. What we *are* doing is preparing the reader to dive into some study that frankly some people are unwilling to undertake. Some folks like everything as simple as it can be. When they graduated from school they threw the big learning switch to "off." The complex frightens them. Uncertainty upsets them. Mystery confuses them. But the Bible demands our *study*, not just our memorization or repetition. In this book so far, we have attempted to study, to pore over, the curious stories of the Bible, and this chapter is no exception. We're going to dig into the meaning of this nearly unbelievable tale of God's intervention in a battle fought by his people, and try to understand what exactly he did that enabled them to be victorious. There might be a lesson or two awaiting us.

Discovering the Text

Context

Just previous to our focus story, the five kings of the Amorites—the kings of Jerusalem, Hebron, Jarmuth, Lachish and Eglon—joined forces to attack Gibeon, which was allied with Israel. In response, Joshua took all his forces and marched up against them. He surprised them with an early morning attack (10:9) and the enemy armies fled. But as they did they were caught in a terrible hailstorm (10:11) with hail so large that it killed more of them than the Israelites had.

It is at this point that the narrative abruptly changes subjects, telling us about the sun and moon standing still or stopping.

We are likely encountering one of those points in the book of Joshua where the writer who compiled the accounts from Joshua's day also consulted other sources and calls our attention to that fact in his reference to the Book of Jasher (10:13). And the abrupt end to the first part of the story, about a battle near Gibeon and a hailstorm, probably is meant to disconnect the two and switch from prose to poetry. The writer shifts into a poetic mood and gives us a conclusion to the larger story where short phrases in prose are mingled with classic Hebrew poetry.

Who's talking?

One of the first issues we must confront in v12 is who is doing the talking—who is it who addresses the sun and moon?

In our scripture above from the HCSB, it certainly appears that Joshua was speaking—or at least he spoke to God *about* the sun and moon. But HCSB, NIV, GNT and others make an interpretive call about how to group the words in the Hebrew. Compare how these translations phrase the verse with how the King James, the NASB, ESV and others render it, and it isn't so clear who's doing the talking by the time the sun and moon are addressed.

In Hebrew, a word for word rendering (which sounds a little choppy in English) would be: "Then spoke Joshua to Yahweh in the day when delivered up Yahweh the Amorites before the sons of Israel, and he said in the sight of Israel sun over Gibeon stand still and moon in the valley of Aijalon." In the Hebrew, the distance between "Joshua" and "he said" is great enough that some scholars have suggested that the words to the sun and moon may have been spoken by God instead of Joshua. The New American Commentary notes that the grammar and word order of v12-13 allow for those verses to be spoken by God, which would make more sense than Joshua's speaking to the sun and moon.[128]

That's a valid point, but there certainly are examples in the Bible of God's people speaking to things—spiritual beings, elements, diseases, etc.—especially *in the name of the Lord*, where miraculous events then take place. The seventy disciples of Jesus reported after they went out and came back that **"even the demons are subject to us through your name"** (Luke 10:17). They apparently spoke directly to demons and cast them out. And Jesus specifically told his disciples (though using hyperbole), that **"if ye shall say unto this mountain, Be thou removed, and be thou cast into the sea; it shall be done"** (Matthew 21:21). For Joshua to speak to the sun and moon *in the authority of the Lord* was not unbiblical *per se*.

Further, as often happens when interpreters grasp at minute points in an attempt to support an interpretive thesis, they may disregard or downplay other parts of a text that conflict. In this case, the summary of the little story is that God paid attention to the words of a man—Joshua—which most certainly refers to the words spoken in v12.

It would appear, then, that translations that switch around the word order to make it conform more nicely with modern English have not confused things; Joshua addressed the sun and moon as a prayer to God, who alone had the power, as Joshua knew, to effect what he asked.

What was asked

The content of the request made to God seems simple enough: **"Sun, stand still over Gibeon, and moon, over the Valley of Aijalon"** (v12). The Hebrew has only the one verb, "stand still" (דום - *dowm*), and it applies to both sun and moon in this sentence.

---

[128] David M. Howard, Jr., *Joshua*, The New American Commentary, (Nashville, Broadman & Holman Publishers, 1998), 241.

The focus of translators for centuries has been on the possible meanings of the verb, which include: stand still, stop, be dumb, be silent, rest, forbear, perish, hold (your) peace, and even relax. A modern colloquialism that fits nicely is "chill."

Two issues affect the translation in v12. The first is the fact that *dowm*, or *dom*, has something of a parallel root word in Babylonian cuneiform that is used in connection with eclipses. More on that momentarily. The second issue is the fact that the next sentence in the text, v13, tells us what happened in fulfillment of Joshua's prayer, and two words are used, one of the sun (*dom*) and one of the moon (*amad*). We must assume that those words parallel the expectations of the prayer. So if we concentrate on v13, we'll be focusing on the heart of the matter.

What was done

Verse 13 tells us what happened in response to Joshua's prayer. Considering the linguistic issues involved, what exactly *did* happen?

Let's look at the basic interpretations that have been offered over the years. We can't cover them all, but most of them fit into one of these. Evaluations follow after the list.

1. **The completely literal view: the earth stopped rotating and the moon stopped rotating.**
2. **The hailstorm blocked the sun's light.**
3. **A solar eclipse blocked the sun's light.**
4. **A localized miracle took place due to natural reasons.**
5. **The sun and moon specifically refer to pagan deities.**
6. **The passage is figurative, referring to the divine efficiency of Israelite warfare.**

Entire books have been written about these three verses of scripture. We don't expect to cover every argument, every theory, every fascinating possibility about this passage. But let's look at each proposal for interpreting it and see where it takes us.

Interpretation 1, the completely literal interpretation, takes the words at face value *only*, discounting the effect of any poetry or symbolism. It depends upon a reading of the Hebrew verb *dom* that means "stop moving." Joshua prayed the sun would stop moving, and the sun stopped moving. We described this view as one that "the earth stopped rotating" only because for centuries we have known that the sun does not rotate around the earth but the other way around. However, in our day we still say that "the sun sets," and we don't apologize for the expression. A long time ago, the completely literal interpretation had to change to fit Galileo's discovery, but the view still held that astronomical bodies stopped whirling in space.

The main strength of this view is its sheer simplicity. It also plainly states the all-powerful nature of God. And, it comes out of a very high view of the inspiration of scripture. But the weakness of this view is that it totally disregards the highly relevant fact that the passage is loaded with poetry, and that Hebrew poetry is frequently filled with wild hyperbole and exaggeration.

Further, Interpretation 1 goes against a principle that can be derived from scripture itself, namely what this author calls **God's self-limitation of supernatural intervention.** A study of the miracles of the Old and New Testaments shows that when God intervenes in a miraculous way in human affairs, he does so with economy: he doesn't cancel, pause, interrupt, or interfere with his own laws of nature more than he needs to in order to accomplish his purpose. He limits his supernatural deeds to the task at hand.[129] Examples:

- The parting of the Red Sea did not involve the cessation of the flow of all rivers or the tides of all seas on earth, just the flow of the inlets to the Red Sea and the Sea itself right where the

---

[129] The author has put forward this theory after significant review of the scriptures. He is open to anyone's citation of a supernatural event clearly disproving the theory.

Israelites were gathered looking for a way across.

- Jesus fed 5,000 (and since that referred to *men*, the number was really more like 10,000 plus) from 5 loaves and 2 fish, but the pantries of the neighboring towns did not burst at the seams at the same time.
- In the sign given to Hezekiah (2 Kings 20:8-11), the shadow went back ten steps *on Ahaz's stairway*, not everywhere in the world, country or even the city. Whatever caused it was limited to the site of the sign for which Hezekiah had asked God. (The fact that inquirers from Babylon later visited Hezekiah to ask about this sign is no disproof of its limitation. The scripture says they asked him about **"the sign that happened in the land"**—i.e. the land of Hezekiah, not the Babylonians.) Reports of this amazing event had reached them far away.
- In the crowd where a woman thought if she could just touch the hem of Jesus' garment she would be healed, he turned and asked, "Who touched me?" His disciples asked how he could say that, when dozens had touched him in the press of the crowd. But even when Jesus didn't know at first how his power had been applied, he knew it was just the one whose prayerful and faith-filled touch reached him who had received supernatural healing. The rest of the crowd went home with their arthritis and gout.

As Howard puts it: "while God certainly is capable of performing a miracle on such a grand scale as stopping the earth on its axis, this is out of proportion to his normal ways of working, and so other naturalizing explanations are advanced."[130] If the earth stopped rotating such that the sun didn't "move" in the sky for *any* length of time, much less twelve or twenty-four hours, the direct implication would be that it didn't move forward, either, along with the rest of

---

[130] Howard, *op. cit.*, 242-243.

the solar system, around the galaxy. And even if the rotation were the only thing interrupted, the laws of physics concerning gravity and other things would have to have been suspended, or else everything on earth would have flown out into space.

In other words, a great deal more than God *had* to have done to ensure Israelite victory would *have* to have been done, and it would have affected not just Joshua and the armies of both sides, but the entire globe as well.

Scientific "proofs." Not bothered by the super-extensive involvement of the very solar system in a literal view, the proponents of this view have come up with "discoveries" by scientists that support this interpretation. In 1936 *The Harmony of Science and Scripture,* by Harry Rimmer,[131] purported to document a preexisting story to the effect that a "missing day" resulting from Joshua's experience had been discovered in calculations of various scientists. For Rimmer, that story went back to yet another book published in 1890 by C. A. Totten of Yale University (title not given), saying that a fellow professor (name not given) attempted to disprove the Bible using our story where the sun "stood still."

It's all pretty convoluted, but the upshot of it is that the original accounts of this "proof" can't be verified. But Totten started something rolling, and it got occasional renewals in religious books, newspapers and, ultimately, of course, on the Internet. One of the more recent iterations of the account is that NASA was doing calculations for some space mission when their computers "ground to a halt" and "showed a red flag," when they found a missing day in history, which ultimately traced to Joshua. Computer users, certainly computer experts, will smirk at language like "ground to a halt" and "red flag" to describe what computers do. In other words, the story itself betrays its lack of factual basis. Our understanding is that years ago NASA was queried about this story and confirmed a

---

[131] David Mikkelson, *NASA Discovers a 'Lost Day' in Time?*, Snopes, Accessed August 16, 2024, https:// www.snopes.com/fact-check/the-lost-day/.

name or two involved but disavowed that any "calculations" had been done that proved the literal view of Joshua 10:12-14.

We will not attempt to go any further with the specific claim that "scientists" have proven that a day "went missing" in Joshua's time. To trace all these claims to their sources would, in fact, be impossible, because so many of them would lead to dead ends. To be blunt, the entire effort to cite scientific studies as verification for a two-day-long day is what we call **urban legend.** Most of the stories have just enough truth to make eager searchers believe them, but they are myths laced with lies. As one author put it, "[W]e cannot find sources which support these claims, and other Christians believe that they are most likely fraudulent."[132]

After careful consideration and warning himself against it, this author will admit to having been sucked in by such an urban legend in the 1970s (when he was a *very* young man), when looking for material for a sermon to illustrate how miracles are sometimes proven by science. An article in the *Dallas Morning News,* by local WFAA television personality Bob Gooding, retold some of the "scientific" evidence about the missing day of Joshua 10. In spite of the high profile of this particular retelling of the "scientific proof" for a two-day day, the falsity of the report was eventually discovered by this author, and the clipped article was angrily trashed, while a vow was made to be less credulous in the future.[133]

Historical "proof." Another attempt to support the literal view involves the claim that around the world, histories of various cultures contain references to an extraordinarily long day, and that these records correspond to Joshua's time. Chinese, Grecian, Egyptian, Mexican, Aztec, Peruvian, and Babylonian histories

---

[132] "Evidence Unseen," Accessed June 10, 2024, https://www.evidenceunseen.com/bible-difficulties-2/ot-difficulties/joshua/josh-1013-how-could-the-sun-stand-still-without-destroying-life- as-we-know-it/.

[133] A photograph of the article can be found at https://www.worthpoint.com/worthopedia/vintage-article-missing-day-bob-1866806714.

purportedly say such things—with appropriate adjustment for whether the extra time was light or dark.

An Internet search will yield perhaps hundreds of sites where these reports are repeated, but getting to the root of them will prove impossible. However, consider just one supposed historical source, that of a Chinese Emperor named Yao, said by many of these reports to have been emperor when Joshua prayed for the sun to stop. Actually, a very reliable source, the *Encyclopedia Brittanica*, says that Yao was a *mythological* emperor, who was supposed to have lived in the 24th century B.C., not the 12th (give or take a hundred years). And the details of his mythological life are brimful of wild but symbolic fiction about how wonderful things were in his day and time in China.

Bernard Ramm summed up his justified skepticism of one of these "proofs:" "This I have not been able to verify to my own satisfaction."[134] Nor have we.

Anyone—individual or group—can be the victim of the negative effects of urban legend and Internet hoaxes. The fact that someone makes up a story supposedly to help a cause, and that later it is disproved and actually hurts that cause, does not mean that the cause itself is invalid.

In spite of the weakness of the literal view—principally that it assumes God acted way out of proportion to what was necessary—we wish to sum up this interpretive approach by asserting the truth that lies at the heart of it:

God, who created all that is, is infinitely powerful and can do anything he pleases in an instant, perfectly, and without any negative effect.

If God wanted to stop the earth's rotation, effectively freezing

---

[134] Ramm, Bernard L., *The Christian View of Science and Scripture*, (Grand Rapids, Michigan, W.B. Eerdmans Publishing, 1954), 109.

the sun and moon in the sky, while maintaining all other principles of astrophysics for the preservation of the earth's people, and without affecting the "space-time continuum," he could do it. Perhaps he did and the literal view is right.

Meanwhile, let's review another view that has been advanced.

Interpretation 2, that the hailstorm (v11) blocked the sun's light, is effectively the suggestion that the day was not lengthened at all, but instead that it only became hard to tell the time because of the storm.

This view has very little to recommend it, but surprisingly it has been promoted by a few devotees for years. It depends on a reading of the aforementioned Hebrew verb *dom* that means, not stop in the sense of ceasing to move, but stop in the sense of ceasing to shine. The key to the meaning of the event, according to this view, is found right there in the text, in a natural event, albeit one divinely timed. And not only did the hailstorm make the day seem longer (or of questionable length), but it also killed more enemy soldiers than the Israelites had killed with their weapons.

This supposed, scriptural support of the hailstorm view is really its chief strength. And we know that when human beings are deprived of the rhythm of day and night, they lose an accurate sense of time. Still, it's a stretch to think that a little midday darkness because of a storm would leave the distinct impression in the Israelites' minds that two days had passed instead of one. Not only that, it's hard to see how time disorientation could have made the battle more successful.

Interpretation 3, that a solar eclipse blocked the sun's light, is similarly based on a reading of the Hebrew verb to the effect that "the sun and moon just stopped doing what they normally do: they stopped shining."[135] This interpretation of the sense of the Hebrew is strengthened by what we said earlier about the similarity of that word with a Babylonian root used to refer to eclipses.

But the view is similarly defeated—and rather easily, we think—and for the same reasons as Interpretation 2. Additionally, it's worth asking if the kind of darkness that an eclipse produces helped the Israelites in battle, wouldn't it have helped their enemies to the same degree?

And finally, the eclipse view contradicts what seems to be the plain sense of what Joshua was said to have been asking for: *more time.*

Interpretation 4 holds that a localized miracle took place, due to natural events. These events, however, were divinely timed and probably divinely exaggerated—made worse or better or more extensive or more concentrated—than they ordinarily would be, resulting in whatever it was that Joshua and his armies experienced.

As to these natural events, those who hold this interpretive view mean absolutely no diminution of God's involvement or power. Readers will remember that in the parting of the Red Sea (Exodus 14:19-31) God used a "strong east wind" to drive the waters upstream (14:21). The film, "The Ten Commandments," didn't quite depict the miracle this way, though it was an impressive visualization.

The strength of this view is first its recognition of the principle described above, God's self-limitation of supernatural intervention. The view posits that God acted in the vicinity of Joshua's battle and nowhere else, doing so by natural events.

This view is characterized by the noticeable vagueness of its proponents as to just what those natural events were. Some scholars

---

[135] David Sedley, "'Joshua stopped the sun' 3,224 years ago today, scientists say," *The Times of Israel,* Accessed June 18, 2024, https://www.timesofisrael.com/3224-years- later-scientists-see-first-ever- recorded-eclipse-in-joshuas-battle/.

suggest some kind of refraction of light, but they are generally not specific about where and how such a refraction could have taken place. Some sources offer the possibility that this localized miracle might have been paired with an eclipse. That suggestion runs into the same, significant weakness of Interpretation 3.

However, this vagueness should not be read as a weakness of this view, exactly. One might as easily ask *how* Jesus multiplied the loaves, or *how* he healed people, or *how* he rose from the dead. One might also ask, about Old Testament miracles, *how* God made an ax head float, or *how* a donkey was able to talk. We've dealt with those last two miracles in this book, but not by trying to explain the "mechanics" of the miracles. After all, if we can fully explain *how* a miracle happened, it probably wasn't a miracle. One of the major characteristics of a miracle is that it defies natural explanation. In the Bible, "a miracle is always a 'sign' of an extraordinary divine intervention which imparts a grace unmerited by man and inconceivable in any other way."[136]

What really defines Interpretation 4 is that it posits no less a miracle than Interpretation 1, but only limits that miracle to a few square miles instead of involving the entire earth, the moon, and who knows what else. We think that's its strength, and it's probably why this view has had so much support over the years.

Interpretation 5 is somewhat non-specific about any supernatural event during Joshua's battle, but what it says is that whatever did or didn't take place was due to the nature of Joshua's petition, which was addressed to pagan deities. This view rests on the claim or assumption that for "Israel's neighbors…the moon and sun would be seen as gods."[137] "Sun and moon are supposed to have

---

[136] J. Alberto Soggin, *Joshua, A Commentary*, (Philadelphia, Westminster Press, 1972), 123.

[137] Trent C. Butler, *Joshua*, The Word Biblical Commentary, General Editors Bruce M. Metzger, David A. Hubbard and Glenn W. Barker, (Waco, Texas, Word

been the tutelary deities of Gibeon and Aijalon, respectively, and they are enjoined here not to take part in military action."[138] The authors quoted above were careful about wording what they said because other scholars have asserted that we have no certain knowledge that the enemies of Joshua and Israel on the day in question were worshipers of the sun and moon. They may have been. They may not have been.

It is this uncertainty that constitutes a major weakness of Interpretation 5. The other weakness is the rather glaring fact that it offers no other explanation for the sense of what happened in v13, just that whatever happened, it happened because the deities of the sun and moon were incapacitated as a result of Joshua's prayer, *or* that the enemy was discouraged or psychologically defeated by that prayer against their gods. As to the latter, however, left unexplained is how the enemy knew about Joshua's prayer, in order to have been psychologically defeated by it. The petition was uttered in the hearing of the Israelites, but not that of the kings and armies they were fighting.

We think the ultimate weakness of this view is that even if Joshua had been addressing the sun and moon because his enemies regarded them as deities, Joshua himself would not have believed them to be such, and they weren't. His prayer, therefore, wouldn't have kept the sun and moon from helping the enemy as deities, because they weren't personal beings with heavenly powers in the first place.

Interpretation 6, the figurative view, is logically on the other end of where we started, Interpretation 1, the completely literal view. We listed them that way to begin with for just that reason.

Books, 1983), 117.

[138] Marten H. Woudstra, *The Book of Joshua*, The New International Commentary on the Old Testament, (Grand Rapids, Michigan, William B. Eerdmans Publishing Company, 1981), 175.

The figurative view holds that the assertion that the sun and moon both stopped is figurative or symbolic of other, more deeply important realities. One of the major supports for this view is the fact that half of v12 and most of v13 are in the form of poetry in Hebrew, and thus are highly likely to consist of figurative speech.

Consider perhaps most significantly a similar use of poetry to communicate a spiritual idea about the sun and moon in Habakkuk 3:11. The prophet there has been talking about an appearance of the LORD—a theophany—and he says, **"The sun and moon stood still in their habitation: at the light of thine arrows they went, and at the shining of thy glittering spear"** (KJV). The appearance of the LORD in the previous verses outshines even the sun and moon—the greater and lesser lights God created—and they stand still in awe, dumbstruck. "Stand still" in that verse is *amad*, just as in Joshua10:13. Ellicott says, "[T]he conception is that the surpassing brightness of the theophany shames the heavenly bodies, which accordingly cease to pursue their journey."[139]

Note also Judges 4-5, where a prose, historical account is followed by a poetic representation, with figurative language that— if the history hadn't already been recounted—might have led to a questionable reconstruction of the events that had occurred.

There are literally hundreds of examples of Hebrew poetry with figurative language that cast historical events into the realm of hyperbole, making it the stuff of myth, if we weren't already aware of the actual events the poetry memorialized. The Psalmist is one of the major users of hyperbole and symbolism in the Bible.

In Joshua, the poetic response of the sun and moon is to stand still or do nothing, in response to the fact that God is intervening in a battle and waging war for his people. This would be one of the major ways the commander of the LORD's army took charge of

---

[139] C. H. Waller, *Joshua*, Ellicott's Commentary on the Whole Bible, Accessed Jun 10, 2024, https:// biblehub.com/commentaries/habakkuk/3-11.htm.

Israel's warfare and guaranteed their success.[140]

One of the linguistic features of the poetry in v13 that may tip us off to a figurative meaning is the verb in the phrase, **"delayed going down"** (NIV). The King James has "hastened not" and the International Standard Version has, "seemed not to be in a hurry." A modern rendering faithful to the Hebrew, which is (אֵת - *as*), would be, "took its time" going down. It's not a word meaning simply "didn't" go down, but a more subjective word suggesting people's *perception* of what was taking place rather than an objective measurement of it. That would lead to the conclusion that as the Israelites fought, it seemed they never ran out of time to do what needed to be done to defeat the Amorites. Their plans were being carried out methodically and unhurriedly.

Some scholars also translate the final phrase of v13 as "did not hasten to go down as a perfect day."[141] Nothing went wrong, not even to a degree that everyone on Israel's side might have resigned themselves be expecting. Instead, everything went perfectly, every phase of the battle plan was carried out with sufficient and precise timing, and God's hand was evident in it all.

Some sincere believers fear that taking a scripture passage to be figurative instead of literal somehow constitutes acquiescence to theological liberalism, as if they had abandoned belief in the Bible itself. Considering how much of the Bible is bathed in metaphor and symbolism, that fear is really unfounded. "The suggestion of a figurative interpretation is not a denial that God could perform such a miracle, and one does not need to accept the figurative view

---

[140] In Joshua 5:13-15, this commander turns out to be a theophany, a pre-incarnation appearance of God the Son. Note that thereafter in the book the LORD spoke to Joshua periodically, led Joshua as he led Israel's armies, and fought for Israel in their campaign to conquer the holy land. Behind the scenes we read about where Israel fights physical enemies on all sides, but the LORD is in charge, fighting the spiritual enemies and the nations who serve them.

[141] J. J. Lias, *Deuteronomy, Joshua and Judges*, The Pulpit Commentary, (New York, Funk & Wagnall's, 1895), 167.

because of any concern over scientific problems."[142] As we stated categorically, with bold and italic emphasis above, God, who created all that is, is infinitely powerful and can do anything he pleases in an instant, perfectly, and without any negative effect. The question for this passage in Joshua, as with all accounts of miracles, is not whether God *could* do a thing in a particular way, but whether he *did* do that thing in the way that this person or that person insists that he did.

Learning the Lessons

Christians wanting to apply the Old Testament's lessons to their lives should remind themselves that it's easy to make a direct application that is unrealistic or even entirely unjustified by the scripture in question. For instance, a Christian cannot depend on God's actually performing a miracle every time that Christian faces spiritual enemies, and base that expectation on this passage in Joshua. And before a defensive Christian starts referring to New Testament passages about the power of God for Christian living —such as 2 Corinthians 10:4-5, etc.—let's agree that a "miracle" is not merely the experience of spiritual power possessed by the believer in Christ, and not even the spiritual warfare that goes on invisibly around the believer's visible life. We reserve the word "miracle" to refer to those incidents in which God makes exceptions to the laws of nature that *he himself* put in force, for the benefit of his people and the accomplishment of his kingdom plans. After all, if "everything" is a miracle, nothing really is.

Nor should a Christian be disappointed to the point of discouragement or abandoning the faith just because he or she prayed for a miracle and it didn't happen. Sometimes God wants us to struggle through. Sometimes he wants us to come closer to him

---

[142] Howard, *op. cit.*, 249.

precisely because of our suffering. Sometimes he uses our difficulties to purge us of sinful thinking or behavior. Not always will he step in, interrupt the laws of nature, or even defy "the odds,"[143] in order to deliver us from having to go through tough times.

Perhaps the first lesson, then, would be cautionary:

1. Realism
An Attitude to Develop ☑

When faced with opposition in your life, be realistic about whether God will deliver you from all trouble by way of miracle.

Joshua faced what we would have to call a monumental task in his day. It truly was of gigantic historical proportions. What happened not only in this battle with the Amorites but also with all the other enemies that both inhabited the Promised Land and also surrounded it would resound down through history to this very day. It shaped the way history developed in that region and around the world. If ever there were a time for a miracle, that was it. But not all Joshua's battles would be fought with miracles happening left and right. Sometimes it was divine strategy that won the battle, directions revealed by God and followed faithfully by Joshua and his armies.

The point for the Christian is that *we* are not in charge of how God will act: *he* is. We are to turn to him, stay turned to him, pray continually, and seek his direction and power. If he does something that defies physics, well and good. If he doesn't, he will still be faithful; **"he cannot deny himself"** (2 Timothy 2:13).

---

[143] The use of this phrase should not be taken in any way to suggest that there is a "force" called "chance." The author vigorously denies that there is. What is valid, however, is the fact that certain processes ordinarily result in predictable results. It is not likely, for instance, that a baseball pitcher will hit a bird with a fastball, but it has happened. Randy Johnson did it in 2001.

2. Expectancy

Notwithstanding the wisdom of realism, the Christian should expect God to act in his life.

It was William Carey (1761-1834) who famously said, "Expect great things from God; attempt great things for God." Note the order of the two phrases. In the context of our lives for him in discipleship to Jesus Christ, we are always to expect God to do great things; such an expectation is preliminary to any and all of our efforts for him. However, we are to act in light of our expectancy, and to be bold in our attempts to carry out his will and leading in our lives. We may not know how he is going to accomplish his purpose in us, but we may go forward expectantly, because he has repeatedly proven that he will demonstrate **"the immeasurable greatness of his power toward us who believe, according to the mighty working of his strength"** (Ephesians 1:19).

3. Timing

Know that in God's time, and in God's timing, there is all the time you need to do his will if you keep doing it without stopping.

Among other things, Joshua is famous for the instruction given to him, **"Be strong and courageous"** (Joshua 1:6,9, Deuteronomy 31:7,23). It became a byword for leaders in subsequent generations, as in 1 Chronicles 22:13 and 2 Chronicles 15:7, 32:7. The instruction continues to be a challenge expected of every follower of Christ. And in the believer's commitment to be strong and courageous, he may fully expect that God will make available every resource to him necessary for doing his divine will, including time.

Have you ever wondered why it's so difficult to swat a fly with your hand? It's partly because of the fact that your hand displaces a lot of air, which the fly feels, and he has time to fly off in a flash. Fly swatters have holes in them to displace much less air. But the other reason you miss them is that the fly is so much faster than you. He has less mass to move, and his motions are all quicker. It's true with many small insects. Some spiders move with almost incredible speed. And how do spiders see *you?* They think you move like a slug.

The opposite is true of an elephant, who can run (really just walk fast) at about 15 mph, while a man can usually outrun him, but not by much. But as for swatting a fly with his trunk, an elephant would be even less successful than a human being.

When movie makers depict the movements of fictional super heroes who have the speed of insects, they often don't attempt to show the actor playing the super hero moving very quickly; instead, they may show attackers and enemies moving in slow motion. The super hero shifts into insect mode and everything around him slows down. He is able to see incoming fists and ducks them. He sees approaching bullets and dodges them. He sees attackers running at him, and trips them or uses their weight against them with lightning speed.

No suggestion is being made here that what happened that day when Joshua prayed for God's intervention was that time slowed down for the enemy or speeded up for Israel, or both. What is intended is an illustration of the possibility that the enemy was so predictable, so plodding, so uncoordinated, and that Israel was so fast and efficient, so instantly effective, and so speedily active and reactive, that it was like they had all the time in the world to apply divinely inspired and infused strength, and they kept on attacking until there was no one left to fight. Poetically, the battle was over before the sun and moon had time to move. It was a perfect day for battle.

When it is God's time for you to act, *act,* with strength and courage. God will make certain you have all the time you need to do his will if you keep at it. Time may run out on physical life before what a believer may have *assumed* was God's will for his life has taken place. Consider Stephen, the first Christian martyr. Or read the story of Jim Elliott, a young man who less than a year into his bold missionary venture into Ecuador, was murdered by Huaorani warriors. These men's lives were cut short—but were they? Not in God's timing. The accounts of their bold witness have inspired generations of believers.

God's timing is perfect, and he gives us all the time we need to do all that he has planned for us. Trust his timing, and keep going in his strength.

FAT MAN DIES BADLY

Judges 3:14-25

Some Bible stories are memorable for their striking details even when there isn't anything mysterious or obscure about them. Such is the story of an assassination that took place in the early days of the Israelite Judges.

[14]The Israelites were subject to Eglon king of Moab for eighteen years.

[15] Again the Israelites cried out to the LORD, and he gave them a deliverer—Ehud, a left-handed man, the son of Gera the Benjamite. The Israelites sent him with tribute to Eglon king of Moab. [16] Now Ehud had made a double-edged sword about a cubit long, which he strapped to his right thigh under his clothing. [17] He presented the tribute to Eglon king of Moab, who was a very fat man. [18] After Ehud had presented the tribute, he sent on their way those who had carried it. [19] But on reaching the stone images near Gilgal he himself went back to Eglon and said, "Your Majesty, I have a secret message for you."

The king said to his attendants, "Leave us!" And they all left.

[20] Ehud then approached him while he was sitting alone in the upper room of his palace and said, "I have a message from God for you." As the king rose from his seat, [21] Ehud reached with his left hand, drew the sword from his right thigh and plunged it into the king's belly. [22] Even the handle sank in after the blade, and his bowels

discharged. Ehud did not pull the sword out, and the fat closed in over it. ²³ Then Ehud went out to the porch; he shut the doors of the upper room behind him and locked them.

²⁴ After he had gone, the servants came and found the doors of the upper room locked. They said, "He must be relieving himself in the inner room of the palace." ²⁵ They waited to the point of embarrassment, but when he did not open the doors of the room, they took a key and unlocked them. There they saw their lord fallen to the floor, dead (Judges 3:14-25 NIV).

This is the story of the initial exploits of Israel's second judge, Ehud. As was true in a number of cases, the judges were people who attained that distinction after, or in the process of, delivering the Israelites from oppression under one of the surrounding peoples. In the case of Ehud it was the Moabites who had invaded and conquered the Israelite tribes.

As our story opens, the Israelites have been in this oppressed condition for eighteen years. Apparently, all that time they had been sending tribute to Eglon, the king of the Moabites. Also apparently, as we may reasonably induce, for most if not all those years the carrier of tribute was Ehud.

Discovering the Text

The characters: Ehud

The text says simply of Ehud that Israel **"sent him with tribute to Eglon king of Moab"** (v15). The Hebrew verb is the simple past, but it does not necessarily refer to only the last year he made the trip to Moab, nor the first trip. It may be taken to refer to the decision the Israelites made to select Ehud as their perennial envoy to Moab, leading a contingent of Israelites, carrying the tribute, in whatever form that tribute took.

As we consider who Ehud was, we are introduced to two salient facts about him in the biblical record. The first is his name itself. The two syllables of the name Ehud are two Hebrew words "which together denote 'Where is the splendor, majesty?'" suggesting that the "name reflects the despondency of the times."[144] The name calls attention to itself for another reason. Ehud is described as **a Benjamite.** Daniel Block remarks that, first, "if the events of chaps. 19-21 belong to the time of the prologue or shortly thereafter, we do not expect much from the Benjamites. The tribe has been decimated by intra-Israelite warfare. Second, the name 'Benjamin' means 'son of the right hand,' that is, 'right-handed.' …But [Ehud] is left handed!" This fact was significant, perhaps symbolically as well as literarily, to the author of Judges, and it will play into one of our takeaway lessons in the conclusion.

Of the Bible's statement that Ehud was left-handed, Block thinks it means he was ambidextrous. The New International Commentary mostly disagrees, saying, as all commenting sources do of the Hebrew words, that they mean "[l]iterally, 'a man restricted in his right hand' *(is itter yad-ye mino)."* Some soldiers were taught to be left handed as well as right handed by binding their right hands during training. While this is possible, it is not the point of the text, which is in fact that Ehud was left handed and that everyone knew it. Specifically, the court of Eglon knew it.

The characters: Eglon

Eglon, king of Moab, according to the Bible was **"a very fat man"** (v17). A nice word would be "corpulent." In today's super-sensitive culture calling someone fat is "fat shaming" and the political correctness police will loudly publish their condemnation

---

[144] Daniel I. Block, *Judges, Ruth*, The New American Commentary, General Editor E. Ray Clendenen, (Nashville, Broadman & Holman Publishers, 1999), 160.

of anyone who calls attention to someone's being fat. In the days of the Judges, and pretty much ever since until the first few years of the 21st century, if you were fat you could expect people to describe you that way. After all, it wasn't like it was an accident.

However, there is some question about the degree of the word. We have medical words and a range of words in the vernacular to refer to varying degrees of fatness. Does the Hebrew word here, *bārī*, mean "somewhat overweight," "pleasingly plump," or "morbidly obese?" Or something in between? The Bible itself uses the adjective *m^{e}ōd* - "very." That should be enough. However, as Trent Butler points out, in the Bible "wicked people whose bodies are [fat] gain worldly admiration (Ps 73:4). Daniel and his friends proved their good health with their [fat] (Dan 1:15). ...Most often it [(fat)] signifies good-quality animals, ready for sacrifice (Gen 41:4 [*et al.*].)"[145] What controls the meaning is, in fact, the context. Here, the blunt statement that Eglon was **"very fat"** invites the reader to picture someone who, while his subjects may not have publicly ridiculed him for his corpulence for fear of swift consequences, was nevertheless grossly, morbidly obese. "By fattening himself on the tribute...Eglon has turned himself into a large, slow-moving target and a helpless sacrificial animal."[146]

The plan of Ehud

The text tells us that Ehud planned to assassinate Eglon with a long knife. The length of it was **"about a cubit,"** which was the length of a typical man's arm from elbow to knuckles, or about 18". Scholars debate, as scholars will do, whether it was the "long cubit" or the "short cubit," but it little matters. Ehud strapped the knife on his right side under his robe. A right handed man would be expected—if armed—to be carrying his weapon on his right side.

---

[145] Butler, *Judges*, 70.

[146] Webb, *The Book of Judges*, 165.

Ehud's plan was to give the impression that he was not armed: if Eglon's staff or guards "patted him down" (we don't know what they did in those days), they would have concentrated on his *left side,* knowing him to be a left-handed man. This is where Ehud's familiarity at the court of Eglon came into play. He had been there repeatedly and had always come with respect and obeisance. Nobody expected him to cause trouble. He was being a dutiful subject of Moab. "Apparently Ehud had the full confidence of the Moabite court."[147]

The plan called for Ehud to find a way to be alone with Eglon so no one would rush to defend the king when Ehud struck. The Bible describes what he did and there is little to no debate about what happened.

The tribute was presented as a matter of routine, and the delegation from Israel left. They traveled some distance to what the text calls **"the stone images near Gilgal"** (v19). This detail in the story may provide us more understanding of why Ehud's plan was successful.

The Broadman Commentary says that these "stone images" were "[p]robably a well-known landmark"[148] But what kind of landmark? The King James translates the word *hap·p^e·sî·lîm* as "quarries." Oddly enough, the New King James renders it "stone images." But as translators have looked into this word more thoroughly, other ideas about what it means have emerged. The Amplified Bible says "sculptured stones"—a sort of neutral term that could be taken one of two ways. The Christian Standard Bible says "carved images," taking the term as more likely a reference to idols. Young's Literal Translation has "graven images." Several modern translations drop all pretense and just say "idols."

The term "graven image" (KJV) goes back to Exodus 20:4,

---

[147] Edward R. Dalglish, *Judges,* Broadman Bible Commentary, General Editor Clifton J. Allen, (Nashville, Broadman Press, 1970), 402.

[148] Dalglish, 401.

Leviticus 26:1, Deuteronomy 7:25 and other texts, where the reference is to idols the Israelites are commanded not to worship. They weren't to worship idols made by other nations or make them for themselves. The Hebrew word is the same in all these texts as here in Judges. Commentators who point out for us that these stones "Probably were sculpted images of the Canaanite gods the Israelites were openly worshiping"[149] appear to be on the right track. While the Tyndale volume on Joshua suggests that the stones were the ones Joshua set up after crossing the Jordan (Joshua 4:19-24), this wouldn't seem to have any significance in the story. But if they were idols, their meaning in the story would be interesting. When Ehud returned from this place and reported to the royal staff that he had a message for the king from God, he used the word *elohim,* which Eglon would have heard as "god," since Ehud did not say, "*yhwh*" — the LORD. At that point, Eglon stood up, apparently in reverence to whichever god Ehud meant. As the Word Biblical Commentary notes, if the place of images was of Canaanite images, "[t]he Moabites would see the place of idols as an appropriate and likely place to receive such a divine secret."[150]

In other words, it would appear very likely that stopping at the *stone idols* on their way back from giving tribute was part of Ehud's plan, to give the impression that their passage through that place, perhaps stopping briefly for effect, was the occasion of Ehud's getting 'a message from a god.' We may supply the detail, altogether likely, that the delegation from Israel had probably been followed, if not overtly escorted, from the border of Moab to the royal city and from the royal city back at least as far as the idols.

The assassination

Doing the deed itself was straightforward. As the text says, Ehud

---

[149] Block, 165.

[150] Butler, *Judges,* 71.

came back to the royal complex, gaining entrance by his report of having a divine message. The king dismissed everyone else (the Hebrew word for "Leave us" is *has* and means simply, "Silence!" or "Hush!") They took it as a command to leave, or he gestured for them to do so, and while they were leaving he went up to what Tyndale calls a "summer chamber,"[151] an airy upper room where he and Ehud could be alone. Ehud followed.

When Ehud said, "a message from [G]od, Eglon stood, prepared to hear the sacred words. Instead, as the text so clearly says, Ehud reached with his left hand to his right thigh, underneath his robe, which may have been parted there instead of in the front, and he retrieved his double-edged sword and swiftly plunged it into Eglon's fat belly, before the king could even react. It went in so far it buried itself, possibly coming out Eglon's back. The description suggests strongly that the knife had no hilt.

Ehud left it there, and fled via the porch, using whatever method was available to him to get down to the ground. Possibly he had done reconnaissance the previous year and had planned his escape route well in advance.

The wound was fatal virtually instantly. The language suggests that the knife was moved enough sideways or up and down to have opened up enough of Eglon's abdomen to allow severed intestines to spill out, with their contents. That the court staff or attendants thought **"he must be relieving himself"** may be due in part to their having smelled the results of Ehud's gruesome deed.

Learning the Lessons

What is most remarkable about this story is not some ancient secret that we have to decode, but rather the dramatic and picturesque details in which it has been transmitted to us. Obviously

---

[151] Cundal, *Judges and Ruth*, 77.

Ehud himself, who was alone from the point of his return from the idols until he rejoined his delegation, recounted the story to them and to others, so that it was passed down as we have it—plus details from the Moabites. The story provided the launching point for the writer of Judges to tell us that Ehud rallied Israel, defeated Moab, and turned the tables on them and made them subject to Israel.

Not all the tales of the individual judges are stories of spiritual experience with God. In fact, few of them are. Nevertheless, there are lessons to be learned from them, and there are important lessons to be taken from this story of Ehud.

1. Left-handed deliverance — A Truth to Believe ☑

Even in times of our spiritual obtuseness, God may use left-handed ways to deliver us or position us where he wants us.

The term "left-handed," according to Merriam-Webster, when not referring to actually being done with the left hand, means "clumsy, awkward," or even "insincere." But this author has found the term to be useful to convey what a person will do *if he must,* in order to do what *he needs* to do. It's similar to having something come "out of left field," which means it's unexpected or doesn't appear (at first) to make sense. "Left" has been shortchanged a lot in history.

But God sometimes must do something in a left-handed way if it's going to get done at all. The period of the judges was such a time. It is noted frequently in the book that "there was no king; everyone did what was right in his own eyes" (Judges 17:6 *et al.*). That generalization describes the lack of spiritual moorings during the era. The accounts of the individual judges describe a wide array of warriors, not many of whom would have made good candidates for spiritual reformers. As we said in the previous chapter about Lot and his daughters, God has used some crooked sticks to hit straight licks.

For each of us, that means that we should anticipate that God will not limit himself to burning bushes to guide us, or dreams of ladders to heaven to reveal his plans, or parting waters to give us a means of escape, or any other kind of supernatural means of getting his will done in our lives. Sometimes, because of the general depravity of our situations or because of our own obtuseness, God will use some highly unlikely event or person to put us where he wants us or to deliver us from where our situations were deteriorating.

Realizing that God's means and methods are unlimited inspires us to develop our faith and to believe in the imminency of his moving in our lives when otherwise hopes seem dim. The chief lesson of Ehud's rise to leadership is to expect the unexpected, to hold out for what God is going to do when it seems that nobody else is apparently going to be able to do anything for us.

2. God's timing An Attitude to Develop ☑

Always be ready to act when God gives the word, and commune with him continually so you will know when he says, "Go!"

We don't know what kind of spirituality characterized Ehud's life. The description of him is brief. We do know that he planned, and that he waited. He waited possibly for the entire eighteen years the Bible says the Israelites were under the Moabite king's thumb. And we know that once Ehud acted, he told the Israelites that the LORD had given Moab into their hands. Nothing in the text suggests that he wasn't certain of God's involvement.

We may not know any more about the spirituality of Ehud, but we do know that we are divinely commanded to "walk in the Spirit," to "abide in me [Jesus]" and to "grow in the grace and the knowledge of our Lord and Savior, Jesus Christ" —among other biblical admonitions. In other words, we know we are to be constantly communing with God through the Holy Spirit. We never know when the Lord is going to use us, or for what. We must be ready to act at a moment's notice.

Each of us probably has some pretty good idea of how the Lord will lead. His moving will probably involve one of our spiritual gifts, or a talent we have, or life and work experience. *How* God will give any of us the "go" signal is impossible to say. *When* he will do so—in our youth, in our middle years, in old age?—is not something this book, or *any* book, or anyone else, can tell you. It may be a moment of circumstantial intersection unique to your life and impossible to anticipate. What you *can* know is that God will make his voice heard, his hand felt, his direction clear, *to you.* Your responsibility is to be *ready* to act, and *to act* when the word comes.

SISERA GETS THE POINT
Judges 4:17-22

Every country has beloved stories of the heroes who founded it, fought for its existence, and championed its causes. Often those stories resemble myth more than history, but strange things really do happen in history, and sometimes remarkable tales probably reflect exactly what happened. As the saying goes, truth is often stranger than fiction.

Such is one account of an individual contribution to the Israelite resistance against the Canaanites during the early period of the Judges. As our story opens, Israelite forces have just attacked Canaanites led by Sisera and are in the process of routing them completely.

[17] Howbeit Sisera fled away on his feet to the tent of Jael the wife of Heber the Kenite: for there was peace between Jabin the king of Hazor and the house of Heber the Kenite. [18] And Jael went out to meet Sisera, and said unto him, Turn in, my lord, turn in to me; fear not. And when he had turned in unto her into the tent, she covered him with a mantle. [19] And he said unto her, Give me, I pray thee, a little water to drink; for I am thirsty. And she opened a bottle of milk, and gave him drink, and covered him. [20] Again he said unto her, Stand in the door of the tent, and it shall be, when any man doth come and inquire of thee, and say, Is there any man here? that thou shalt say, No. [21] Then Jael Heber's wife took a nail of the tent, and took an hammer in her hand, and went softly unto

him, and smote the nail into his temples, and fastened it into the ground: for he was fast asleep and weary. So he died. ²² And, behold, as Barak pursued Sisera, Jael came out to meet him, and said unto him, Come, and I will shew thee the man whom thou seekest. And when he came into her tent, behold, Sisera lay dead, and the nail was in his temples (Judges 4:17-22 KJV).

Quite a few sources identify this story as one of the strange tales in scripture, though it really doesn't stand out from its context in an odd way. What marks it in the minds of many Bible readers is apparently the subterfuge of Jael and the somewhat unexpected violence wreaked upon Sisera. Otherwise it seems straightforward. But we'll let a little basic Bible study turn up helpful truths leading to personal challenges.

Discovering the Text

The characters

Sorting out the characters in Hebrew stories is often a challenge, and this story is no exception. Let's mix up the order in which they appear in Judges 4 and group them by which side they were on:

The Bad Guys

First is Jabin, which v1 of this chapter tells us was the king of the Canaanites, who had begun oppressing Israel and had pillaged them at will for twenty years. Jabin's seat of power was at Hazor, about 15-20 miles due north of what later was called the Sea of Galilee or the Sea of Tiberias.

Second is Sisera, the commander of Jabin's armies, who lived in Harosheth of the Nations, which scholars tell us was near Hazor. He had some nine hundred chariots at his command for the exploits of Jabin.

The Good Guys

First is Barak, who lived in Kedesh, The current judge of Israel, Deborah, had him in mind as a military leader to go over the mountain to confront Jabin and free Israel of his continual, menacing raids.

Second is Heber, the Kenite, formerly aligned with the family (and possibly forces) of the father-in-law of Moses. He was not a Canaanite but also not an Israelite, and he had managed to maintain a neutral status, kind of like a one-man Switzerland, and had no quarrel with King Jabin. Somewhere in these twenty years of skirmishing, raiding and constant tension between Israel and the Canaanites, Heber had taken his family and moved near to Kedesh, about seven miles north of Hazor, just over a mountain.

The Surprise Element

Jael, the wife of Heber, was the unknown quantity who brought surprise to the story. Heber may have kept himself in relatively good relations with King Jabin, but Jael herself had other political persuasions, which she managed to keep to herself—that is, until the time of our story.[152]

The encounter

It didn't take long after Barak had gotten on the move for Sisera to learn of it, and he moved his forces to the wadi (river) at the base of the mountain on the other side of which Barak was amassed. Deborah, who had accompanied the somewhat fearful Barak, gave the order, and Barak came over top of the mountain and descended at speed to Sisera's forces. For some reason—ultimately it was God who was in charge—Sisera was not able to repel this highly motivated, divinely imbued force of Israelites, and he was routed.

---

[152] Trent Butler discusses two schools of scholarly thought. One is that Jael feared that whoever defeated Sisera would come to capture and rape, and that she would be endangered. Another is that she heroically acted to save Israelites.

The Hebrew word for "routed" is *hamam,* and Keil & Delitzsch say the word "places the defeat of Sisera and his army in the same category as the miraculous destruction of Pharaoh and of the Canaanites at Gibeon."[153] Sisera's men were killed in astounding numbers, but Sisera himself managed to get away—without even a horse, much less a chariot—almost to Kedesh, where he knew Heber lived. The text implies that Heber was not at home at the time, but his wife Jael came out to greet Sisera—apparently he was unaccompanied— and she had him come quickly into the tent, out of sight. Certainly, she figured, whoever had attacked him and their chariots would be in pursuit.

There is no specific description in the text of Jael's knowing Sisera, but since Sisera apparently came directly to Heber and Jael's home tent complex, it seems likely that the two were previously acquainted.

Jael escorted Sisera to a place in the tents where he could hide, and she gave him a blanket to cover himself, probably in a corner, on the ground. She played the perfect ally and friend, assuring him he needn't be afraid (v18) and giving him milk to drink, though he asked only for water (v19). He was exhausted, but just before he collapsed into sleep, he told her if someone came to the tent and asked if there were 'a man' here, she should say No. We can imagine her agreeing earnestly—the accomplished actress she was—and leaving him to rest from his flight.

But when Sisera began, as he likely did, to breathe audibly as he lay there on the ground, Jael got a tent peg and a hammer, went in to Sisera, gently lifted the blanket where his head was, and drove the tent peg—likely a foot or more long—through his temples and into the ground. For those modern readers who wonder if the tent peg was an unlikely weapon, Butler says "the task of pitching the tent was the woman's responsibility, so we should not be surprised

---

[153] Keil & Delitzsch, *op. cit., Vol. 1,* 1405.

that Jael has 'the instruments of murder at her disposal.'"[154]

Not just anyone from Barak's forces but Barak himself came to Heber's tents and Jael went out to meet him, and then showed him his enemy, dead.

Like numerous exploits in the book of Judges, this tale recounts a violent act that played a major role in freeing the Israelites from oppression. Critics of the Bible today sometimes condemn such acts by Bible characters, ultimately finding fault with God for sometimes giving specific orders to carry these acts out. No such divine directive is explicitly given here, but we're left to wonder if what Jael did was justified in God's sight. Certainly what Deborah ordered Barak to do had the implicit imprimatur of God (see Judges 4:6,14). Why would Jael's act be any different? Some scholars are hard on her. Keil & Delitzsch say "her heroic deed cannot be acquitted of the sins of lying, treachery, and assassination, which were associated with it."[155] We will not be so quick to make that judgment. What else should she reasonably have been expected to do, considering all the circumstances?

The victory Barak won that day was the opening salvo in what the text implies was a brief conflict that resulted in Israel's not only fending off the Canaanites' oppression, but also defeating them soundly.

Learning the Lessons

It's a challenge sometimes to get spiritual lessons for churches or individuals from stories like this, but it's possible. We can suggest a couple.

---

[154] Butler, *Judges*, 107, quoting Mieke Bal, *Murder and Difference: Gender, Genre and Scholarship on Sisera's Death*, Indiana Studies in Biblical Literature, Pp x + 150, Bloomington, Indiana University, 1988, Cloth, 60.

[155] Keil & Delitzsch, *op. cit. Vol. 1*, 1407.

1. *God can use you*

Don't let the views of culture or critics keep you from believing that God can use you to do something important.

We intend to fall just a bit short of suggesting that God might want you to put a tent peg through anybody's head! But let us suggest that as a Christian, you are not only God's child but his potential instrument, wherever you are.

One scholar says of this story that it "downplays the role of a hesitant male leader...and highlights the role of a cunning and daring woman."[156] Cultural prejudices often make some people feel they are less likely to be used of God than someone else. Age, gender, education, sophistication, ethnicity, experience—all these are factors some people misuse to denigrate others or make them feel less likely to be God's instruments to do important things in his will. If negative expectations of others sometimes make you feel you aren't as useful to God as someone else, consider reconsidering!

2. *Just war*

The concept of "just war" is important to understand. While no one likes war, sometimes it's necessary to defend or free people.

Each of us needs to have not only a spiritual view of things, but also a realistic one. Jesus taught personal peacefulness, but he did not tell his future followers that they should never answer their nation's call to defend itself or to go to the deliverance of others. In the United States, we can hardly imagine what would have happened in the world had America not joined the forces fighting World War 1 or World War 2.

While there are some small groups of Christians who would find fault with international conflicts, most believers accept the reality

---

[156] Butler, *Judges*, 100.

that some threats *must* be repelled and that sometimes people who are threatened *must* be saved. Sometimes in order to love one person you must fight the one threatening him. Loving your enemies doesn't mean letting them kill your friends.

JEPHTHA SACRIFICES HIS DAUGHTER
Judges 11:29-40

Many a father emotionally facing a daughter's leaving the home in order to become a wife has heard the friendly counsel, "You're not losing daughter; you're gaining a son!" We suspect it's not entirely helpful—though this author had only sons and wouldn't know.

But in the case of this particular curious Bible account, if anyone had tried to console the star of the story with similar advice, it might have gone this way: "You're not losing a daughter; you're—oh, wait—you *are* losing a daughter." This chapter's strange account is about Jephthah, one of the judges of the Old Testament book, Judges, who made a dangerously odd promise to God, which cost him—and his daughter—dearly.

²⁹ The Spirit of the LORD came on Jephthah, who traveled through Gilead and Manasseh, and then through Mizpah of Gilead. He crossed over to the Ammonites from Mizpah of Gilead. ³⁰ Jephthah made this vow to the LORD: "If You will hand over the Ammonites to me, ³¹ whatever comes out of the doors of my house to greet me when I return in peace from the Ammonites will belong to the LORD, and I will offer it as a burnt offering."

³² Jephthah crossed over to the Ammonites to fight against them, and the LORD handed them over to him. ³³ He defeated 20 of their cities with a great slaughter from Aroer all the way to the entrance of Minnith and to Abel-keramim. So the Ammonites were subdued before

the Israelites.

³⁴ When Jephthah went to his home in Mizpah, there was his daughter, coming out to meet him with tambourines and dancing! She was his only child; he had no other son or daughter besides her. ³⁵ When he saw her, he tore his clothes and said, "No! Not my daughter! You have devastated me! You have brought great misery on me. I have given my word to the LORD and cannot take it back."

³⁶ Then she said to him, "My father, you have given your word to the LORD. Do to me as you have said, for the LORD brought vengeance on your enemies, the Ammonites." ³⁷ She also said to her father, "Let me do this one thing: Let me wander two months through the mountains with my friends and mourn my virginity."

³⁸ "Go," he said. And he sent her away two months. So she left with her friends and mourned her virginity as she wandered through the mountains. ³⁹ At the end of two months, she returned to her father, and he kept the vow he had made about her. And she had never been intimate with a man. Now it became a custom in Israel ⁴⁰ that four days each year the young women of Israel would commemorate the daughter of Jephthah the Gileadite.

Unlike some of the other strange tales in this book, this one is not just a couple of verses long, and we won't try to exegete every verse. Much of the story is self-explanatory, anyway. What may confuse the modern reader, especially if he or she is new to the faith and the Bible, is what a story like this means in the first place. Why is it in the scriptures?

Discovering the Text

The Judges

First, we need to review the subject of the judges of Israel. The judges were those people who were responsible for pronouncing God's wisdom between Israelites and determining guilt in criminal matters, after the basic conquest of the Promised Land and before the first king was chosen. How long that was is a subject of some disagreement among scholars, some calculating it to be as little as 180 years and others as many as 400 years or more. It little matters for our story.

As to the matter of "judging" Israel, little is said about the specific judicial function of the judges. Mostly what we have are accounts of their military or quasi-military exploits during those years. Some scholars would minimize their judicial role and suggest that it was much less important than the deliverance these men (and one woman) carried out. If the book of Judges is meant to represent their activities on balance, this is a fair observation. In fact, some translations render the Hebrew word for "judge" (*shaphat* - שפט), as simply "led." It may be that these judges were accorded the status of "chief justice," so to speak, since there were other judges, including most prominently the chief priest.

The first of the judges listed in the book of Judges was Othniel, a nephew of Caleb. The judge of our curious story was the ninth person to be called by that title, which apparently was not the result of any sort of vote, but rather public acclamation after a first feat of military deliverance. In Jephthah's case, he defeated the Ammonites, peoples east of the Jordan who had resisted the passage of the Israelites through their land to get to Canaan. Jephthah had proved his military worth as a young man, but he was looked down on by family and apparently community, because he was the son of a prostitute his father Gilead consorted with, and Gilead had other sons by his proper wife. Gilead, in fact, lived at the edge of Ammon, and at some point his legitimate sons drove Jephthah out (Judges 11:2) and he went to the land of Tob, just east of the Jordan. There he attracted the friendship of men the Bible says were "scoundrels" (NIV), "worthless fellows" (ESV *et al.*), "lawless men" (HCSB), who traveled with him. The suggestion is that they made themselves into a raiding party, and one may infer that they raided the Ammonites, who had made Jephthah—and probably his band of lawless men—unwelcome.

For probably a period of years they gained a kind of mixed notoriety: fame as fighters who knew how to win, and scandal as men who weren't always principled. It was this reputation that led the Israelites of Gilead to seek out Jephthah and his band, when war broke out with the Ammonites. On terms that he would be named their commander, he came on board.

Jephthah first tried negotiations with the Ammonites (Judges 11:12-28), which failed. So he, presumably his worthless fellows as newly promoted officers, and Israelite armies went to war against the Ammonites (vv29-33) and subdued them victoriously.

Somewhere in this process of deliberations with the Israelites about leadership, Jephthah acquired the status of their next judge, succeeding Jair, with a period of some years during which the Israelites had become idolatrous again and had brought on themselves the judgment of God represented by the pestilence of the Ammonites.

A Rash Vow

As Jephthah was vaulted to status as Israel's hope of deliverance, he apparently thought it was wise to make some sort of vow to God, a promise on which he would carry through if God, for his part, would grant victory to the Israelites over the Ammonites. Just as he crossed over from Mizpah (in Gilead) into Ammonite territory, he made the vow to God we read in the text above:

...If You will hand over the Ammonites to me, [31] whatever

**comes out of the doors of my house to greet me when I
return in peace from the Ammonites will belong to the
LORD, and I will offer it as a burnt offering** (Judges 11:30-
31 HCSB).

The first thing most readers would think would be in the form of
an incredulous question: Why would anybody ever promise such a
thing!? Admittedly, people—then and now—often attempt to make
deals with God, and some of them are somewhat patterned on
legitimate, spiritual covenants. 1 Samuel begins with such a vow,
when Hannah, a godly woman, vowed in prayer that if God would
give her a son she would "give him to the Lord all the days of his
life," which meant that after he was weaned he would grow up in
the service of God at the Lord's house in Shiloh. God granted her
request and Hannah honored her vow, which gave the Israelites a
great leader in Samuel.

People in great distress of some kind often think of costly things
they would be willing to give, give up, or do if God would heal them
or save them in some way, but usually, if not almost always, those
things are costly to *them alone,* not to others around them. In the
case of Jephthah, however, his vow was to take the life of **"whatever
comes out of the doors of my house to greet me when I return"**
from defeating the Ammonites. What in the world, we say to
ourselves, was he thinking!?

We could answer that he *wasn't* thinking. Sometimes people
make rash promises they haven't thought through. It's quite possible
that Jephthah just said the first thing that came to his mind. The
Proverbs would later memorialize the caution: "Think carefully
before you promise an offering to God. You might regret it later"
(Proverbs 20:25 GNT).

It's also possible that he had a passel of pets or other animals
that wandered in and out of his "house," which might have meant
a sprawling complex not entirely unlike the typical family dwelling
of modern people. We should note that he said "whatever comes

out" (aser) of the door, not "whoever" (kal). It might not have occurred to him that the first being to come out of his house "to greet" him would be a *human* being. But this possibility is not high on a scale of likelihood; the text clearly says that he described such a being as one who would "greet" him, normally an activity of people.

This brings up the possibility that Jephthah wasn't entirely fond of most of the people in his household and thought that perhaps a disliked servant would see him through a window and make a show at the door of welcoming him home. But we would have to have some evidence that this was the case, and we don't.

The bottom line is that we have no idea why anyone would make such a rash and bizarre promise, especially if he thought he might actually have to carry it out—if God gave him what he asked for. We can fully explain the meaning of what he promised—i.e. just what the text says, that he would **"offer it as a burnt offering"**— but we can't explain why he said it in the first place.

Possibly some sense can be made of it in an inspection of the moral and social culture of the period of the judges in the first place.

A time of turbulence and lawlessness

There have been times in history in which in some cultures there was significant order, a common sense of morality and decency, and behavior largely governed by an internal compass of natural law and respect for other people.

Then, there was the period of the judges.

The scripture is quite clear that the period between the death of Joshua and the selection of Saul as the first king was a time often, if not usually, marked by turbulent, unruly and uncivilized behavior. In fact, Judges tells us repeatedly that Israel had no king: everyone did as they saw fit (Judges 17:6, 18:1, 19:1, 21:25). Ellicott says these verses were written "by way of apology for the lawless crimes, terrible disasters, evaded vows, and unhallowed excesses of retribution"[157] that mark the period of the Judges. It is our duty in the interpretation of the book to come to a sober realization of the often unfathomable evils that emanated from not only the cultures surrounding Israel, but also Israel itself. The books of Moses containing the law had been completed, for the most part, but were not well known. With almost ridiculous ease the people were led into the idolatry their ancestors had conquered other nations for being engaged in. Immorality of all kinds was rife. And apparently good sense was not a common attribute of the people.

If the reader has difficulty imagining such a time, he need only look at the emerging picture of cultural immorality in the United States. At the time of this writing people are not only tolerating transsexual behavior but celebrating it and making laws guaranteeing that it will be taught as perfectly sensible behavior in young children's schools. Children are being counseled in how to "become" the opposite gender. In some cases they are being given drugs to keep them from maturing into what they were born as, later to be surgically altered (we would say mutilated) to resemble it as well. There have always been transvestites—the Bible outlaws their behavior in Deuteronomy 22:5—but never has trans-behavior of all kinds risen to the level that people actually believe a man can become a woman or vice versa. Yet that is what is happening in 21st century America and some other western nations.

Where do such unconscionable ideas come from? Where is common sense? Apparently, as Nicholas Amhurst is credited with first saying in 1726, common sense isn't so common.

In the period of the judges, law was—popularly, at least—a concept of the individual mind, not the collective wisdom. A reading of the book of Judges reveals a sordid assortment of behaviors that illustrate how unhinged and untethered to fixed morality and ethics people's behavior could be. Perhaps this

---

[157] Charles John Ellicott, *Ellicott's Commentary for English Readers*, Accessed June 9, 2024, https://biblehub.com/commentaries/judges/21-25.htm.

widespread corruption and excess partly explains the context in which someone like Jephthah would propose a deal with God in which it was very likely that he would have to kill someone in his own family—which, in fact, he did.

Why God agreed (?)

It's reasonable to ask at this point why God agreed to grant Jephthah his request for victory against the Ammonites. In fact, we are convinced that he would have granted that request entirely without Jephthah's rash vow. In other words, God didn't decide to give Jephthah the victory so he could watch Jepthah suffer for his impulsive promise. We have no evidence here or anywhere else in scripture that God wants people to promise him agonizing remittance in exchange for his blessing. In other words, we may be assured that God did not inspire Jephthah's vow.

God didn't make a deal with Jephthah at all. The tone of the entire narrative leads to the firm conclusion that God would have sent his Spirit upon Jephthah anyway. As Butler puts it, "God's coming is to give the enemy into Jephthah's hand, not to justify Jephthah's pagan vow."[158]

In fact, the pattern God set for his people in Exodus and then throughout the Old Testament is that he would conquer their enemies and give them natural and supernatural blessings if they would devote themselves to him and worship and serve him faithfully. That kind of "deal" was a win-win. And the service he wanted was not focused on sacrificial offerings but on obedience in living (Micah 6:8).

Keeping the vow?

If God didn't ask Jephthah to promise him a burnt offering, but Jephthah made such a vow anyway, was he obligated to keep it?

---

[158] Butler, *Judges*, 287.

Certainly he believed so (v35). Deuteronomy 23:21 had stated in no uncertain terms, "If you make a vow to the LORD your God, do not be slow to keep it, because he will require it of you, and it will be counted against you as sin" (HCSB). This may have been a solemn saying in the era of the judges. The Law had spoken of paying vows of sacrifices (Leviticus 7:16, etc.). Later Bible writers would continue to sound this note of keeping promises to God (Psalm 50:14, etc.).

But taken out of the context of legitimate vows to do *holy* things, to obey God in what he had already instructed, or to make personal commitments of faithfulness, any number of outrageous vows might be made that certainly should not be kept. There is nothing in scripture to suggest that God holds people to their promises to do evil things. The bottom line is that Jephthah was not beholden to God to kill his daughter, even though he was convinced that he was.

Submission of the daughter

In a previous chapter we looked at the experience of Balaam when confronted with his talking donkey, and we suggested that while the account of the confrontation at that moment moved quickly to Balaam's response and the conversation with the donkey, we're certain there was a significant time of shock and disbelief. Similarly, here in Judges we think it's patently obvious that Jephthah's daughter didn't say, 'Okay, dad, let's go get it over with.' While we won't present another film script to illustrate, we encourage the reader to play the scene in his or her own mind, to imagine the entirely likely moments of shock and fear experienced by the daughter, as well as the reported surprise and anguish of Jephthah.

We imagine that the two of them stood stock still near the door of the house, Jephthah's daughter's eyes wide with incredulity and panic as she tried to make sense of this unthinkable vow and then began to imagine rapidly what would take place. She had no doubt seen animals sacrificed. Was that really going to happen to her? Would someone slit her throat? Was she going to be burned? Should she run? Could she get away? Was this some kind of cruel joke?

Arthur Cundall thinks that Jephthah's reported words, without details, were followed immediately by his daughter's acceptance of whatever he had promised, without knowing what it was, "only anticipating with feminine insight the content of her father's rash vow."[159] We think Cundall's view fails to take into consideration the controlled, literary brevity of the narration, which most certainly leaves out comments about pauses and silent thoughts—details the reader may easily and justifiably infer.

Jephthah's sudden, overwhelming grief is described in the text (v35). The verse does not say that he repeated to his daughter all the details of his vow, but obviously at some point in that conversation he did. By that time it must have been evident that this was no joke.

It is likely that some period of time elapsed between the initial confrontation at the doorway and the daughter's expression of submission to her father. Nothing in the text suggests that he ordered her bound then and there; in fact, their subsequent agreement about a two-month delay strongly implies a period of time during which Jephthah probably brooded in discomfort and his daughter tried to come to terms with the unimaginable.

The daughter's ultimate acquiescence reveals, unfortunately, that she didn't have any greater understanding of the amorality of his having made such an obscene vow than he did. Daniel Block points out: "Apparently this innocent child knew nothing of the Mosaic allowance for the annulment/transformation of vows involving human objects"[160] [Leviticus 27:1-8]. She was less to blame for this ignorance than he, but the reader is shown a tragic

---

[159] Arthur E. Cundall, *Judges*, The Tyndale Old Testament Commentaries, (Downer's Grove, Illinois, Inter-Varsity Press, 1968), 148.

[160] Block, *Judges, Ruth,* 373.

consequence of parents raising children in an environment of savagery and brutality inspired by idolatry, and thus perpetuating these evils through their progeny. Jephthah's daughter's support of her father's vow in no way excused it, but "her portrayal as loyal, obedient, brave, courageous, a bit independent, and loved by her friends makes her by far the most sympathetic character in the Jephthah narratives and possibly in the last half of the book of Judges."[161]

Jephthah's regret

The scripture says that Jephthah was shocked and thrown into sudden grief and despair over the fact that his only child, a daughter, had been the first to come out the door of his house to greet him. Obviously, he never imagined this is what would happen.

But look carefully at what he said: **"You have devastated me! You have brought great misery on me. I have given my word to the LORD and cannot take it back"** (v35). Notice: **"You...You."** He blamed *her* for his sudden undoing! He blamed *her* for his misery! We believe the writer of this account preserved the story that came down to him with the very specific words credited to the rash mouth of Jephthah. To him, his predicament was not so much his fault for his foolhardy vow as it was his daughter's, for a mistake of timing or for her hapless naiveté.

The agreement

Ultimately, Jephthah's daughter submitted to her father, while asking for one last favor. The reader should be duly impressed with the apparent maturity of this girl, who was likely a mid-teenager, compared to the immaturity of Jephthah himself, who had not grown out of his impetuous youth. After some time to come to grips with what was going to happen to her, the daughter proposed a

---

[161] Butler, 293-4.

delay while she prepared her mind and spirit for what was coming. **"Let me wander two months through the mountains with my friends and mourn my virginity,"** she said.

The Hebrew word for "wander" means basically to "go down," or in context, "up and down." She wanted to take a road trip in the beautiful surrounding mountains, which she may not have seen other than from a distance. She might have spent time in a garden or field gazing at the mountains and wishing she could go up some of them and peer down at the beauty of the valleys. She had friends who wished the same, and perhaps they had talked together about wandering about in their glorious land.

The Hebrew word for "virginity" (בתולי - *betulay*) means not only non-existent sexual experience but stands for the entire ancient concept of a daughter's being under her father's rule until transferred to that of a husband.

That Jephthah's daughter brought into her negotiation with her father her going somewhere with her friends suggests even further that there was some time, perhaps a matter of days, during which her becoming a human sacrifice was not finally decided. During that time she probably actually discussed the subject with said friends, who no doubt were as appalled and shocked as she was, but who, as would have been consistent with the culture of the day, were reared in submissiveness to their fathers and, indeed, to men in general. But she retained the dignity and self-worth to propose this variance to the plan, that she be allowed to take two months in a mountain retreat, during which time she would reconcile herself to what was going to take place, and be settled in her heart that whatever came after death would make up for her never having the opportunity to fulfil the common desire of women to marry and to bear children.

It is notable, as well, that Jephthah agreed to the plan and expressed no apprehension that his daughter might simply run away. Whether this suggests that he knew her well enough to trust her cannot be said. There is also the possibility that he thought that if she *did* run away, that would solve his dilemma—no daughter, no sacrifice! There is no evidence to support either idea.

The unspoken deed

We should note that the author of Judges does not give any details about Jephthah's carrying through with his vow, but merely says that **"he kept the vow he had made about her."** The author spares us any description, but it is a somber and grim statement of the simple fact that a father killed his daughter and had her body burned, believing somehow that he had to do it because he had foolishly promised it.

In light of the fact that God had specifically said that the sacrifice of children was abominable (Leviticus 20:1-5), and had never, ever, suggested in any way that his people should offer their children as sacrifices,[162] Jephthah should have known that his vow was a promise to do something immensely evil and that God would not hold him to it because he should never have made it in the first place. Later prophets would repeatedly condemn Israel for child sacrifice (to Molech - Jeremiah 32:35), adding that God said, "I had never entertained the thought that they do this detestable act causing Judah to sin!"

Added to this is the fact that Leviticus 5:4-6 had specifically addressed the matter of thoughtless or rash oaths and the procedure for extracting oneself from them through confession, animal sacrifice and forgiveness pronounced by a priest. Why Jephthah didn't avail himself of this remedy is likely due to his unawareness of it. While the books of Moses would have been complete, as we have previously noted, they were not on the lips of the people or their

---

[162] We have no real opportunity here to discuss the instruction God gave Abraham to sacrifice his son Isaac as a burnt offering (Genesis 22:2). Though, briefly, we should say that God's having kept Abraham from doing it and having provided a ram as an offering instead made the point precisely and powerfully that God had other plans for payment for sin, which every person owes but none can pay himself except by death.

leaders, else such tragic circumstances as this would have been avoided.

Human regret

A brief note in v39 says, **"And she had never been intimate with a man."** The modern reader might be tempted to make light of this ancient lament. But even today children who face imminent death, such as those with cancer, have been known to express to parents or others their regrets about things they would never experience— romance, marriage, sex, children, growing old. That a young girl in ancient Israel lamented her dying as a virgin was not to be dismissed or ridiculed.

In fact, the legitimacy of regretting the lack of fulfillment of basic human expectations was sufficient for the young women of Israel to come to observe a custom, a solemn, four-day remembrance of Jephthah's daughter, who never got to marry, be one with a husband, bear children, or grow old.

And we never knew her name.

Learning the Lessons

This story is full of lessons, some of them sad, and all of them applicable to not only the day in which the writer of Judges lived but also to our own day and time.

1. Corruption without truth   A Truth to Believe ☑

A culture not anchored in the eternal truth of God will sink into corruption, perversion and ultimately brutality.

The superficial reader of the Bible constantly criticizes it as being full of awful tales of immorality and brutality, implying that the Bible supports or condones social evils such as slavery, abusive patriarchy, polygamy, etcetera, etcetera. The folly of such superficial interpretation is in failing to learn that many of the Bible's most exalted and perfect lessons in holiness are delivered by way of accounts of the perfectly awful way people lived and behaved. One of the powerful lessons of Judges as a whole is that a people who are not anchored in the word of God and governed by his eternal truths will ultimately become corrupt, perverse, and brutal. This story of Jephthah illustrates the decline of the morals and ethics of the very people God selected to advance the continued claim he had on the land he wanted them to possess fully.

Any nation that ever had a sense of divine destiny and at some point realizes that their future is at risk, or worse, would do well to inspect its lost moorings in the truth of God. And for the individual Christian, this is the advisement: don't expect a culture that worships at the altar of pleasure, money, and self to enthusiastically adopt laws that reflect the divinely given word of God. Instead, seek the Kingdom of God first in your life and spread the gospel of the Kingdom to others. Only in the conversion of a nation's people will there be a conversion of that nation's guiding principles, leading to a return to God's truth.

2. Providential guidance
through imperfect people
A Truth to Believe ☑

God always must use imperfect people to effect his plans in this sinful world.

In 21st century America, there has developed a phenomenon known as the cancel culture, a social movement led by self-appointed arbiters of the moral and ethical character and behavior of, particularly, persons in the past who deserve to be stricken from commemoration—if not from memory altogether. The social and political character of these judgmental agents of the cancel culture is mostly leftist or liberal.

The self-righteousness of those who promote the cancel culture is frequently appalling. But it has been surprisingly effective. Their bullying has resulted in: the change of sports team names with "pejorative" monikers for "native Americans" (Indians); the removal of statues of American Civil War heroes from the south; the renaming of grocery products like "Aunt Jemima" because of claims of racism; disapprobation for most if not all the founders of the United States, over charges of being slave owners or for other disapproved beliefs; and numberless other changes, boycotts, and public disparagement. The movement is in the hands of people of varying, but usually extreme, political or anti-religious viewpoints.

What the agents of cancel culture fail to reckon with is the unavoidable fact that history is full of heroes of social, educational, military, national, scientific and other kind of ventures and successes who were seriously imperfect people. Present history in the making is no exception. And those who from pulpits of sanctimony presume to purify the public by eliminating the past or present influence of those who violate their standards will ultimately learn two lessons: first, that there are no perfect people and never have been (except Christ); and second, that they, the culture cancel-ers, may eventually be cancelled themselves, for flaws they failed to recognize in their own lives.

The history of Israel during the period of the Judges is a vast illustration of the intent and power of God to use some of the most egregiously imperfect people to advance his purposes. "It has been observed repeatedly that little in the Book of Judges is normal or normative."[163] But the book's lessons do not depend on the example of moral normalcy, much less the ideal behavior of morally superior persons. Instead, the story of Judges teaches us to expect some of the most valuable lessons to come from the most abominable failures—some of them our own.

---

[163] Block, 378.

3. Making deals with God

The only "deals" God makes are to deliver blessings he has already prepared, for our living as he has already planned.

The Bible contains examples of many people attempting to make deals with God. Usually the idea is expressed as a holier matter— making vows. One of the earliest is Jacob's vow in Genesis 28. Jacob slept with his head on a stone and had a vision of heaven and God. When he woke, he said that if God would provide for him, the LORD would be his God and he would give him a tenth of his increase. Even a casual reading of the history of Jacob's family reveals that it had always been God's plan to bless Abraham and his descendants and for them to worship him and live for him. Jacob wasn't vowing to do anything God hadn't already planned for him to do, and God wasn't agreeing to bless Jacob in any way he hadn't already planned to bless him. What was happening in this vow —and in any vow with a basis in holy purposes and living—was that Jacob was in the lifelong process of discovering God's leadership and will. The vows were memorializations of these timely discoveries, like the pillow/stone Jacob set up like a pillar on this occasion.

The history of the nation of Israel was, as is true of any nation in any age, discovered at every moment as it was taking place. The book of Judges describes a period of several hundred years during which Israel discovered continually its desperate need of the dynamic Lordship of Yahweh God. In the particular story of Jephthah and his daughter, we are confronted with a true tragedy. Thinking to advance the cause of Israel, Jephthah attempts to strike a deal with God, making a vow in what he assumes [wrongly] would be in exchange for divine assistance. As a result, a deeply flawed hero conquers the enemies of the public but is defeated by his own corruption in private. His leadership guarantees the continuation of his country, but his foolishness brings about the discontinuation of his family, through the death of his only child.

Vows are not verboten *per se*. But God doesn't make deals. He carries out his plans in our lives, period. If we make a vow to God, let it be at his leading, in his timing, and for his purposes. And let us follow through with *holy* vows, in the power of the Spirit of God.

4. Taking blame for our mistakes An Attitude to Develop ☑

Only when we mature and own up to our own sins will we be able to grow spiritually.

Usually because of pride, embarrassment, or potential repercussions to ourselves, we are tempted to blame others for bad things that happen to us, when perhaps we are solely responsible.

- Thieves often blame their behavior on law-abiding people who have more money, more education, more privilege, more fulfilment in life. "It's *their* fault I steal for a living."
- Violent people often blame their conduct on anyone who "makes" them mad: parents, ex spouses, political opponents, religious groups, police, government, etc.
- Sexually perverse people often blame anyone from family members to friends to religion—whoever they think "pushed them over the edge."

These "macro" examples are joined by all the "micro" examples in all our individual lives where we suddenly come face to face with the results of our misbehavior, foolish living, or rash boasts. Tempted to blame others, we not only short-circuit the learning and maturing process of our own lives, we may hurt those we blame by smearing their reputations or worse.

The story of Jephthah and his daughter teaches us to accept and absorb the consequences of our foolish words and actions. Perhaps the price we pay for our excesses, indiscretions, and evils will make less likely our repeating them.

GRAB YOUR PARTNER
Judges 21:15-25

The wrath of man has a way of going overboard whereas the justice of God does not. In this chapter's curious story, The tribes of Israel turn on the tribe of Benjamin, to punish them for a reprehensible event one of the Levites had experienced at their hands.

The larger story takes up three chapters, Judges 19-21. It begins with a scene so reminiscent of what happened to Lot (see our chapter, "Lot Offers Up His Daughters") that the NET Bible's heading for the section is, "Sodom and Gomorrah Revisited."

A Levite traveling with his concubine comes to Gibeon, a town in Benjamite territory. A kind resident takes him in for the night, but the town perverts come to the door and demand the resident turn over his male guest, the Levite. As Abraham's nephew Lot had done many lifetimes before, the host pled with the men, **"Don't do such a disgraceful thing to this man!"** (Judges 19:24). Then the Levite himself grabbed his concubine and forced her out the door, hoping to appease the men.

Unlike the ancient event in Sodom, on this occasion the men at the door accepted the offer, gang raped the concubine and left her dead at the threshold. In the morning the Levite took her body and finished his journey home. There, he cut her body into twelve pieces and sent one each to the twelve tribes.

The response was immediate and overwhelming. The tribes decided to engage in a civil war against the entire tribe of Benjamin. They conducted a campaign focused on Gibeah, where most of the Benjamites had amassed. The forces of the other eleven tribes

219

soundly defeated the Benjamites. Not satisfied to simply win a battle, the united tribes went from town to town in Benjamite territory, burning down their cities and killing nearly everyone there —men, women and children—especially women.

Then, reality set in. They were on the verge of wiping out the tribe of Benjamin. They stopped and took stock of what they were doing. And they had a problem. Here's where our story becomes downright curious!

[15] The people regretted what had happened to Benjamin because the Lord had weakened the Israelite tribes. [16] The leaders of the assembly said, "How can we find wives for those who are left? After all, the Benjaminite women have been wiped out. [17] The remnant of Benjamin must be preserved. An entire Israelite tribe should not be wiped out. [18] But we can't allow our daughters to marry them, for the Israelites took an oath, saying, 'Whoever gives a woman to a Benjaminite will be destroyed!' [19] However, there is an annual festival to the Lord in Shiloh, which is north of Bethel (east of the main road that goes up from Bethel to Shechem) and south of Lebonah." [20] So they commanded the Benjaminites, "Go hide in the vineyards, [21] and keep your eyes open. When you see the daughters of Shiloh coming out to dance in the celebration, jump out from the vineyards. Each one of you, catch yourself a wife from among the daughters of Shiloh and then go home to the land of Benjamin. [22] When their fathers or brothers come and protest to us, we'll say to them, "Do us a favor and let them be, for we could not get each one a wife through battle. Don't worry about breaking your oath! You would only be guilty if you had voluntarily given them wives.'"

[23] The Benjaminites did as instructed. They abducted two hundred of the dancing girls to be their wives. They went

home to their own territory, rebuilt their cities, and settled down. ²⁴Then the Israelites dispersed from there to their respective tribal and clan territories. Each went from there to his own property. ²⁵ In those days Israel had no king. Each man did what he considered to be right (Judges 21:15-25 NET).

The author of Judges ends this story, and Judges, with the byword that appeared repeatedly in his book, that everybody just did what he thought was right. Clearly, such a philosophy of governance often led to what was wrong.

Oddly enough, the leaders of the eleven tribes had sought the Lord for guidance, in consultation with Phinehas, the priest (20:18, 20:23, and 20:28) and the Lord had given them the go-ahead for this campaign. But obviously, God was positioning the tribes, during this tempestuous time of moral and spiritual conflict, for purposes they could not fathom. Frankly, we have our own difficulties in fully understanding those purposes, too.

Perhaps the greatest purpose of God, a purpose uniting the entire message of Judges, was to demonstrate that the historical people of God's choice did not possess within themselves the ability to rule themselves righteously without the hand of the Almighty King.

Discovering the Text

A troublesome vow

We've run into some troublesome vows elsewhere in the Bible, where someone makes a solemn promise that he will do or not do something, and later regrets it—see the previous chapter, "Jephthah Sacrifices His Daughter." In this present chapter's story, the eleven tribes aligned against Benjamin apparently unanimously vowed not to give any of their daughters to the men of Benjamin as wives. Their intent was for the Benjamites to die out.

Notice v15 says **"the Lord had weakened the Israelite tribes."** The word for "weakened" is actually two words: *āsāh peres* - "made a void." The people were confessing that in his sovereign manner of dealing with Israel, God was in the process of erasing 1/12th of it.

We can't offer here a thorough treatment of the sovereign actions and plan of God or how his sovereignty intersects with the free will and choice of man. But a short explanation is in order.

God the Ultimate Cause

The overarching principle the Israelites believed was that God was the first or ultimate cause of everything. This was true not only in the physical world but in the spiritual one. Even though other spiritual entities existed, they were created by God and acted only with his permission. As an example, read the opening verses of Job to see how God permitted the Accuser to plague Job's life almost mercilessly. And as an example of seeing temptation from both sides, read 2 Samuel 24:1 vs. 1 Chronicles 21:1, one of which says that God incited David to take a census of fighting men, and the other saying that it was Satan who did the inciting.

James 4:13 says that we should not say that God is tempting us because he doesn't tempt people to do evil anymore than he is tempted to do evil himself. But that is an example of the difference between the *ultimate* cause and the *efficient* cause (or the *immediate* cause), where the specific actor who attempts to induce people to do evil is the latter.

The doctrine of the ultimate cause holds true because a deity who is not ultimately in charge of everything is not the ultimate deity. The Jewish and Christian concept of God is that he is one greater than whom cannot be imagined.[164]

We might have trouble explaining to ourselves, much less to others, how God's allowing Satan to tempt—or even directing

---

[164] Something close to this statement was articulated by Anselm of Canterbury (1033-1109).

him to tempt—is no contradiction of his holy nature. The Israelites were not any better at explaining it. They were simply so unswervingly devoted to the absolute sovereignty of Yahweh that they were untroubled by his ultimately being in charge of the length of leash on which he allowed Satan to operate.

We'll just say that the Israelites who responded to the heinous act upon the Levite recognized that God was using the larger context of these events to reposition and perhaps resize the tribes involved.

But the eleven tribes fell under some degree of conviction about what they were doing; they relented and realized that **"an entire Israelite tribe should not be wiped out"** (v17). However, spending their anger against the Benjamites had practically done just that, and so many Benjamite women in particular had been killed that it was going to be hard for Benjamite men to find wives with whom to raise families.

It was certainly possible for the eleven tribes to revisit their vow to withhold any of their marriageable girls from the Benjamites. The context of the Torah's commands about keeping vows was certainly about vows to do righteous things, not evil things. In consultation with priests, the eleven tribes might well have gotten divine direction that they could be released from their pledge. Apparently, however, they didn't consider looking into that possibility. Perhaps they simply didn't want to appear in any sense capricious.

A technicality

Whoever came up with the specific plan of how to do some matchmaking between Benjamite men and marriageable girls from the other eleven tribes deserves a gold star for one of the greatest examples of "a technicality" ever devised. The Benjamite men were to hide in the vineyards along the road to Shiloh where a festival would take place. They were to wait for the virgin girls who (probably) led the way in a procession going to that festival to come along the road, singing and dancing. Then they were to jump out, each grab a girl, and hurry back into Benjamite territory.

They did just that, carrying off **"two hundred of the dancing girls to be their wives"** (v23). If the fathers or brothers of these girls mounted a protest to any of the leaders of the eleven tribes, they would be told (1) there wasn't any other way to preserve the tribe of Benjamin, and (2) not to worry about their vows, because they didn't actually *give* their daughters to Benjamites; the girls were *taken* from them. It was a technicality, but an important one. Everybody could save face.

There were disappointed mothers and fathers, to be sure—no nuptial celebrations and the like. There's also nothing in the account about the hapless girls' reactions. We might imagine they kicked and screamed. This wasn't exactly the dream every girl had about getting married. It was more like the quintessential image of a caveman using a club to subdue a woman and then dragging her off by her hair. Perhaps, however, a few of these couples eventually found the incident oddly romantic in retrospect.

Learning the Lessons

We hinted at one of the main lessons of this story at the first of this chapter, and perhaps there is one more to be garnered.

1. Judiciousness   An Attitude to Develop ☑
The godly person will learn to control the desire for revenge and to avoid rash vows and actions.

The actions of a few Benjamites did not justify the reactions of a whole country against the entire Benjamite tribe. In our own experiences, likewise, the offenses of other people often do not merit the kind of anger that frequently mounts in our emotions. Some of us are hot tempered by nature or we learn the behavior from parents or other early influences. But ultimately we cannot blame our responses on others: we are responsible for our reactions to what other people do. A Christian certainly should be always in the process of growing in the likeness of Christ. That takes self-inspection. Colossians 3:8 mentions **"such things as anger, rage, [and] malice"** that we should identify and address in our lives.

If there is truly a question of justice's being done in response to the wrongful actions of others, invariably it calls for us to be judicious in our responses. And we should always consider the element of mercy and forgiveness in how we determine to act.

2. Disappointment of second best   A Truth to Be Believed ☑

Making the best of a bad situation we ourselves created is far less satisfying than having acted righteously to begin with.

While we can often, to some extent, repair the damage we do by our injudicious actions, it is never as satisfying as having done the right thing to begin with, and often our excesses or "tit for tat" responses to other people damage relationships in ultimately irreparable ways.

In reality, of course, people being who we are, and sin being as pervasive as it is, all our relationships are marred by numerous disagreements, hasty accusations, overblown reactions, selfish deeds and hundreds of other things. Even in the best of friendships or marriages there are repairs that have been done to wounds inflicted and second-best solutions found to situations for which ideals were long ago lost. And yet, the grace of God can heal and bless.

But when faced with the next challenge, see how fast you can do the *right* thing, rather than having to make up for the wrong thing later with something that is second best.

THE PRICE OF A BRIDE
1 Samuel 18:25-29

In western culture today, the notion of a "bride-price"—money or possessions offered to the father of a prospective bride in order to secure his permission and blessing—is strange and even repugnant. Yet it is still practiced in some Asian cultures. It's based on the concept of a daughter's belonging to her father (in particular) and a prospective husband's having to earn her transfer to his household and family.

Bride-price was practiced with some consistency in Old Testament times. We run into it with Jacob, who agreed to work for seven years for Laban in order to secure Rachel as his wife. You remember how that worked out. He wound up having to contract for seven more years for Rachel, after Laban did a switcheroo and sent Rachel's older sister Leah into the pitch black marital tent on the wedding night.

In the biblical history of Saul, the first king of Israel, we are introduced to David, who, before he eventually became king himself, became Saul's armor bearer and then led troops in daring raids on Israel's enemies. Saul became intensely envious of the acclaim given to David by the public, and he ordered him into increasingly dangerous situations hoping he would be killed. He offered him his oldest daughter, Merab, for the bride-price of just generally heading up his international skirmishes—which he hoped would result in David's demise. But David avoided such nuptials, until one day things changed. In coming to and going from the royal court, David met and fell in love with another of Saul's daughters, Michal.

When Saul saw that David was smitten with Michal, he put out the bait once again. 1 Samuel tells us how it went:

> ^{25} Then Saul replied, "Say this to David: 'The king desires no other bride-price except a hundred Philistine foreskins, to take revenge on his enemies.'" Actually, Saul intended to cause David's death at the hands of the Philistines.
> ^{26} When the servants reported these terms to David, he was pleased to become the king's son-in-law. Before the wedding day arrived, ^{27} David and his men went out and killed two hundred Philistines. He brought their foreskins and presented them as full payment to the king to become his son-in-law. Then Saul gave his daughter Michal to David as his wife. ^{28} Saul realized that the LORD was with David and that his daughter Michal loved him, ^{29} and he became even more afraid of David. As a result, Saul was David's enemy from then on (1 Samuel 18:25-29 CSB).

Two things make this story curious to the modern reader. The first is the bride-price just discussed. The second is the somewhat startling fact that David actually paid it.

Discovering the Text

Saul's bride-price

Few translation difficulties exist in this story. In fact, the Hebrew passage yielding the widest range of translations in modern Bibles is in v27. Otherwise, the story is straightforward.

Saul, as we described above, initially offered his eldest daughter, Merab, to David. But David simply demurred, saying he was a nobody and shouldn't be marrying the king's daughter.

But Saul wasn't just mildly interested in getting rid of David.

Even before he tried sending David out repeatedly into battle, Saul had tried pinning David to a throne room wall with his spear. Twice. The scriptures say an evil spirit was active upon Saul, causing this kind of behavior. But the evil spirit didn't originate the idea of killing David; Saul's desire to eliminate David simply gave the spirit the entrance it needed to bring the king under the influence of its evil power and suggestion.

So Saul was committed to seeing David die. The opportunity came when he realized that David and Michal were in love. The text actually says that **"Saul's daughter Michal was in love with David"** (v20). The Hebrew just says, "loved," but "was in love with" is a defensible translation for the modern English reader. David's being in love with her as well is a reasonable inference, because although David repeated his self-deprecating excuse (v18), he changed his mind when Saul made the bride-price a difficult military exploit. David wanted to marry Michal; he just wanted to feel that he had earned the right.

Saul set the bride-price the way he did because he realized that David wanted to feel he had accomplished something worthy, something daring, something significant. Saul's idea was that while David had been successful in his previous raids, this particular battle plan would be especially dangerous. It would require killing a hundred Philistines whose bodies could not then be defended by other Philistines against the Israelite soldiers' performing the circumcisions. So David had to somehow isolate a hundred Philistines, and with his men, kill them all. Then they had to circumcise them and return to Jerusalem. David agreed.

Accordingly, the wedding day was fixed. Verse 26 has a somewhat obscure Hebrew phrase, *wᵉlō mālᵉ'u hayāmīm*, which some translations render, "before the time (or time limit) had expired," and others, "before the days expired." The Contemporary English Version expands it to say, "King Saul had set a time limit, and before it ran out…" In other words, David didn't have all the time in the world to find a Philistine contingent of a hundred men, kill them all, circumcise them, and return with this somewhat gruesome bride-price. If he failed to do it in the "allotted time" (NIV), presumably the wedding was off.

David's daring exploit

The text tells us very simply in v27 that David promptly went out and killed not just 100, but 200 Philistines, circumcised them posthumously , and brought the foreskins to Saul.

Just a bit of difference exists here in the details as scholars see them. First, the Septuagint has "100" instead of "200," but it is alone in that variation. The detail seems to have been included by the writer of 1 Samuel specifically to make the point that David exceeded expectations.

Second, some commentaries point out that the Hebrew verb for "killed" is singular, and that therefore David himself killed all 200. Perhaps he did, but it would have been virtually impossible without help. If men with him subdued all 200 and held them to be executed there on the battlefield by David, that would suffice. However, it makes more sense—especially in the absence of any mention of a miracle—to assume that David had a contingent of men and that all together they killed the 200. David then may have been the one to harvest the foreskins.

David brought his grisly trophies to Saul. He laid them out before the king. Several versions say he counted them out. The KJV says, "in full tale." The Amplified says, "presented every one of them to the king." David was not letting the opportunity escape him to make a full showing of his accomplishment. He was *doubly worthy* of Michal's hand and the position of son-in-law to king Saul.

But if David earned every bit of the right to marry Michal, he also earned the permanent enmity of Saul. As hard as Saul had attempted to rid himself of the young man who had won the hearts of the nation with his victories, it seemed that everything he tried backfired. This bitter animus against David would ultimately play into Saul's undoing and death.

Learning the Lessons

Stories with bizarre details like this one leave the reader feeling variously: surprised, mystified, mildly horrified (or more than 'mildly' depending on the sensitivity of the reader), or disturbed; or impressed, amused, or entertained. Perhaps most people would cheer for David, but some would wonder if his actions weren't morally offensive. There are all kinds of readers, and all kinds of reactions.

But what can Christians get from this curious story that they can apply to their lives? If we expand the story to just a little more than we've quoted above, but which we have summarized, we can derive at least two lessons.

1. *Humility pays*   A Teaching to Obey ☑

Humble yourself. If you deserve honors, you will receive them, if not here, then hereafter.

Jesus told a parable about a man who seated himself at a wedding banquet and then was told he had to give up his seat for an important guest—more important than he! It embarrassed him. So Jesus gave the lesson of the story: "For everyone who exalts himself will be humbled, and the one who humbles himself will be exalted" (Luke 14:11 CSB).

We're all eagerly tempted to accept accolades and take promotions. Sometimes we rush the proper time for our recognition or advancement, instead of remaining humble. It may be that we should resist praise and reward, more than we do.

A student of acting had performed numerous roles in his college theater but had never received an award at annual ceremonies. In advance of those awards presentations one year, he began dropping hints, where they might do the most good, that he really was deserving of an award and hoped he'd get one. Awards night came.

He didn't expect "Actor of the Year." But awards included "Excellence in Acting," and numerous students received them. Finally the MC, a theater professor, called our student's name and said, "to him goes an Excellence in Acting Award," and then with a wry smile he added, "because he wanted it so much." The silver award bowl graced a shelf in the star of our story's home for years to come, but the humbling memory of being ever-so-deftly put in his place came to mind every time he looked at it. It reminded him to be more humble. Eventually, if a reward was deserved, he would receive it.

2. Be wise about "impressing" people   An Attitude to Develop ☑

It isn't always wise to "go over the top." Weigh carefully whether to do more than required, just to impress someone.

David's decision to bring 200 foreskins instead of 100 may have resulted from his finding 200 Philistines he could isolate and kill instead of only 100. But the story gives the detail in a way that certainly suggests he did it to impress Saul. And we can easily deduce that what it did was merely showed up the king, who hadn't even thought David could come up with 100.

We can't use this passage to come up with a hard-and-fast rule to never seek to impress people. Surely an employee who goes beyond the required to do the unexpected is not always—maybe not even usually—being foolish. Most people who have a right to expect from us our best performance are happy to have us go the extra mile. But occasionally the motive to impress is sinful, and it backfires.

Every Christian must make this decision when the situation comes up. Think about it. Pray about it. Seek guidance from the Holy Spirit. Be wise.

Saul Gets in the Spirit
1 Samuel 19:18-24

Saul, the first king of Israel, was an interesting character. He was strong and imposing in stature, though contradictorily a bit shy. But he had what in literary terms is called a tragic flaw: He was prone to intense jealousy and envy, and it got him in trouble repeatedly. Having the temperament he did, he could become quite violent when he was convinced someone was eclipsing him. Specifically, once David came on the scene, even as Saul's armor bearer, king Saul began to be insanely envious of the attention he received, and the more that attention increased, the angrier and more sullen Saul became, and the greater his drive to eliminate his competition.

This bent toward envy was in sharp contrast with a very positive character trait, even a very spiritual one. Saul was at heart a man inclined toward spiritual experience, and disarmingly vulnerable to the moving of God's Spirit.

- In 1 Samuel 10:6, after anointing Saul as king, Samuel told him to go to Gibeah, where he would be met by a procession greeting him. Samuel told him the Spirit of the Lord would come upon him powerfully and he would become a transformed man. It happened just that way, and Saul "prophesied" with the other prophets in the procession. And people began to say, "Is Saul also among the prophets?"
- In 1 Samuel 11:6 we read that Saul was outraged by the Ammonite siege of Jabesh-gilead, and that "the Spirit of God suddenly came powerfully on him," and he launched into a frightening demonstration of holy anger that brought a terrified

unity of support from Israel behind him.

- And in our curious story in this chapter, Saul was overcome by the Spirit of God, began to "prophesy," and people said more than ever, "Is Saul one of the prophets, too?"

This is all fascinating drama, but not especially curious. The curious element in focus in this chapter is in the odd details recounted as part of an interesting scene in Saul's life, as he is pursuing David. The scene opens with David fleeing from the royal court after being warned by his wife Michal that her father was going to kill him. —David could have guessed this on his own by the fact that Saul had tried for at least the third time to pin him to a wall with a spear.

> [18] When David had fled and made his escape, he went to Samuel at Ramah and told him all that Saul had done to him. Then he and Samuel went to Naioth and stayed there. [19] Word came to Saul: "David is in Naioth at Ramah"; [20] so he sent men to capture him. But when they saw a group of prophets prophesying, with Samuel standing there as their leader, the Spirit of God came on Saul's men, and they also prophesied. [21] Saul was told about it, and he sent more men, and they prophesied too. Saul sent men a third time, and they also prophesied. [22] Finally, he himself left for Ramah and went to the great cistern at Seku. And he asked, "Where are Samuel and David?"
>
> "Over in Naioth at Ramah," they said.
>
> [23] So Saul went to Naioth at Ramah. But the Spirit of God came even on him, and he walked along prophesying until he came to Naioth. [24] He stripped off his garments, and he too prophesied in Samuel's presence. He lay naked all that day and all that night. This is why people say, "Is Saul also among the prophets?" (1 Samuel 19:18-24 NIV).

Our concentration in this account will be on the unusual elements, namely the somewhat surprising, "charismatic" experience of Saul's men, and then of Saul himself.

Discovering the Text

Prophesying

In 1 Samuel 19:20, as Saul's contingent nears Naioth, where David has gone for refuge, they find Samuel and a group of prophets "prophesying." What happened was that **"the Spirit of God came on Saul's men, and they also prophesied."** Our first question will be to determine, as much as possible, what "prophesying" means.

The word "prophesying" translates the Hebrew *nib^e'im* (נבאימ) —the word in all four instances in this story. It's also the same word found throughout scripture to describe what prophets did when they both declared God's judgment and foretold future events. When Bible readers read the word "prophesy" they think of what Old Testament prophets said—men such as Isaiah, Jeremiah, Ezekiel, Daniel, Hosea, Joel (and the rest of the names many readers can recite in order). We know they got energized about the sins of Judah, and they preached about God's demand for repentance. And we know they felt God's anger at the surrounding nations that attacked his people, and they warned those enemies that judgment was coming upon them. We hear the word "prophesy" and we also recall predictions of the distant future—still beyond us—when God's absolute kingdom will come.

So when we read the word "prophesy" in this description of Saul and Samuel and the men at Naioth, we're confused. What are they doing? Are they all preaching to Israelites and predicting the future?

Quite apparently we are encountering a different sense of "prophesying" in 1 Samuel.

Most scholars seem to agree that what we're reading about in this story is ecstatic utterance. Let us offer a working definition:

ecstatic utterance : speech that, while perhaps not *entirely* immune to the speaker's control, is largely spontaneous, is inspired by an ongoing emotional and spiritual experience, and is addressed to divine entities if not to witnesses present.

We decline in our definition to say that the utterance is addressed to the Lord God, Yahweh, because ecstatic utterance has been a part of cultures around the world and has been addressed to all kinds of spiritual entities.

Most scholars agree that the prophesying spoken of in this passage of scripture was ecstatic utterance. Difference of opinion exists among major scholars as to the nature of these utterances, however, especially whether the speaker was caught up in something from the true God. A sampling of opinions:

- "Incapacitated by a 'prophetic seizure'…Saul brought reproach on himself and his family by associating with the undignified ecstatic prophets."[165]
- "[N]o techniques used to get into an ecstatic state as in other extra-biblical religious practices are noted; the verbal phrase suggests it was an unexpected event."[166]
- "…the gift of prophecy. It could result in mere 'raving' …and uselessness, hence the need to be discerning" (1 Jn. 4:1).[167]
- "Saul became 'beside himself' (*cf.* the etymology of our word ecstasy)…The evaluation in chap. 19 is negative, though even

---

[165] Ben F. Philbeck, Jr., *1-2 Samuel*, The Broadman Commentary, Edited by Clifton J. Allen, (Nashville, Broadman Press, 1970), 60-61.

[166] David Toshio Tsumura, *The First Book of Samuel*, The New International Commentary on the Old Testament, Edited by R. K. Harrison and Robert L. Hubbard, Jr., (Grand Rapids, Michigan, William B. Eerdmans Publishing Company 2007), 497.

[167] Joyce G. Baldwin, *1 Samuel*, Tyndale Old Testament Commentaries, Edited by D. J. Wiseman, (Downers Grove, Illinois, Inter-Varsity Press, 1988), 133.

here the proverbial question has a certain ambiguity."[168]

Some scholars lean strongly towards identifying this instance of ecstatic utterance as evidently from the Lord. One commentator says the phrase "came upon" (vv20,23) in the Bible is not associated with anything negative[169] and that we should definitely disassociate this experience of Saul's from non-Israelite—i.e. pagan—experiences of ecstasy.[170] And another scholar connects the Old Testament experience of "prophesying" to the New Testament gift of prophecy, where that gift is not debated as to its origins in the Holy Spirit. In fact, the New Testament says that the spirits of the prophets are subject to them (1 Corinthians 14:32). This would undergird our definition of ecstatic utterance.

Few scholars think Saul's ecstatic utterance was meaningless, or, even worse, pagan in content. But some do reflect an opinion that Saul's experience was not of the sort that followers of God would want to seek for themselves.

But there are at least two very significant factors in this account that demand our attention when we try to interpret the nature and origin of Saul's "prophesying:"

One is the fact that **"Naioth at Ramah"** (vv22-23) was likely a compound of prophets in the town of Ramah, either frequented by or under the control of Samuel, sometimes called the last of the judges and the first of the prophets. This is the Samuel who heard from the Lord that Saul should be anointed as the first king. This is

---

[168] Ralph W. Klein, *1 Samuel*, Word Biblical Commentary, edited by David A. Hubbard and Glenn W. Barker, (Waco, Texas,Word Books, 1983), 199.

[169] We should note that this is true even of 1 Samuel 16:14:" Now the Spirit of the Lord had left Saul, and an evil spirit sent from the Lord began to torment him." This allowance of tormenting spirits access to Saul was analogous to the Lord's permitting the Accuser to torment Job with financial and family loss and physical disease. All rebellious spirits are still under the sovereignty of the Lord and serve his good purposes.

[170] Tsumura, 497.

the same Samuel who would disqualify Saul and anoint David, all on the revelations of the Lord to him—revelations which he received with apparent frequency. In other words, the presence of Samuel in this religious community means it was certainly not a den of practitioners of unholy worship. Just the opposite is the case. In fact, the text says that Samuel was **"standing there as their leader"** (v20). Samuel wouldn't have associated himself with unholy fits of ecstasy. So when Saul's men got near to Naioth and suddenly fell under the influence of the Spirit of God (v23), their subsequent ecstatic utterance must have consisted of praise and thanks to the Lord and related things.

The other controlling fact is that just as Samuel was present when Saul's three contingents of men fell under the control of the Spirit, Samuel was present when Saul himself came to Naioth. Samuel witnessed Saul's ecstatic fervor for an extended period of time. Surely Samuel would not have countenanced Saul's behavior at his enclave had Saul been dabbling in the area of pagan practices.

The bottom line for us:
Saul's "prophesying" was holy in nature.

The reader is probably urgent to listen in on Saul's utterances and get some hint of what he was saying, but the Bible doesn't give us any clues as to specifics. Unless, that is, we want to compare Saul and these prophets at Naioth to later prophets who sometimes fell into trances and saw visions and then wrote what they saw. The differences between such prophetic visions and the prophesying going on in our story in 1 Samuel are considerable. Still, in each there is a detachment from the constraints of the moment, and a connection of the human spirit to the Spirit of the Almighty.

One wonders as well if some of the poetic writings of the Old Testament might have had their roots in extended periods of their writers' spiritual ecstasy, even if not in the context of a public display.

Naked all night

The second of two curious features of this story about Saul is what happened when he got to Naioth and seemed to be nowhere near running out of ecstatic utterances. Verse 24 says, **"He stripped off his garments, and he too prophesied in Samuel's presence. He lay naked all that day and all that night."** A quick survey of twenty-seven Bible translations from The Geneva Bible to the King James to the RSV and beyond shows that every one of them renders the Hebrew word *ārōm* (ערם) as "naked." The same word is in Genesis 2:25 where Adam and Eve are described as "naked and unashamed." Our question is: does "naked" here mean totally unclothed?

With what we've already said about the word, it might seem difficult to understand it any other way, but we must explore the possibility because of the implications that might inhere.

Most commentators say naked means naked. The New American Commentary says, "Saul remained 'naked'…a grave shame in the ancient Near East)"[171] But others allow that the word might mean something else in context: Tsumura says, "Naked ('arom) is not necessarily totally without any clothes. As Driver observes, Saul could have worn his inner tunic and still be described as naked (see Isa. 20:2; Mic. 1:8)."[172] Many scholars seem content to understand Isaiah's being "naked" in public as consisting of merely walking around in his underclothes. Similarly, they generally say Micah (in the work cited) was without his upper clothing or without an outer garment.

Indeed, similar to the previous issue of ecstatic speech, it is difficult to imagine that Samuel would have allowed any of the members of the conclave of prophets at Naioth to run around totally

---

[171] Robert D. Bergen, *1, 2 Samuel*, The New American Commentary, Edited by E. Ray Clendenen, (Nashville, Broadman & Holman Publishers, 1996), 211.

[172] Tsumura, 499.

naked, much less the king of Israel. We hold that:

Saul shed his outer, royal robes and lay in his undergarments throughout the night, caught up in a state of spiritual ecstasy.

The iffy proverb

The only other question we need to address is whether what was said after this incident by the unidentified **"people"** of v24 was meant in a positive or negative way. People said, **"Is Saul also among the prophets?"**

The New International Commentary takes the question to be a proverb,[173] perhaps adaptable for various occasions by inserting the appropriate name. The issue is whether the people repeating this proverb thought of it as a rhetorical question with the understood answer of "No" or "Yes." Word Biblical Commentary largely avoids taking a position but says a survey of opinions shows some think that "[b]eing numbered with such prophets [would be] bad news, not good."[174]

The question was asked previously, in 1 Samuel 10:10-12. The Broadman Commentary takes that earlier question as meaning that "Saul brought reproach on himself and his family by associating with the undignified ecstatic prophets."[175] We don't concur. The prophets in both cases would appear to have been the Lord's prophets, not pagan ones, and Saul's participation is cast as godly ecstasy.

The bottom line for our interpretation is that Saul, out of his spiritual experience so far in his lifetime, exhibited the capacities of a prophet. As we said at the top of this chapter, Saul was vulnerable to intense spiritual experiences with God. These experiences

---

[173] Tsumura, 499.

[174] Klein, 199.

[175] Philbeck, 361

occasionally broke forth in ecstatic utterances, especially in the company of others who were intensely focused on communicating and communing with God.

Some readers almost certainly feel in this story reverberations of spiritual experiences some Christians report having in modern times. We've already noted that the Tyndale Commentary connected the Old Testament experience of "prophesying" with the New Testament gift of prophecy. Many readers will expand the connection to include what the New Testament describes as the gift of languages.[176] The reader might wonder if what is represented today as this legitimate gift is consistent with what was being described in 1 Samuel 19, and earlier in 1 Samuel 10. More broadly, modern readers wonder if Saul's and the other prophets' experience could legitimately be described as "charismatic" in the same sense the word carries in today's Christian context.

It would be hasty to conclude that it is, especially since nothing in the 1 Samuel texts suggests that the prophesying done by Saul or the prophets was foreign or unintelligible in any way, while what is represented in the present day as a spiritual gift is always something other than in the language spoken by those who hear it.

Learning the Lessons

We can derive at least two lessons from this story.

1. Unexpected deliverance

A Truth to Believe ☑

Against our temptation to be pessimistic, God often surprises us in the ways he delivers us from opposition or danger.

Remember how this story about Saul came about: David was

---

[176] We've intentionally not said, "the gift of tongues." The Greek word means both the biological part and a spoken language.

fleeing for his life from a king mad with envy. Put yourself in David's shoes for a moment. David could have been very pessimistic about his chance of always outwitting Saul. He could have thought, 'I run and hide, run and hide, but eventually he's going to get me. It's a losing battle.' Why didn't he think that? It was because of the attitude he expressed in Psalm 56:3: **"When I am afraid, I put my trust in you"** (NIV). Just how God was going to deliver him, David didn't know. Would he have guessed that it would be through overcoming Saul and all his men with the Holy Spirit, sending them into holy rapture? I doubt it occurred to him.

And that's the point. We don't know how God is going to interrupt the flow of bad things happening to us and deliver us. Actually, we don't know *if* he's going to do so, in this world and time. But if you've been a Christian long, think back on difficult places you've been in your walk with Christ. Likely you'll remember that something unlikely took place somewhere along the line to free you from temptation, deliver you from opposition, save you from danger. God is full of surprises. Some of them he plans for you!

2. Be vulnerable to God · An Attitude to Develop ☑

Learn to be, and continually be, vulnerable to the moving of God.

This author's father, a pastor for many years, once preached the annual sermon to the South Carolina Baptist Convention entitled, "Open on the Godward Side." While the adjective "Godward" is not very common these days, it simply means "toward God." The sermon described that area of one's life characterized by having the greatest potential for communication with, and influence by, God. Ideally, of course, the whole of our lives should be open to God, but the concept of that sermon communicated the need of Christians to develop sensitivity to God's leading and moving and to remain in such a state always.

Saul, over the forty years of his kingship, became less and less the kind of man people should imitate. But he was only one of several others who fell under the influence of the Spirit of God at Naioth. His men, just regular people, also experienced the powerful moving of God. And the prophets at Naioth were continually experiencing the dynamic and dramatic presence of the Lord. It seems like everyone who even got close to the enclave of prophets began to experience "revival!"

There are certainly times when God stirs communities and acts in unusual ways to revive his people as a whole and to move specially in the lives of a few. But *every* Christian *every* day can and should be vulnerable to the moving of God. You never know when he wants to show you something, tell you something, teach you something, use you for something, or give you something. Be ready to encounter the Lord at any moment. And when he begins to speak, move or work, don't shut him down. Let him have his way. It can only bring you blessing!

DISOBEDIENT MAN OF GOD
1 Kings 13:1-34 (11-24)

When most Bible commentators come to 1 Kings 13, they remark that it tells a strange tale. A prophet contrives a way to discredit and bring the downfall of a man of God, for reasons not stated at all. When he is successful, a remarkable divine execution of the man of God takes place. The tale raises many questions that beg to be answered, not the least of which is whether there is a good guy and a bad guy. And if so, which is which?

This perplexing story is actually a subplot within a more major story that is less strange. The chapter begins with a "man of God"[177] from somewhere in Judah coming to the scene of idol worship in the northern kingdom, Israel, at an altar in Bethel, where he confronts king Jeroboam, who is about to offer sacrifices there. The man of God pronounces a curse on the altar. Jeroboam points to him and orders him arrested, and Jeroboam's hand shrivels up. Jeroboam begs the man of God to pray for his hand to be restored. He does, and it is. Jeroboam then offers him a meal and a reward. The man of God vociferously refuses, and the reason he gives Jeroboam is the key to understanding what happens next: **"I was commanded by the word of the LORD: 'You must not eat bread or drink water or go back the way you came'"** (1 Kings 13:9 CSB).

So far, the story is fairly straightforward. While it is dramatic and

---

[177] The writer of Kings was careful to call the divinely sent messenger from Judah the "man of God," while calling the other prophet, from Bethel, merely that: "the prophet," or "the old prophet," to distinguish them. We have names for neither.

certainly presents a powerful message for the times—theirs and ours—there is nothing odd about it. The Bible is filled with prophets preaching against idolatry and the leaders who promote it. The odd part of the account is what happens after the man of God leaves Jeroboam's presence to return home.

Here's what the Bible tells us happened next:

[11] Now a certain old prophet was living in Bethel. His son came and told him all the deeds that the man of God had done that day in Bethel. His sons also told their father the words that he had spoken to the king. [12] Then their father said to them, "Which way did he go?" His sons had seen the way taken by the man of God who had come from Judah. [13] Then he said to his sons, "Saddle the donkey for me." So they saddled the donkey for him, and he got on it. [14] He followed the man of God and found him sitting under an oak tree. He asked him, "Are you the man of God who came from Judah?"

"I am," he said.

[15] Then he said to him, "Come home with me and eat bread."

[16] But he answered, "I cannot go back with you, eat bread, or drink water with you in this place, [17] for a message came to me by the word of the LORD: 'You must not eat bread or drink water there or go back by the way you came.'"

[18] He said to him, "I am also a prophet like you. An angel spoke to me by the word of the LORD: 'Bring him back with you to your house so that he may eat bread and drink water.'" The old prophet deceived him, [19] and the man of God went back with him, ate bread in his house, and drank water.

[20] While they were sitting at the table, the word of the LORD came to the prophet who had brought him back,

²¹ and the prophet cried out to the man of God who had come from Judah, "This is what the LORD says: 'Because you rebelled against the command of the LORD and did not keep the command that the LORD your God commanded you— ²² but you went back and ate bread and drank water in the place that He said to you, 'Do not eat bread and do not drink water'—your corpse will never reach the grave of your fathers.'"

²³ So after he had eaten bread and after he had drunk, the old prophet saddled the donkey for the prophet he had brought back. ²⁴ When he left, a lion attacked him along the way and killed him. His corpse was thrown on the road, and the donkey was standing beside it; the lion was standing beside the corpse too (1 Kings 13:11-24 HCSB).

Interpreters have struggled to offer definitive answers to a number of questions raised by this story. Possibly the modern reader cannot presume to reach revealing conclusions where others have been befuddled, but the lessons we *can* perceive on good evidence will help us to derive the main thrust—the answer to *why* this story is in the Bible in the first place.

Discovering the Text

The old prophet

The questions this story generates begin with the very first verse that recounts it, v11: **"Now a certain old prophet was living in Bethel."** Who was this "old prophet?"

It should first be noted that the divinely sent messenger from Judah is called "a man of God" (Hebrew, איס אלהימ - *ish elohim*), a person wholly devoted to God's service. The shorter term, "prophet," was used of true prophets, false prophets, spokesmen of Ba'al, and others. Not only is a distinction made between the two characters in this story who otherwise are not identified by name, but a general difference in character is unavoidably implied. From the start, then, the "old prophet" and the "man of God" are assumed not to be spiritual equals.

The chief question that arises about the old prophet is whether he was complicit in the idolatry Jeroboam was aggressively promoting. The venerable Adam Clarke remarked that the old prophet was "probably once a prophet of the Lord, who had fallen from his steadfastness, and yet not so deeply as to lose the knowledge of the true God, and join with Jeroboam with his idolatries."[178] Somewhat counter to that opinion, Matthew Henry commented: "If he had been a good prophet he would have reproved Jeroboam's idolatry, and not have suffered his sons to attend his altars, as, it should seem, they did."[179]

The prophet's sons

Of relevance to the issue of the old prophet's character is the question of why his sons[180] were at the scene of the idol worship and the man of God's message to the king. Had the old prophet merely sent his sons to later report the goings on, or had they simply happened by the event? More interestingly, had they been there because they were involved somehow in the idol worship, if only as congregants at the event? Earlier Bible stories such as that of the judge and prophet Eli, whose sons were spiritually profligate, carry a similar theme of children who bring shame to more honorable, but probably permissive, parents.

---

[178] Adam Clarke, *Commentary on the Holy Bible*, (Kansas City, Kansas, Beacon Hill Press, 1972), 348.

[179] Matthew Henry, *Commentary on the Whole Bible, Vol. II, Joshua to Esther*, (MacLean, VA, MacDonald Publishing Company, n.d.), 647.

[180] While two sons were involved, only one is said to have brought up the matter of what had taken place at the altar scene. Scholars generally conclude that nothing significant is intended by this minor, supposed discrepancy.

The fact is—and we will repeat this admission later about other issues—we don't know the status of the sons. If their presence at the event in Bethel compromised them spiritually, that fact might imply something about their father's spirituality, faithfulness to his prophetic calling, etc. The very fact that the old prophet was not, himself, at the scene of the idol worship condemning it might suggest that he was living in unfaithfulness to his role as a spokesman of God's word—or not, as the case may be, for not every prophet or preacher is led by the Spirit of God to go condemn every public evil act.

One modern preacher said, "You still have to ask why a god-fearing prophet would stay in such a godless place"[181]—meaning the city of Bethel. But we suggest: what more useful place for a prophet to be than in a place where prophecy is most needed? And as the Apostle Peter later wrote, "righteous Lot" endured the hideous sins of Sodom, living there as a de facto witness to God's truth.

The bottom line on this "old prophet" is that we have little but opinions, and those opinions range widely. Essentially we're left to guess about the spiritual status of either the father or the sons, and we're better off, when interpreting scripture, to require at least *some* evidence before offering an interpretation that holds any import.

This lack of understanding on our part may, in fact, be evidence itself, of the author's intended meaning. File that suggestion away for a moment.

The sons' report

What the sons further told their father, the old prophet, generates another set of questions:

"His sons also told their father the words that he had

---

[181] Greg Tabor, Sermon Central, Accessed May 1, 2024, https://www.sermoncentral.com/sermons/sermons-about-1-kings- 13/?searchPhrase=1%20kings%2013&search Phrase=1%20kings%2013.

spoken to the king" (13:11 CSB).

It was this part of the sons' accounting that apparently got the old prophet actively interested in what had happened, because in response he asked them, **"Which way did he go?"** and they told him. It is at least a minor question how they knew which way he left town unless they followed him a ways, or unless the roads in and out were blatantly obvious as to their destinations. The text plainly says they **had seen the way taken by the man of God.** Everybody at the scene of the idol sacrifice would have watched the man of God leave the presence of Jeroboam. These sons apparently had slightly more knowledge, suggesting that they may have trailed him at least far enough to know by what route he was going to leave the city.

But of more interest is why the old prophet responded the way he did to what his sons told him. There is urgency in his immediate question, "Which way did he go?" Did he have some internal revelation at the moment to the effect that God wanted him to go after the man of God? Or was it just curiosity about the man who confronted Jeroboam? Was his interest piqued for reasons purely related to their both being prophets—possibly the Bethel prophet was one of few left and he missed the company of fellow men of God. 2 Chronicles tells us that Jeroboam refused to let Levites serve as priests and that they had almost uniformly abandoned Israel for Judah (11:14). Had the prophets mostly left, too?

At least some scholars think his interest was spiritual: "[W]hat the man of God had said …alarms him so much that he resolves to find him and determine whether he has authentic, authoritative revelation."[182] Apparently neither the priests, who had possibly been run out of the north by this time, nor any prophets remaining in that region had mustered the courage to confront leadership as it rushed into idolatry. Perhaps the old prophet thought, 'Can this man of

---

[182] Simon DeVries, *I Kings*, Word Biblical Commentary, (Waco, Texas, Word Books), 171.

God be the real deal?'

Indeed, it seems likely the immediate response of the prophet—"Which way did he go?!"—suggests an instant spiritual impression. If so, we might draw the tentative conclusion that the old prophet was not entirely untethered from his profession. On the other hand, Henry says "one may hope" his motives were good, but that considering the whole picture, "I suppose it was done with bad design, to draw him into a snare."[183] Here, again, we have no outright or definitive clue what was in the old prophet's mind as he hurried off to intercept the man of God.

Intercepting the man of God

The old prophet found a man he presumed to be the man of God, and then questioned him to be sure. The man of God was **sitting under an oak tree** (1 Kings 13:14).

It would be easy to take potshots at the Judean prophet at this point. One commentator says, "It must be considered significant that the man of God was idly resting under an oak tree instead of returning to Judah, and the man could not have been blameless, because God had dearly instructed him to waste no time on his mission. Many a servant of God has been overcome with disaster in a moment of idleness."[184]

But the story contains nothing we can see that demands that we regard the man of God's resting under an oak tree as pregnant with significance, or that he was "wasting time." In fact, he had been divinely instructed to go back to Judah—we don't know where in Judah—by a route other than the one he took to Bethel. If he went the most direct route *to* Bethel, which some commentators say was a main highway, it would have been some 12-15 miles. The way

---

[183] Matthew Henry, *Commentary on the Whole Bible, Vol. II, Joshua to Esther,* (McLean, Virginia, MacDonald Publishing Company, n.d.), 647.

[184] James Burton Coffman, *Comemntary on 1 Kings 13*, StudyLight, Accessed May 13, 2024, https://www.studylight.org/commentaries/eng/bcc/1-kings-13.html.

back—which was *out of the way*—would have been over mostly un-traveled territory, and very hilly. Anyone would tire easily and no one would be castigated for stopping for a breather. *Maybe* he was being a little lax, but there's nothing to support this conclusion with certainty. It is *possible* that the directive about not eating or drinking on the way implied that he wasn't to stop, but exhaustion might just as well be a plausible reason.

The man of God's being where he was, allowed the old prophet to catch up with him: that's just about all we can conclude with assurance. For a writer, it would be simply a device to advance a plot. Of course, we're not reading a parable, constructed by a writer out of whole cloth, but a historical incident. So, whatever happened took place because of the inscrutable providence of God. Of that much we can be absolutely certain. And the meeting of the man of God with the old prophet brought about an event in which the former was tested as to his commitment to obedience.

The meeting of the prophets

The instrument of testing was to be another prophet, the old (and we assume, older) prophet, who for reasons we have not been able to discover so far, wanted the younger man to come aside and share a meal.

He first invited him directly: **"Come home with me and eat bread"** (v15). The man of God's answer first seems firm: **"I cannot go back with you, eat bread, or drink water with you in this place, for a message came to me by the word of the LORD: 'You must not eat bread or drink water there or go back by the way you came.'"** (vv16-17). This is a nearly verbatim repetition of what he had told king Jeroboam (vv8-9). It strongly suggests that the man of God had received some visionary kind of revelation, or an audible word, which he had committed to memory. What he had come to Bethel to tell the king was probably uttered word for word from what he had heard in the divine communiqué, and he simply repeated the Lord's travel warning to the old prophet.

So far, so good. The man of God has been faithful to what he was sent to do. We have no indication that he is wavering or looking for an excuse to do anything less or anything else until his mission is finished by stepping foot on his home turf.

But then the old prophet, almost inexplicably, contrives to trip him up. Whatever reasons he had for rushing off to find the man of God, whatever the condition of his heart or his prophetic ministry up to this point, whatever he may have felt or thought about a Judean prophet venturing into the nascent northern kingdom, and whatever legitimate desire he might have had—or *not* had—for fellowship with a visiting prophet, the old prophet undertook as if by well-thought-out plan to trick the man of God into straying from his mission directives:

> **He said to him, "I am also a prophet like you. An angel spoke to me by the word of the LORD: 'Bring him back with you to your house so that he may eat bread and drink water'"** (v18).

This is arguably the core of this strange story within a story: the lie told by an old prophet to trick a younger man of God into deviating from his mission. We know it was a lie because the narrator of the story tells us: **"The old prophet deceived him"** (v18). We have already asked why he did it, and we have been unable to give a definitive reason. Some clues as to the spiritual state of the old prophet are yet to come. But so far, it's a mystery why he wanted to trip up the prophet who had just boldly confronted the wicked king—something the old prophet probably wished somewhere in his heart he had the courage to do himself.

The man of God had probably not seen anything like this coming. If he was a much younger man than the old prophet, it is possible that he, as many young men called of God to preach, was heady with the honor and challenge of preaching fearlessly. But he was a bit naive about the tendency of some older proclaimers to become jaded and perhaps somewhat contemptuous of newcomers to the calling, whom they might see as proud novices.

Some commentators observe that a shift takes place at this point in the story:

> From this point on we will watch the man of God's tragic destiny unfold...Our attitude toward the [old] prophet changes too. We see him as evil, and perhaps our antipathy is the stronger because we have for so long entertained the possibility that he is good.[185]

Remember what we said at the beginning of this chapter, that there is a question of whether there is a good guy and a bad guy—and if so, which is which! Perhaps not all of us readers have assumed so far that the old prophet was good, but we have not seen strong evidence that he was up to *no* good.

Until *now*. He tells a blatant lie, and his intent is to get the younger prophet to be untrue to his mission.

Some scholars, however, think it just possible that the old prophet himself had been deceived first, that there was in fact an **"angel [who] spoke to me by the word of the LORD"** and that it was a lying spirit, and that the old prophet reported what he said for the truth.[186] The problem with this view is that the narrator says *specifically* that the old prophet "deceived him," which unavoidably indicates volition. Someone who tells you something that is untrue when he isn't aware he is wrong has not lied to you, has not deceived you. Only if he *knows* he is telling an untruth for the truth has he crossed over into lying. The narrator of this story has settled

---

[185] Jerome T. Walsh, *1 Kings*, (Collegeville, Minnesota, Liturgical Press, 1996), 185.

[186] See Adam Clark, *Commentary on 1 Kings 13*, 349.

that issue for us: the old prophet was lying.[187]

Now, the young man of God has two claims that something is "the word of the LORD," namely his own experience of revelation and the claimed experience of this older prophet.

Men engaged contemporarily in the divine calling to preach prophetically, often disagree on many things. Christian theology in the 21st century is rife with disagreement on things large and small. It is no surprise, then, that ministers would disagree on other matters such as the nature of divine calling, the genuineness of personal revelations, visions, and the like. It was no different 2,500 years ago when prophets appeared and other prophets called them liars, and people were left to guess which were the truly called men of God.

There is no question here, however—*at least for the reader*—that the man of God from Judah had a genuine, divine call, a very specific one, and that the old prophet from Bethel was lying through his teeth in saying essentially that God had changed his mind and rescinded the part about the younger man's needing to go home by another route and not eat or drink on the way. In the story, however, it is at this point that our main character—looked at from at least one perspective—faces a crisis. He must decide whether what he thought was God's fixed direction for him in the next few hours has quite unexpectedly changed. The main part of his mission has been accomplished. Could God be accommodating him at this point, since, after all, he *is* tired; he stopped to *rest*; and who *wouldn't* be hungry?

Many commentators, following the respected lead of older scholars, suggest that the young man of God should be cut some

_____

[187] DeVries thinks this comment about the old prophet's deceiving the man of God was a textual gloss, but he doesn't explain why he thinks so. This is a matter of more interest to textual critics than for the ultimate interpreter. What the communities of Jews and later Christians accepted as the word of God included this inside revelation by the narrator of 1 Kings.

slack for taking the old prophet at his word. After all, he *was* older, he shared a prophetic calling, he claimed to have an experience of supernatural communication, and he didn't seem otherwise to be one of Bethel's idolaters. But against that, F. B. Meyer, no theological slouch himself, insists that "he had a word from God to guide his actions, and should receive no other word except through dramatic and direct confirmation by God's Spirit."[188]

Most scholars agree that the man of God fails the test of his complete commitment to obedience when he declines even to question the older man further to see if his claim is true, and then accedes to the old prophet's invitation. As John Whitcomb wrote:

> The unnamed prophet knew God's command. He also knew that God does not contradict His own Word. So when a prophet said that an angel said that he could eat and drink in Israel, his heart should have detected the hiss of the Serpent ('you shall not die' Genesis 3:1ff) and his lips should have cried out, No!![189]

Another writer says:

> "Would God have told the man of God one thing and then have contradicted it by sending an authentic word by another? 'Beloved, believe not every spirit, but try the spirits whether they are of God'" (1 John 4:1).[190]

The bottom line is that the younger man of God **"went back with him, ate bread in his house and drank water"** (v19)—exactly

---

[188] F. B. Meyer, *Our Daily Homily: Samuel-Job, Volume 2,* (Westwood, New Jersey: Revell, 1966), 68.

[189] John C. Whitcomb, *Solomon to the Exile: Studies in Kings and Chronicles,* (Winona Lake, Indiana, BMH Books, 1971), 26.

[190] Coffman, *op. cit.,* 200.

what *he* said he wasn't supposed to do according to the **"word of the LORD."**

The old prophet didn't say anything right away. It appears he was astounded that his ruse had worked, and he may have been waiting for the right chance to say, "Aha!" When that opportunity came, it was a surprise, even to him. **"While they were sitting at the table, the word of the LORD came to the prophet who had brought him back"** (v20). A while ago, he had lied in saying that he had a word from the Lord. But now, he really did. It may have been the first genuine word from the Lord he had received in quite a while. We don't know this, but we might suspect it because of his easy willingness to put a lie in the mouth of God in telling the man of God it was okay for him to scrap what the Lord had said about not eating, etc. At any rate, a word comes to him powerfully while they're eating together, and he blurts it out: the man of God will die shortly, because of his failure to obey what the Lord had told him.

From this point, the story becomes less abstruse, though still fascinating:

- The old prophet predicts the younger one will not be buried with his fathers;
- as a friendly gesture he saddles his own donkey for the man of God to return home—perhaps suspecting he will not get there;
- the man of God is attacked by a lion on the way home and killed but not eaten;
- responding to the report of the incident, the old prophet goes and finds the younger one dead on the road, the lion merely guarding him, and the donkey also unharmed, standing nearby;
- the old prophet has the man of God placed in his own tomb;
- he tells his sons to bury him with the man of God when he dies;
- and he confirms that the prophecy of the man of God—about a descendant of David named Josiah and the future of the idolatrous altar—would indeed come true, as it did 340 years later!

The old prophet's attitude of respect and reverence for the younger man of God is all occasioned by the very fact of God's discipline of him for disobeying the final part of his instructions about returning home. Ironically, it was that very failure, and God's holding the man of God to account for it, that convinced the old prophet that his "brother" (v30) was genuinely sent from the Lord.

It is very likely that this story was told by the old prophet, with notes of wonder, regret, and solemnity, to his family and others, and became known by the community. Not only would it have served as a powerful sermon to them all, but it would have been preserved in that way for later recording by the author(s) of 1 & 2 Kings.

Learning the Lessons

The larger story, which is about the progressive decline of God's people—north and south—in their faithfulness to him, arguably begins in 1 Kings 11 and concludes at the end of 2 Kings. But this little tale about the interaction of two prophets captures our interest, challenges our understanding, and illustrates what is going on in the newly formed northern kingdom of Israel and the southern kingdom of Judah. The author of 1 Kings has told the story, first because it happened, and second because it encapsulated the spiritual truths that would reverberate throughout this period of divided tribes and their separate but similar decline and eventual overthrow. What were the lessons of this story that the author meant his readers to gather?

1. Obedience
An Action to Take ☑

God requires complete obedience to his word.

This is the chief lesson of this story, as nearly every commentator agrees. The man of God had received a revelation that was quite specific. The word from the Lord told him to go to Bethel (v1), to cry out against the altar (v2), to prophesy a future king who would put the idolatrous prophets themselves on their altar (v2), to retreat from the altar scene and return to Judah by a route other than the one he had taken to Bethel in the first place (v9), and not to eat or drink on the way (v9). When Jeroboam tried to get him to accept some sort of reward for healing his withered hand, the man of God refused by repeating verbatim what God had told him to do. He repeated it a *second* time to the old prophet when he invited him to go eat and drink with him.

But the man of God *let his guard down* in the presence of a fellow prophet, based on nothing more than the latter's claim to having gotten notice of a change of plans from **"an angel…by the word of the LORD"** (v18). *Perhaps* weakened by lack of food and the length of his journey, *perhaps* swayed by a natural inclination to trust his elders, he detoured from the precise plan he had received and which *he did not have adequate reason to believe had changed.*

Ironically, the old prophet emphasized the extreme importance of the word the man of God had received. When he quoted his revelation back to him, the older man said the younger one had gotten his instructions from "Yahweh's mouth" (Masoretic Text, פי יהוה, *pi yahweh*),[191] graphically depicting what the man of God must have experienced. Why, when he got it directly from the mouth of God, did the man of God revise his directions when they came from the mouth of merely another man?

This is the critical point for the reader of the Bible in every age since this story was penned. God's specific instructions to us are not amendable by lesser voices—whether **"an angel from heaven"** (Galatians 1:8-9), a persuasive professor, an older minister, or a soft-spoken "friend." If the revelation of God is undeniable, nothing less than complete obedience to every part of it is required.

---

[191] DeVries, 166.

Now, few of us receive unique, personal, supernatural revelations giving us instructions for our living. But *all* Christians have the Bible. And while some of its accounts are laced with mystery, quite enough of it is clear and undebatable and constitutes the kind of "word of the Lord" that should be obeyed without exception, day after day, for as long as we live.

2. Discipline   A Teaching to Obey ☑

God punishes or disciplines according to his own purposes and is never unfair.

It will be quite obvious to every Christian reader that the occasions of his disobedience to God in the years since becoming a follower of Jesus Christ are innumerable, and many of them are knowing and deliberate. As punishment, why have we not been attacked by lions—or killed in car crashes, or stricken with debilitating diseases, or subjected to some other horrible circumstances that we would realize were God's judgment on our sins?[192]

Clearly, the answer is that the way God disciplines or punishes is entirely up to him. There is no rule that one kind of sin results in immediate execution while another kind of sin merits only a slap on the wrist, with various levels in between. In fact, there would be few of us left—make that *none* of us left—if God sentenced us all to death for any disobedience. He would have run out of lions a long time ago.

The story of the man of God and the old prophet illustrates, in

---

[192] The words "discipline," "punishment" and "judgment" generally are of distinguishable meaning in the scriptures. But some overlapping use of the terms takes place. We do not mean "judgment" here as equivalent to final judgment, as in the loss of eternal life. It may be taken in the sense given to it by the Apostle Peter in 1 Peter 4:17, where God's judgment comes first upon "God's household." We could as easily have spoken of Gods punishment for our disobedience.

fact, the apparent disparity of punishments, a disparity that can be explained only by understanding that no divine code of punishments exists obligating God to mete out specific things. Remember what Exodus 33:19 says: **"I will have mercy on whom I will have mercy."** Paul quotes this verse later in Romans 9:15. It is the truth underlying God's actions toward us *before* salvation through Christ and *after* salvation when we sin—in fact, it is true of his actions always and everywhere. What he does about our sins is entirely up to him, as it suits his purposes.

Reading the story of the two prophets may tempt us to say of the death of the man of God, "That's not fair!" That's simply not true. God is never unfair. If he gave us all what we deserved, we would all *already* be dead and beyond hope, outside God's presence forever.

What this story shows us is that sometimes radical obedience is so vital that, in order to teach or warn observers, God will require a price for disobedience that he might not demand of most others. Our not knowing when our complete obedience to God's clear instructions might be of such consequence is all the more reason to adopt an overarching rule: no matter what, obey everything God has said.

3. *Good guys and bad guys* An Attitude to Develop ☑

God uses the lives and history of flawed human beings to communicate his truths and direct his people.

This third lesson we can quite obviously draw from this remarkable story is one we hinted at from the beginning. Sometimes there are no completely good guys or completely bad guys. It may depend on who is being compared to whom, of course: in the larger story, Jeroboam is not a good guy. But of the two prophets, the guy who starts out pristine eventually trips and falls, and the guy we believe was already compromised softens and confirms the godliness of the one who fell.

We don't get all our good lessons from perfect people, perfect prophets, or perfect ministers. In fact, we don't get any lessons at all from perfect people except from Jesus Christ, because there aren't any others. And sometimes we get truths about God's working, his will, and his purposes through history, from the interplay of good guys who aren't all good and bad guys who aren't all bad. That's what biblical history is, after all: the story of sinful people, chosen of God, redeemed through his mercy, guided by his Spirit, and people who aren't redeemed but are providentially used of God anyway to bring about his purposes in spite of themselves.

This is part of what is meant by God's providence. The forefathers of America commonly referred to the Almighty as "Providence," not to avoid saying "God" at all, but simply to acknowledge that whatever might have been happening in human history, God was at work in it all and was sovereign over it.

4. Other possible lessons

While the foregoing three lessons seem to be the main ones intended by the author, some other, less direct, but supportable lessons should be considered as applications.

ONE IS THAT the prophet and the man of God may be "emblems of larger realities,"[193] namely Israel and Judah, and that their disobedience to God was simply on a different time line. Israel was speeding away from God, but Judah was headed the same direction eventually. The more modern lesson is that no matter how much a nation might consider itself blessed of God, its people cannot afford to think that God will not hold it accountable for departing from his word. And those nations that long ago abandoned godliness cannot assume they will skirt responsibility simply because they haven't encountered God's full judgment so far.

---

[193] Walsh, 185.

THERE MAY ALSO BE a message here to that class of God's people we call "ministers" today, notwithstanding the general sense in which all Christians are ministers. Those who are called to career ministry, those identified by the New Testament as elders or bishops or pastors, in particular, have a heightened responsibility for obedience to God. In part because of the visibility of their lives to churches and communities, and in part because of the purity of life that affects their very ability to sense God's leading and inspiration for their tasks, preachers and teachers must hold themselves to high standards. God already does. They have been called not to follow the people but to lead them. Their obedience should set them apart as **"examples to the flock"** (1 Peter 5:3). And that obedience is doubly important for them because they are warned: **"Not many should become teachers, my brothers, because you know that we will receive a stricter judgment"** (James 3:1, CSB).

IT IS ALSO VITAL that the church acknowledge the divine calling only of those who have proven their maturity and commitment. While the "man of God" in this story in 1 Kings was selected directly by God for his role, the claim of divine calling is common and not always genuine. For this reason Paul told Timothy to **"lay hands suddenly on no man"** (1 Timothy 5:22)—not to ordain ministers without a thorough vetting and spiritual testing. If even genuinely called prophets can violate or merely vacate their mission, certainly those who *call themselves* to ministry are likely to go astray and lead others with them.

A FINAL LESSON seems very possible, and it is one that would apply to any Christian, minister or not: Live up to the mission God gave you—*all the way home*. God has called you to follow Jesus Christ. He has set standards for you and given you a commission. Keep fulfilling it. The "man of God" in our story didn't, and it was his downfall.

A reader in his or her senior years may be especially attuned to hear this message. After the callings of life—education, marriage, rearing children, career—are in the past, and the "golden" years themselves are shortening, coming toward the end, *don't stop following the Lord.* Don't stop being faithful. Don't take liberties with the way God has taught. Continue to be a 100% disciple. Do things God's way, *all the way home.* Not only is it important for its own value to be faithful, but no Christian knows for sure that there's nothing of any kingdom value for him or her to do in the very twilight of years, even if it seems that way because of advanced age or incapacity.

A man who was stricken with pancreatic cancer entered a nursing home where he wasted away because he couldn't eat. He had been a pastor and had visited others in that facility hundreds and hundreds of times, and now pastors and others were visiting him. But they came away repeatedly saying that he ministered to them more than they to him.

He had a poster made by his son and positioned on the wall next to his bed, with a familiar list of "Things That Cancer Can't Do." And he shared the gospel with all the nursing home staff and others. He told his son he had probably done more personal witnessing since being in the nursing home than in several years before. Reflecting on all this later, the son adopted a motto for his own rapidly advancing senior years: **Finish strong.** Keep doing God's will. Keep looking for opportunities to fulfill your calling. Keep following the divine plan, all the way home.

PLEASE DON'T BURN ME UP
2 Kings 1:9-15

On one occasion when Jesus was headed to Jerusalem with his disciples, they stopped in a Samaritan village. The people there apparently were not very welcoming, and two disciples—James and John, whom Jesus called 'the sons of thunder'—suggested, "Lord, do you want us to call down fire from heaven to consume them?" (Luke 9:54 CSB). Fire from heaven wasn't some random idea that one of them came up with. It had some history in their Bible, the Old Testament:

- The Lord rained burning sulfur and fire from heaven on Sodom and Gomorrah to destroy them.
- King David built an altar to the Lord at the threshing floor of Araunah the Jebusite and fire came from heaven to consume his sacrifices.
- Fire from heaven consumed the bull Elijah had put on an altar in the contest with the prophets of Baal.

And it wasn't the only time something like this happened in Elijah's own experience. This chapter's curious story is about the misfortunes of King Ahaziah's soldiers in trying to capture Elijah and usher him to the king. The account is in 2 Kings 1:

> ⁹ So King Ahaziah sent a captain of 50 with his 50 men to Elijah. When the captain went up to him, he was sitting on top of the hill. He announced, "Man of God, the king declares, 'Come down!'"

¹⁰ Elijah responded to the captain of the 50, "If I am a man of God, may fire come down from heaven and consume you and your 50 men." Then fire came down from heaven and consumed him and his 50 men.

¹¹ So the king sent another captain of 50 with his 50 men to Elijah. He took in the situation and announced, "Man of God, this is what the king says: 'Come down immediately!'"

¹² Elijah responded, "If I am a man of God, may fire come down from heaven and consume you and your 50 men." So a divine fire came down from heaven and consumed him and his 50 men.

¹³ Then the king sent a third captain of 50 with his 50 men. The third captain of 50 went up and fell on his knees in front of Elijah and begged him, "Man of God, please let my life and the lives of these 50 servants of yours be precious in your sight. ¹⁴ Already fire has come down from heaven and consumed the first two captains of 50 with their fifties, but this time let my life be precious in your sight."

¹⁵ The angel of the LORD said to Elijah, "Go down with him. Don't be afraid of him." So he got up and went down with him to the king (2 Kings 1:9-15 CSB).

Anytime fire rains from heaven, it's an amazing thing! Perhaps no reader has ever seen such a thing—this author either!—but it would stir the curiosity of witnesses: where did it come from? How did it happen?!

In this story about Elijah, there's nothing particularly surprising about the king's purpose of shutting down Elijah's prophetic ministry or Elijah's resistance to being apprehended. What's curious is the fire from heaven and the fact that it came not just once, but *twice*, and it almost came *three times*.

Discovering the Text

The king and the prophet

Essential to understanding the thrust of this story is the relationship between king and prophet. King Ahaziah was not a godly king. After an injury he had sent messengers to inquire of Baal-zebub about whether he would recover. The name Baal-zebub literally means lord of flies. It referenced a god that was supposedly in charge of either sending or withdrawing pestilential flies, and more generally a god of medicine. It was this more general responsibility that Ahaziah had in mind, no doubt.

But the Lord told Elijah to intercept the messengers. He told them the king would not recover, but would die, and he chided Ahaziah for inquiring of one of the gods of the land instead of the Lord, Yahweh. The messengers told the king about this and the king ordered a captain and fifty men to go get Elijah. This is where our story comes in.

Clearly Ahaziah and Elijah were not friends. The pagan religion of Ahaziah set him at odds with any true prophet, in the first place. He was one of *many* kings of Israel of whom the historian of the books of the Kings said, **"He did what was evil in the LORD's sight. He walked in the ways of his father, in the ways of his mother, and in the ways of Jeroboam son of Nebat, who had caused Israel to sin. He served Baal and bowed in worship to him. He angered the LORD God of Israel just as his father had done"** (1 Kings 22:52-53 CSB). While the specific record of Ahaziah's kingship doesn't contain all he did that was sinful and evil, the list of Jeroboam's sins—which Ahaziah continued in—is extensive elsewhere. Elijah and other true prophets during Ahaziah's reign would have been calling him out on his iniquities regularly and with vigor.

So when we read that Ahaziah sent a contingent of soldiers to go get Elijah, we know he was not asking the prophet to make a social call. He intended to arrest him and take him out of commission. As many scholars admit, we can only infer what Ahaziah's specific plans for Elijah were.

The result of the king's dispatching soldiers to get Elijah was the first of two miraculous heavenly assaults on Ahaziah's men, which would have been three, but for the circumstances.

The story is straightforward and needs no in-depth linguistic studies. The first group of soldiers came and their captain said, **"Man of God, come down!"** (v9). The key to understanding what Elijah said in response is the tone of the captain's words. It wasn't a request; it was an order. So Elijah answered him, **"If I am a man of God, may fire come down from heaven and consume you and your 50 men"** (v10). The author of the account probably meant to juxtapose the irony of the expectation the captain had, that Elijah would "come down," and the fact that something else deadly would "come down" instead.

The author of this account is making the point that Elijah did not take orders from the king, but from God. The fact that the captain called Elijah "man of God" did not mean he recognized or respected Elijah's divine calling, only that the soldier used the proper terminology. It was protocol and nothing more. But Elijah's repetition of the title pointed to the fact that *it meant something,* and the captain was about to find out just what that was. When the report got back to the king, he would be on notice that he had attempted to exert earthly authority over a heaven-called messenger.

Nevertheless, when Ahaziah heard about what had happened to his fifty men, he simply sent another contingent of fifty men with a captain who made the same mistake. If there was any difference, it was only in the addition of one word: **"immediately!"** This captain attempted to be even more authoritative, like yelling the order instead of just speaking it. But Elijah's response was the same. He called on God to respond with fire from heaven, and he based this request on his being exactly what the captain of the fifty had said in a *pro forma* way: **"If *I am* a man of God…"** (v12, emphasis ours). And the fire fell again. Ahaziah hadn't gotten the message yet. He was not Elijah's true king.

It is surprising that Ahaziah got the report of the demise of the second contingent of fifty men and sent yet a third one out with the same mission. But while Ahaziah hadn't gotten the message that Elijah reported to a higher authority, the third captain Ahaziah sent to get Elijah had heard the message loud and clear. When he came into Elijah's presence, his approach was entirely different. If we were to paraphrase it: "Man of God—and I know you *are*—I didn't have a choice about coming here. I got orders to bring you to the king. So please be merciful to us and spare our lives. I know you don't have to, but please, *please do!"*

We added a lot to that verse for the sake of drama! But you can almost hear the "please!" between the lines in what this captain said. He was like the man in Jesus' parable about a pharisee and a tax collector who went to the temple in Jerusalem to pray. The pharisee prayed about himself and how worthy he was. The tax collector didn't even come near the actual place of prayer and he didn't look up, but looked down in shame, and begged for mercy because he was a sinner. Jesus said the tax collector went home right with God.

Here in 2 Kings, the first two captains bore the air of the king who sent them, imperious and demanding, proud of their position and confident in their authority. The third captain had been confronted with news that convinced him he was about to be in the presence of someone who got his orders from One higher than the king. So, when he approached Elijah, it was with humility and a request for mercy.

For that reason Elijah consulted the Lord—or the Lord instantly spoke to him; we cannot tell—and the Lord told him to go with the soldiers without fear.

The point of the repeated confrontations was to emphasize that prophets were not at the beck and call of kings. God built into the design of Israel's political structure—both before and after the division of the kingdoms—a necessary tension between those who ruled the kingdom of men and those who spoke for the kingdom of God. The Broadman Commentary notes on this point that "[t]he narrative illustrates the divine protection of the prophet and the fact that his life can only be yielded voluntarily to the king."[194]

Fire from heaven

Quite separate, really, from the drama built around the political and religious realities of Israel in this story is the issue of the fire from heaven. Readers want to know what it was. Anytime a miracle takes place people in an era of vast scientific knowledge, such as we are in, we want to know if it can be explained in some way.

Predictably, readers' interpretations of this account in 2 Kings run the gamut from wholesale disbelief to the envisionment of clouds opening up and delivering flaming masses precisely targeted on the fifty men.

Interestingly enough, scholarly works largely avoid commenting on the actual form of the fire from heaven, or its possible source. Broadman does suggest that the story was embellished by the prophets who preserved the story. But then Broadman expresses an opinion on the appropriateness of the soldiers' punishment as it appears in the story that eventually became part of the book of Kings. "Few persons would defend the morality of calling down fire from heaven upon groups of fifty as in the present narrative. The New Testament certainly repudiates a comparable proposal on the part of James and John…"[195] It's somewhat surprising to this author that Broadman implicitly accuses the Bible of presenting God as engaging in immoral conduct.

---

[194] M. Pierce Matheney, Jr., and Roy. L. Honeycutt, Jr., *1-2 Kings*, The Broadman Bible Commentary, Edited by Clifton J. Allen, (Nashville, Broadman Press, 1970), 228.

[195] Matheney and Honeycutt, 228.

But were the situations "comparable?" We don't think so, and neither does the Tyndale Commentary:

> The morality of the act has often been misunderstood as the "inhumanity of the destruction of the innocent captains and fifties"…Nor should this be measured solely by New Testament standards, for Jesus rebuked his disciples for wanting a similar demonstration of fire (Lk. 9:54-55) though the circumstances differed. A king had no right to ask such allegiance and his actions should always be subordinate to God's word (cf. 1 Sa. 10:25).[196]

In other words, the **"divine fire"** (v12) of 2 Kings was not in the least unjustified.

We can offer no suggestion to the reader *based on any evidence* as to how to envision the fire from heaven. But as to the extremely liberal view discounting any actual fire, it would have to be said that *something* happened that took the lives of fifty men—twice—and that if nothing happened, then the story as a whole falls apart: Elijah didn't say what he said, the fifty men were not killed, and the third contingent was not "spared"—if no one else had died.

This author's assessment of many supernatural events is this:

> Most miracles are the intersection
> of an improbable series of events
> with a situation of great need
> at the most opportune time.

The *rest* of miracles are likely just what they seem to be as described.

----

[196] Donald J. Wiseman, *1 and 2 Kings*, Tyndale Old Testament Commentaries, Edited by D. J. Wiseman, (Downers Grove, Illinois, Inter-Varsity Press, 1993), 194.

Threes

A remaining, brief, third point about this story is its containing the three, repetitious events concerning soldiers and Elijah. It's interesting to note how many times in Bible stories something happens three times before a situation is resolved:

- Balaam beat his donkey three times before God opened her mouth enabling her to speak to him (Numbers 22:28).
- Balaam blessed the nation of Israel three times when he was paid to curse them (Numbers 24:10).
- Samson lied to Delilah three times about the secret of his great strength (Judges 16:15).
- God called to the boy Samuel three times (1 Samuel 3:8).
- God's Spirit came upon three contingents of Saul's men sent to seize David (1 Samuel 19:21).
- Elijah had the prophets of Baal soak firewood three times before he called down fire to consume it (1 Kings 18:34).
- Elijah stretched himself out on the dead son of the widow of Zarephath three times before God raised the boy to life (1 Kings 17:21).
- Jonah was in the great fish for three days (Jonah 1:17).
- Peter's vision of a sheet let down from heaven was repeated three times (Acts 11:10).
- Peter denied three times he knew Jesus (Matthew 26:34).
- Jesus asked Peter three times if he loved him (John 21:15-17).
- Paul prayed three times to be rid of his thorn in the flesh (2 Corinthians 12:8).

There are other instances. In most cases the repetitions are quite intentional by the actors. In the case of our story about Ahaziah and Elijah, the repetition was the result of a determined king, and the only thing that kept the fire from falling a third time was the lesson learned by the third captain and the decision of the Lord to allow Elijah to go without fear. The point is that a thrice-recurring event is no indication of an embellishment in the telling of a story.

Learning the Lessons

As always, the point of the stories of the Bible is not simply to entertain. We've already hinted at the lessons that can be derived easily from this story. They are fairly obvious.

1. *The ministry of word-proclaimers*   A Teaching to Obey ☑
The King of Heaven calls men to speak his word, and human governments must not try to silence God's spokesmen.

The biblical account is about a prophet and a king. The application clearly must apply: to the spiritual inheritors of the prophets, i.e. preachers of the word of God, and more generally the church that proclaims the Bible and the gospel in every country; and to the political inheritors of the kings, i.e. other royalty and rulers of every kind, including parliaments, congresses, republics, and their governors or presidents.

The lesson for present day successors of the biblical characters is identical to what Elijah taught Ahaziah: political powers must not attempt to muzzle the preachers of God's word or God's people in the practice of their faith. This lesson was slowly learned over human history. It is still not acknowledged everywhere, but it is enshrined in the Constitution of the United States. Yet even today there are threats by enemies of God's truth in America to clamp down on the proclamation of that truth to everyone including people in power. The enemy calls truth "hate speech" and attempts to make exceptions to the First Amendment to the U.S. Constitution so as to shut down Christians' preaching and teaching.

The lesson for the Christian, preacher or not, is to be bold in speaking truth, to neighbor or nation, and to take orders in matters of faith from the author and finisher of that faith, God the Son.

2. Coming judgment

Christians persecuted for truth should be patient, knowing that God will soon judge oppressors and vindicate the oppressed.

Fire may not fall from heaven *now* on those who attempt to muzzle Christian witness, but it will eventually, and in no symbolic way. Revelation 8:5 speaks of a vision of fire being cast to earth—a symbol of judgment. But 2 Peter 3:10 says explicitly that **"the day of the LORD will come like a thief. The heavens will disappear with a roar; the elements will be destroyed by fire, and the earth and everything done in it will be laid bare"** (NIV). The repeated descriptions of the Bible concerning the final judgment, while often laced with imagery, are too repetitive in these pictures to be describing anything less than a cataclysmic reckoning on the earth.

Faithful Jews before Christ were sometimes persecuted by sinful kings. Since the time of Christ, Christians who were persecuted frequently had no hope but the last hope, of being delivered through death to the relief and joy of heaven. Christians in our day in some countries and cultures are in little or no different circumstances. Not yet in America are Christians being put to death for their faith, but readers will call to mind some who have been convicted criminally for protesting immoral laws, or sued for following the teachings of scripture. Worse persecution is probably on the way.

The message of the Bible is that the fire is coming. If, in God's inscrutable economy of time and the purpose of his will, he does not relieve this Christian or that one from the injustice of persecution, he will give sufficient grace to overcome from within. And eventually—soon, O Lord!—the fire is going to fall. All who have sought to quiet God's witnesses will be dealt with justly. And all those who have suffered indignities or pain or even death for their obedience to God's word will be rewarded more than sufficiently.

ELISHA AND THE "LITTLE BOYS"
2 Kings 2:23-25

Many people who have read 2 Kings have paused, and perhaps taken offense, at the description in 2 Kings 2 of the prophet Elisha, who encounters some taunting near Bethel and calls down a curse that results in two bears killing forty-two of the offending persons.

Here's what verses 23-25 say in the King James Version:

²³ And he went up from thence unto Bethel: and as he was going up by the way, there came forth little children out of the city, and mocked him, and said unto him, Go up, thou bald head; go up, thou bald head. ²⁴ And he turned back, and looked on them, and cursed them in the name of the LORD. And there came forth two she bears out of the wood, and tare forty and two children of them. ²⁵ And he went from thence to mount Carmel, and from thence he returned to Samaria.

Elisha had just been at Jericho, to which he had returned after going to the other side of the Jordan River where Elijah was taken up to God in a whirlwind. From Jericho, verse 24 says he "went *up* to Bethel." Jericho is a little over 800 feet in elevation, while Bethel is about 2,900 feet, so the description is routinely apt. But this chapter of 1 Kings, which tells a unified story about the transfer of prophetic ministry from Elijah to Elisha, begins by saying that the two of them "went *down* to Bethel" from Gilgal (1 Ki 2:1-2). From the context it is clear that the Gilgal that is meant is the one in the Jericho valley. And here's where the story is curious from the upshot: geographically, it is not "down" to Bethel from Gilgal, but *up—way up.*

If we're going to interpret 1 Kings 2 correctly, and get something out of it, we have to study the question of what Elijah and Elisha were doing when they went "down" to a city that was "up," and what Elisha's encounter near Bethel meant in light of this curious expression.

Discovering the Text

Understanding this strange story relies on our rediscovery of the language of the biblical text. We can probably confidently assume that the first readers of the story in 1 Kings 2 picked up on all the nuances and implicitly understood the symbols or references. How long it took after the original writing for the verses to become obscure, we don't know. Language changes over time. Terms lose meanings they once had or acquire other meanings. Geography that meant something to one generation might fail to mean anything to a distant, subsequent generation. That's what's going on in this passage. On its face it has simply become obscure.

Suppose you read the following in the news: "Washington is a long way from Nevada but it's not far from Vegas. And they're using your greenbacks." You would understand that "Washington" is a metaphor for the U.S. government. You would take "Nevada" literally, but "Vegas" you would understand immediately to mean "gambling." "They're" would imply "Congress," and "greenbacks" obviously means money. The statement would therefore mean, "The U.S. government may be many miles from the State of Nevada, but they might as well be in the middle of Las Vegas, gambling away the money of U.S. citizens" —on some foolish project, perhaps.

Suppose, however, that you read this statement five hundred years from now, after the terms in the statement don't mean what they automatically communicate now. Like as not, you wouldn't know what the writer meant. But with each term you researched and finally uncovered the meaning of, the significance of the statement would unfold.

Geography

Let's unfold 1 Kings 2:23-25. We'll begin with the place name Bethel.

Since early Bible history, various geographical regions on earth have been under the spiritual control of cosmic forces—spiritual beings created by God who became rebellious against him—Satan and other powers and authorities. One of the results of this fact was that many places became inexorably linked with the gods worshiped there, or with the practices of idolatry they were known for.

Many years before the story in 1 Kings, Bethel had been a place where Jacob met God (Genesis 35:15). But it largely lost its positive association and became something far different during the Hebrews' time in Egypt. The people who proliferated in the region of Canaan, where Bethel was, worshiped Ba'al, Ashtoreth and other gods. Bethel was located at a high altitude—2,900 feet as we noted—which made it ideal as a worship site. Even after the armies of Israel had, for the most part, conquered the region, idol worship continued at "high places" such as Bethel. When I Kings was written, to say "Bethel" brought to the reader's mind idol worship, shrine prostitution, and perhaps child sacrifice and other obscene practices, just as "Vegas" is known as "Sin City."

More broadly, Bethel had become for Israel, the northern kingdom, a rival place of worship to Jerusalem. Remember that after Solomon's death the kingdom split and the northern tribes declared their independence of the sons of David by boasting that they would worship somewhere other than the temple in Jerusalem. Through the reigns of various kings, Israel mostly left behind the worship of the LORD altogether and adopted the gods of the nations they had never really defeated. Due to this idolatry, Bethel had become a place of scorn to Judah, the southern kingdom, and to the faithful worshipers of Yahweh.

So, for the opening verses of 1 Kings 2 to say that Elisha and Elijah went "down to Bethel" was like saying they were going to the wrong side of the tracks, or to a bad part of town. It was an opening suggestion that they were headed into (or through) enemy territory in divine terms. So the scene is already set with a righteous prophet going onto decidedly, and famously, unholy ground.

Characters

Now let's tackle the characters involved. We don't especially need more information about Elisha, but the story introduces persons whom the CSV translates as "small boys" and the KJV calls "little children." Several versions, mostly older ones, say just "children," but many modern versions render the term "youths" or just "boys." Who were these characters?

The Hebrew words are *ūnᵉārîm qᵉtannîm*, rendered by the King James as "little boys." *But,* in Gen 37:2 Joseph (the son of Jacob whose brothers sold him to traders going to Egypt) is described with the same word for "boy," and he was seventeen! In 1 Kings 3:7 King Solomon calls himself *na'ar qātōn* (same two root words), "little child or boy" as an expression of humility—Solomon was an adult. In 1 Kings 11:17, Hadad the Edomite is described as *na'ar qātōn* when verse 14 says God raised him up as an adversary against Solomon—he was no mere child, in other words.

"The term [*na'ar qātōn*] is applied to an unmarried male who has not yet become the head of a household."[197] It is not necessarily a "little child" as we understand those words in English.

Then in verse 24, referring to these *na'ar qātōn*, the author calls them *yᵉlādîm*, translated "children" in the KJV (others say "lads" or "boys," etc.). But this term is used twice in 1 Kings 12 to describe King Rehoboam's advisors, who had grown up with him. It is used

---

[197] Michael Heiser, "Naked Bible Podcast," #062, Feb 13, 2018. Accessed June 15, 2024. https://nakedbiblepodcast.com/podcast/naked-bible-62-qa-5/.

to describe royal associations. Scholars say both these terms refer to unmarried, young adult males usually with royal associations.

So what do we have here? Whom did Elisha encounter as he was going up to Bethel, or *down* in theological terms? The group of males in this text were young men of perhaps royal and probably the priestly group at Bethel. Further, they were acting as a quasi gang of idolatrous, priestly protégés, who evidently recognized Elisha—he probably was wearing Elijah's mantle—knew he had been the companion of Elijah, and insulted and challenged him. Elisha had run into ne'er-do-wells who, if they didn't actually plan on attacking him, did plan on deriding and goading him. And the number of them, though not given, was at least forty-two, as we learn in another sentence or two, and probably more than that. Elisha was encountering four dozen or more hoodlums, intent on no good. It would have been thoroughly intimidating to almost anyone.

So, the scene was further set for something dramatic, wouldn't you say?

The provocation

Now we read the next term, the words that provoked Elisha's seemingly drastic response. The gang members began calling out, "baldhead," or "baldy." The Hebrew is *qêrêa*. Now, why did they say that? The most obvious conclusion we can draw is that Elisha was bald or mostly bald. That prompts the question why.

We might think it was a natural, premature condition. Some men lose their hair early in life. Among Jews baldness was actually not very common, so when it did occur, especially in younger years, one of the first possibilities thought of was leprosy, which the law in Leviticus dealt with. But Leviticus also says that if, upon inspection, a man were found to have no indicators of diseases, they were to acknowledge that "he is bald, but he is clean." Probably it was not the first time someone had "noticed" that Elisha was bald or balding, but it's unlikely that he was sensitive about it. That's not what is going on here.

Some believe Elisha was bald because he was old. But estimates drawn from good evidence in 1 Kings 19 and the description of Elisha's "apprenticeship" with Elijah suggest strongly that he was around twenty when Elijah was taken from him. Elisha was a young man. Yet, he was bald—at least when he met these other young men, these "children," near Bethel. We need to look further.

An even more likely possibility is that Elisha may have shaved his head in mourning over Elijah. Shaving the entire head or an area of the scalp was a common practice in the ancient world to indicate mourning to others (see Amos 8;10 or Micah 1:16, for instance). There is no biblical statement to the effect that Elisha had done this, so we can't be certain, but we can't eliminate it. If he had, then the mockery of the "young bucks" was especially disrespectful.

Add to this the fact that Elisha's former master had been described as hairy (2 Kings 1:8). For whatever reason at the moment, Elisha was not hairy, and the taunt of "baldy" was a mocking reproach. Either: the contemptuous cadre said it merely because *they* were young men with glorious, flowing hair whereas Elisha had a "chrome dome;" or they said it because they were familiar with his predecessor's luxurious locks and hoped simply to get Elisha's goat; or they said it making fun of Elisha's mourning. And they said it repeatedly. The idea of the text is that they were chanting it.

But they didn't just say, "Baldy!" They also said, "Go up!" The Hebrew word *'ălêh* has been rendered a number of ways: NIV, GNT—"Get out of here;" NLT, NRSV—"Go away;" but most versions just render it literally: "Go up." The Hebrew word is not known as an idiom for "go away," so what did it mean? Go up *where?* —if we're to take it in its most straightforward sense.

Some people think "go up" meant to go up to heaven, as Elijah had done. If that were what they meant, they might have been challenging Elisha to prove his prophetic status, or even to escape by miraculous means. But there's too little evidence in the text that these irreverent ruffians would have even known about Elijah's whirlwind experience so soon after it took place (2 Kings 2:11-12). The news might have had time to reach the vicinity of Bethel, or it might not. The entire chapter may be an example of a compressed narrative that defies our identifying the proximity of one event to another in time. Without enough evidence to tip the scales, we need to look further.

A few theologians have latched onto the fact that the chapter began with that odd contradiction about "going down" to Bethel when, from where Elijah and Elisha were at the time, Bethel was most certainly *up* in altitude. These theologians think that the taunt of the gang was for Elisha to "go up" to the high place of worship at Bethel, when they knew he was devoted to worship at Jerusalem.

If this is what was going on in their chant, the gang was challenging Elisha to give in to idolatrous worship, to "loosen up!" "Come on, don't be so stuck-in-the-mud! Go up to Bethel! Give Ba'al worship a try!" Or, more menacingly, "Join us, or regret it!"

We may not have the kind of evidence that allows us to be dogmatic about this interpretation, but it's the best candidate we have for the meaning. It incorporates the probable identity of these young men as well as the theological import of Bethel, and it helps explain the curse Elisha called down. It also lends itself to an obvious application of the passage, which is one of the ultimate goals of our study of the Bible.

The curse

Then finally, in response to the taunting of the young men, Elisha turned to them and "cursed them in the name of the Lord" (KJV). This is the part of the story that often offends the casual reader, and sometimes the serious student, as well.

Notice first that Elisha "turned to them," meaning that he was in the process of leaving them behind. In fact, v25 says after this episode he went to Mount Carmel and then returned to Samaria. He wasn't making a stop; he was proceeding to his destination. He had tried to ignore this gang; he went on by them. But then, in response to their epithets, he finally turned. Shortly he would continue going through the area, leaving the scene of abuse; he stopped only to utter a sober word. Under the circumstances, stopping to engage them in conversation would have been akin to what Jesus described as "casting your pearls before swine." It was self-evident that the gang was not open to godly witness.

That sober word Elisha spoke is described by the Bible as a "curse." The Hebrew means simply to pronounce a curse on. To us, "curse" often means profanity, but that's not the case here. This was more like what Paul said to Elymas: "The hand of the Lord is against you. You are going to be blind for a time" (Act 13:11), or what Jesus said to the fig tree: "Let no fruit grow on thee henceforward for ever" (Mat 21:19), or what Noah said to Ham: "Cursed be Canaan: a servant of servants shall he be" (Genesis 9:25, and see our chapter about this story). In each of these scriptures the words were described as a curse. Elisha used words not specifically recorded, invoking the name of the LORD for his authority. Perhaps he said, "May you not leave this place alive." Maybe it was simply, "May the hand of the Lord deal with you severely." We don't know.

It is significant, however, that Elisha cursed them "in the name of the LORD." He invoked the name Yaweh. These young men and all the segment of the culture they represented worshiped Ba'al, Ashtoreth or whatever gods were represented at Bethel, but Elisha worshiped and served Yahweh, the LORD, the supreme being, the creator of heaven and earth, the creator even of the heavenly beings who had rebelled against him and were being worshiped as gods in the nations around Israel. This encounter between Elisha and the Bethel-gang had been dramatically defined as a contest that was in fact no contest at all, between false gods and the one true deity, the LORD. Elisha's words had become necessary, and he called on his authority to utter them: the LORD God himself.

While we don't know what exact words Elisha uttered, we do know what happened next. "Two bears came out of the woods and mauled forty-two of the boys" (v24). The phrasing leaves open the possibility that forty-two wasn't the entire number in the gang, just the number hurt. And the Hebrew is specific that the bears were female. It's a well known fact of biology that the ferocity of the male doesn't compare to the mother bear, especially if her brood is threatened.

If we take the view that these gang-boys were challenging the worship of Yahweh, then Elisha's elicitation of a curse on the young men was a spiritual assault on "the royal household of the northern kingdom and its apostate priesthood."[198] But even if they were only ridiculing a known prophet, their conduct could not be allowed to stand. Elisha's pronouncement of a curse, the fulfillment of which only God knew, was by no means unjust. It was not cruel. It was not mean. It was not ungodly. It was Elisha's putting into the hands of a just God the judgment the LORD himself knew best upon these haughty, abusive, idolatrous young men who were setting themselves against God's prophet, and thus exalting themselves against the LORD himself.

And while we're at it, we should note something about the number mauled (which may mean killed, or may not). *Forty-two.*

- Judges 12:6 tells us the Israelites executed *forty-two* thousand Ephraimites when Jephthah was the Judge in Israel.
- 2 Kings 10:14 tells us Jehu, God's agent of judgment on the royal house of Ahaziah, slew *forty-two* of his relatives trying to get through enemy lines.
- The number of these young men here in 2 Kings 2 was *forty-two*.
- The beast of Revelation was allowed to exercise authority for *forty-two* months, and the outer court of the temple in the vision was to be trampled upon by the nations for *forty-two* months.

Scholars tell us that in near eastern culture, the number forty-

---

[198] Heiser, *op. cit.*

two was symbolic of potential curse or blessing. At least two other scriptures record the number forty-two in reference to potential blessing. The number of these young men mauled by the two bears was not accidental but rather indicative of divine intent. Forty-two said *God's hand is in this.* When rescuers from Bethel counted casualties (or wounded), the number would have meant something to them. *It was a message from God.*

We've uncovered all the terms and we know what the story meant to its first readers:

> The man of God was in enemy territory and was taunted or even threatened by a gang of idolatrous hoodlums; they had the opportunity to back off, but they didn't; in response, the man of God let them know he was leaving in God's own hands what would happen to these vile opponents, and God didn't waste time acting; nor was his judgment mild; it was designed to bring justice to those who persecuted his prophets, and to send a message to Bethel, the capital of idolatry, that the LORD is God, and there is no other.

Learning the Lessons

The exegesis, or exposition of the text, ushers us to the point where we can draw the lessons God has for us in this little story. What does it say to us about what we should know, believe, or do?

There may be more, but here are three lessons this text leaves with us.

1. Persecution   An Attitude to Develop ☑

God's will may bring believers into contact with open challenge to their worship of the LORD. Be prepared for persecution.

In 2 Timothy 3:12, Paul wrote to his young son in the ministry, "In fact, everyone who wants to live a godly life in Christ Jesus will be persecuted." Paul lays out clearly the fact that if a Christian is serious about following Christ—which by definition of becoming a Christian he *must* be—then he should absolutely expect persecution. If not today, then tomorrow. If not always, then sometimes. If not here, then there. Christians in the United States have become accustomed to being relatively free of persecution. That freedom may well be a thing of the past. The tide has turned in America, and Christians here may join the persecuted brethren of many other parts of the world in suffering for their faith.

And in the course of your following Jesus Christ, he may lead you into a place or a situation where your discipleship will be openly, perhaps vilely challenged. When we get out of the church building and away from the neighborhood where our faith is shared, we may find ourselves in front of people who have no use for Jesus and think Christians are fools at best or evil fools at worst. But Jesus told his disciples to expect this. He said, "They will seize you and persecute you. They will hand you over to synagogues and put you in prison, and you will be brought before kings and governors, and all on account of my name" (Luke 21:12). Not all of us will experience resistance, attack, and persecution in this exact way, but "everyone who wants to live a godly life in Christ Jesus will be persecuted." Be ready for it. If it never happens, question yourself as to whether you are a faithful follower.

2. *Witness*   A Teaching to Obey ☑

If God providentially puts you in the midst of a place of ungodliness, stand out for your godliness. Keep up the witness.

As the children's song says, "This little light of mine, I'm gonna let it shine!" Don't give in to the character of the place you may happen to be, or may have to go.

We remember the story of Lot, who lived in a city that became known as the capital of perversion. Sodom was so evil that angels visited him and told him they were going to destroy the city. Many years later, Peter would write of Lot, "that righteous man, living among them day after day, was tormented in his righteous soul by the lawless deeds he saw and heard." We gather by the Old Testament description that Lot was not entirely unaffected by his surroundings, but he remained faithful enough that the Apostle called him "righteous." Follow that kind of example!

For quite a few years the Southern Baptist Convention has conducted a program called "Impact ____" where the blank is filled in with the city of the current SBC meeting. When the Convention met in Las Vegas many SBC messengers intentionally went to "the Strip" after convention sessions and sought witnessing encounters. Similarly, years before, at an SBC meeting in New Orleans, a number of messengers deliberately went down into the French Quarter in the evening, trying to engage people in talking about Jesus Christ. Both these areas in these two cities have been famous for unrighteous activities. *Stand out for your godliness* when you have to be in ungodly places.

3. Persistence
An Action to Take ☑

If, by God's leading, you have to go through a place of testing, by God's leading keep on going; be persistent in discipleship.

Unless you sense God has led you to put down roots in, or otherwise fix your position in, a place or circumstance of terrible evil or unrelenting trial, then determine to keep going until, in the will of God, you make it through. Some things we are not meant to endure for life but only for a time. Some experiences we are meant to have and then be done with. The point is to survive, and to come out on the other side with new wisdom, new humility, new commitment, new confidence in God's power, new holiness borne of difficulty and increased consecration.

Most Christians would not be willing to characterize anything in their lives as being on par with Lot in Sodom or Elisha on the outskirts of Bethel, and certainly not like Paul's being stoned or eventually beheaded. Nor do they wish their trials would intensify, simply to demonstrate how faithful they can be. But if as a Christian *you* have to go through a wicked place in life, keep on going. Follow the Lord through, to survival, and to victory.

In one sense, it seems disproportionate for the average Christian to apply to his life lessons from the lives of famous prophets. Shouldn't those lessons be applied to stalwart figures of the faith, towering examples of Christian witness and leadership? The rest of us are among the countless, the uncounted, the vast bulk of Christ's followers who live our threescore and ten and pass from the scene. After all, the examples of our lives are of value mostly or even only to the three or four, perhaps a dozen who were our families, and a handful who were our friends. Our histories will not be written in a Bible as models for millions. They will not be sung, or recited by generations of people who would know us only by name and exalted reputation. Instead, our stories will be mostly quiet, unpublished examples, spoken and lived out before the few persons we hold dear.

But the relative obscurity that characterizes most of us doesn't relieve us of the obligation to apply the lessons of scripture to the arena of our own influence, small as it may be. Let us live as if we were Elisha: let us not avoid the place of confrontation and persecution if God so leads; let us shine in the darkness while we are there; and let us keep going, keep following, confident of the Lord's power and plan, until we reach victory on the other side of trial, even if that isn't until the other side of this life.

FLOATING AX HEAD
2 Kings 6:1-7

Many of the miracles reported in the Bible involved predicaments of fairly significant import for the parties involved: the ten plagues brought on miraculously from God by Moses'—they were miraculous events that freed a million or so people; the parting of the Red Sea, and later the parting of the Jordan for Israel to cross on dry land; the fire that fell from heaven and consumed Elijah's offering, setting off the defeat of the prophets and priests of Baal; and in the New Testament, Jesus' miracles that gave sight to people born blind, cured leprosy in an instant, and made lame men to walk.

But once in a while a miracle will appear in scripture that—while it does help someone—seems relatively minor. In fact, it may seem solely like a demonstration of the power of man with God more than a tremendous act of mercy to relieve human suffering. Such is a story about Elisha in 2 Kings 7:

> [1] Some of the prophets said to Elisha, "Look, the place where we meet with you is too cramped for us. [2] Let's go to the Jordan. Each of us will get a log from there and we will build a meeting place for ourselves there." He said, "Go." [3] One of them said, "Please come along with your servants." He replied, "All right, I'll come." [4] So he went with them. When they arrived at the Jordan, they started cutting down trees. [5] As one of them was felling a log, the ax head dropped into the water. He shouted, "Oh no, my master! It was borrowed!" [6] The prophet asked, "Where did it drop in?" When he showed him the spot, Elisha cut

off a branch, threw it in at that spot, and made the ax head float. ⁷ He said, "Lift it out." So he reached out his hand and grabbed it (2 Kings 6:1-7 NET).

It is perhaps more difficult for skeptical scholars to dispense with the reality of the parting of the Red Sea or some such major miracle than with a "minor" miracle like this one. Indeed, one of the oldest opinions of this story is that Elisha took a stout stick and fished in the river for the ax head and upon finding it simply lifted it out. If that were what happened, it would hardly rate inclusion in the scripture—there would be no purpose in it. To their shame, we think, the Broadman Commentary argues with itself over whether the account is to be considered literal. Broadman references the "probing/lifting" interpretation in a negative light, but tacitly accepts the idea that the story can't be literally true. But then it argues with its own rationalization, saying that Elisha was very powerful. Was he, or wasn't he?

This fear of acknowledging the factual nature of biblical miracles is characteristic of the scholarship that worked its way through Germany in the late 1800s and crossed the Atlantic to the U.S. in the early 1900s. Ironically, it is a "scholarship" often based on "assuming facts not in evidence," and "calls for speculation," as we say in court. The net result is that scripture is robbed of its basis for deriving spiritual principles: the factual activity of God's working in the lives of human beings. If it didn't happen, you can hardly base much of a theological truth on it.

As to the "probing/lifting" version, one commentator says, "The grammar, however, would argue against such a rationalization."[199]

It is certainly true that the modern reader faces the challenge of reading ancient stories where the authors of them knew little about scientific principles that we take for granted today. We have to take

---

[199] T. R. Hobbs, *2 Kings*, Word Biblical Commentary, (Waco, Texas, Word Books, 1986), 76.

these matters on a case-by-case basis and do our best to understand what may have happened, as expressed in the language of their times and based on their observations. And it is important in this process to avoid two extremes: adopting an attitude of wholesale disbelief; or blindly accepting a simplistic interpretation.

That said, this is a simple story and it appears to mean exactly what it says.

Discovering the Text

Elisha the leader

It's of some importance to look at the relationship of Elisha with "the prophets" described in this story. It was common for a prominent figure such as a prophet or teacher to have a cadre of students or near-peers around him and associated with him. In the case of Elijah, his principle if not only student was Elisha. But a number of probably younger men followed him and made contact with Elisha when he took over. The Hebrew term in 2 Kings 2:15 for this group is $b^e n\hat{e}\ hann^e b\bar{\imath}\bar{\imath}m$, literally, "the sons of the prophets." Recognizing that this is a somewhat representative term rather than a statement about their family connections, some translators render the phrase "group of prophets" or "company of the prophets." The NET version calls this group "the prophetic guild," an apt term, we think.

These other prophets were students and practitioners, if we may use that image. They weren't as seasoned as the more major figures who led them, such as Elisha was by the time this curious story in 2 Kings took place. They looked to him for guidance. They consulted with him about their group activities, as the text shows. Probably they sought Elisha's counsel on their individual ministries, whatever those were, in the places where they established centers or meeting places. They exhibited some characteristics of modern day theological seminarians, some of whom are just beginning students, and some of whom have found places "in the field" where they conduct ministry week by week and return to the seminary for continued training and counsel, and probably a good bit of shared experiences, which help them to grow and develop as ministers.

Like many churches, the prophetic guild faced the challenge presented by growth: they needed a new building. This meant that the number of young men seeking to "enter the ministry," so to speak, was increasing, and they needed space. Their new building was not to be an addition to the current complex, but rather was to be built down by the river (v2). They engaged the help of every man, and they asked Elisha to attend them. Whether they expected him to chop down trees is unclear.

Situation of need

The setup for the miracle event in the story is the scene of the young prophets whacking away at trees to fell logs the size they needed. They were by the Jordan, where there was lush undergrowth and trees to cull. One of the young prophets was using an ax head that was apparently not lashed or affixed to his handle securely, and he accidently slung it off. When he cried, **"Oh, no, my master! It was borrowed!"** (v5), the text says he used the word *sā'ūl* (שָׁאוּל), which Keil and Delitzsch say "does not mean borrowed but begged."[200] The difference is slight, but perhaps somewhat significant. It may point to the amount of 'convincing' the prophet had to do to get the loan of the ax head. The New American Commentary points out that iron was very expensive in Bible times,[201] and it may be that the young prophet had made extensive promises to neither damage nor lose the tool.

---

[200] Carl Friedrich Keil and Franz Delitzsch, *Volume 2, Judges 6:33-Ezra*, Biblical Commentary on the Old Testament,(Lafayette, Indiana, Associated Publishers and Authors, 1960), 771.

[201] Paul R. House, *1,2 Kings*, The New American Commentary, (Nashville, Broadman & Holman Publishers, 1995), 275.

The upshot of the matter was that, to a poor prophet, the loss of a tool he would have to spend more to replace than he may have even possessed, this constituted great personal need.

God's response

The young prophet sounded loudly his need to Elisha, hoping or even expecting the elder would be able to do something. We characterize what Elisha did as God's response, and it was also the response of Elisha, for the elder prophet walked with God in these days in great harmony. The response of Elisha was to ask where the head had fallen into the water—showing that his knowledge of the circumstances was not complete[202]—he was not omniscient, after all—and the younger man pointed out the place.

Elisha's use of a stick or branch has given doubters an excuse to suppose that he fished out the ax head, but there is no evidence of that, as we have said. Throwing the branch into the water was simply the connection of prophet to ax head, like Moses' staff touched to the Nile, or the foot of a priest to the edge of the Jordan, or touch of a woman's finger to the hem of Jesus' robe. Presumably, Elisha could have simply stared at the water at that spot, willing the ax head to rise to the surface of the river. Or he could have spoken a word, or just lifted his hand and pointed. All manner of gestures or symbolic instruments were employed in the Bible by those who, by the power of God, worked miracles. Here, it was just a branch that marked the spot and connected the emission of the power of God to the object to be retrieved. It was no more complicated than that, though it was a profound demonstration of miracle-working power.

House notes that this miracle "parallels the multiplying of the oil (2 Kgs 4:1-7), the curing of the stew (2 Kgs 4:38-41), and the feeding of one hundred (2 Kgs 4:42-44)," and says, "Each of these

---

[202] Hobbs, 81.

stories portrays Elisha saving the prophets or the prophets' families from physical want or financial disaster."[203]

Learning the Lessons

As we advised readers in another chapter, it is important to avoid simply "spiritualizing" the text in order to extract a practical lesson. But it isn't possible, in this case, to port over the story into modern Christian church life or individual Christian life, either. There are no prophets abroad these days on a par with Elisha who can fix what ails a church or replace what a Christian has lost through miracle working—not that *we* know of, anyway!

So, what is the point of this story for the average Christian reader? What can we take away that will help us?

1. God cares about "little" things   A Truth to Believe ☑
God cares about everything that is part of your life; there's no need so small you can't take it to him.

The ways Elisha demonstrated both the will and the power of God to provide for the prophets showed them that he intended to meet their needs as they followed and obeyed him in their ministries. The word "ministry" as we've used it here is not restricted to full time ministers but applies to every Christian engaged in spiritual service as God directs. God showed the prophets that his provision for them wasn't limited to the big picture of their ministry but included also the details of their daily lives.

Losing an ax head was a minor thing, comparatively. But it seemed major at the moment. And where it might have been nothing to someone who had many other ax heads or had plentiful resources with which to replace one, to the unnamed prophet in our

---

[203] House, 275.

story it was not nothing. That fact made something little into something important. When he turned to Elisha for help, the prophet was really asking God for help.

Does God really care about all the details?

Back before his legal troubles of recent years, comedian Bill Cosby cut an album in which he made jokes about people saying, "Oh, God!" —calling on God. He said, "God is busy, man. He's working, trying to solve problems. He's trying to solve the racial problem, trying to solve Vietnam. Trying to solve them so they don't look like it was a miracle. God can hear everything you're sayin', and if you call him in vain that distracts him from what he's doin'."[204] Perhaps his joking was no reflection of Cosby's actual view of God, but it illustrates what a lot of people think. They conceive of God—*if* he exists, they would say—as a being who is too big to care about every little thing in people's lives, or possibly too engaged in the enormous to even be able to pay attention to the minuscule.

Let's be clear about this: the God the Bible describes fills the universe and in fact is not limited by it or by anything in it. And the God of the Bible knows and is aware of every particle in that universe, every atom and subatomic particle, every molecule in every substance, every cell in every living body, and everybody in the world. Jesus said a sparrow doesn't fall to the ground but that God knows about it. And he said God knows every thought and every prayer before you even think or pray it. He knows your every need— including the little ones, the tiny ones. He knows. And he cares.

That means our prayers should include the full range of things that have an impact on our lives, from the professions or jobs we choose, to the people we marry, to the service we render through the church, to the relationships we have with neighbors, to the money we spend on things, to the way we spend our time, to the

---

[204] Bill Cosby, "8:15, 12:15," January 12, 1969, Tetragrammaton, 1969, LP.

decisions we make about each minute of our days.

And of course, if God cares about the little needs we have, he also knows about the little faults we have and the little sins we commit—it cuts both ways.

But there is nothing in your life about which God will say to you, 'Don't pray about that; I don't care about it.' He cares about it all.

2. Be a model

An Action to Take ☑

Teach those who look to you for an example, modeling consecration and power with God.

In our story, Elisha has earned the deep respect of the group of younger prophets whom he mentored. His consecration and the multiple evidence of God's working in his life led them to look to him as their teacher, guide and model. When a situation of need arose, Elisha responded yet again with an implicit appeal to the power of God at work in and among them all. The result wasn't only that the ax head was recovered, but that the company of the prophets saw Elisha model for them the response of a true man of God.

Being an example and model for others may seem a tall order for many Christians who wouldn't consider themselves leaders. But think how many of us have just one someone in our radius of living who looks to us for an example. Every parent has children who fit this description. Many friends are of somewhat unequal status, one being older and more experienced. Siblings usually look to their next older brother or sister as an example of what they should do and how they should develop. In fact *most* of us are leaders to *someone,* if only one. And that person may be counting on us more than we know, to show them what to do, how to behave, what to choose, how to follow God.

ELISHA'S BONES
2 Kings 13:21

For some of the stories so far in this book we have waded very deeply into theological waters, immersing the reader in technical linguistic issues that, while vital for understanding the text, were admittedly heavy reading. We're sorry.

Actually, we're not. But that said, it's time for a simple story that has few or no issues of Hebrew grammar, syntax or vocabulary to explain, and no idioms or cryptic cultural references that need elucidating. It's just a wondrous little tale about the prophet Elisha:

> **²⁰ Elisha died and was buried.**
> **²¹ Now Moabite raiders used to enter the country every spring. ²¹ Once while some Israelites were burying a man, suddenly they saw a band of raiders; so they threw the man's body into Elisha's tomb. When the body touched Elisha's bones, the man came to life and stood up on his feet** (2 Kings 13:21 NIV).

Discovering the Text

A little history

In understanding this story fully, it's helpful to recall a bit of Elisha's history. At the opening of 2 Kings, Elijah, Elisha's mentor, teacher, and father in the faith, goes to see King Ahaziah. He tells him he's about to die, and presently he does. While it's not stated, at that time Elisha was with Elijah, as he was continually since coming on board with the elder prophet in 1 Kings 19. Elijah had famously squared off with King Ahab and had incurred the wrath of Queen Jezebel, who was more than a nasty character: she was a powerful, sadistic and murderous woman who set out to have Elijah killed. As he was in hiding Elijah encountered the Lord in a spiritual renewal. And right after that, he found Elisha and called him to accompany him, by throwing his mantle (or cloak or coat) around him.

Elisha stuck with Elijah devotedly. As 2 Kings begins, Elijah tells Elisha he is going to Bethel, then to Jericho, and then to the Jordan. At each stage he tells Elisha to stay behind, but Elisha declines, vowing to stick with his mentor every step of the way. Finally at the Jordan, Elijah asks what he can do for Elisha before he is taken away from him.

Elisha says, **"Please let me inherit two shares of your spirit"** (2 Kings 2:9). As powerful as Elijah had been in the Lord, Elisha wanted to be even more. That's hard, says Elijah, but I tell you what. If you see me being taken from you (momentarily), you'll have it. If not, you won't. Presently Elijah was taken up in a chariot of fire with horses of fire, in a whirlwind, and Elisha saw it all.

From that point, Elisha immediately demonstrated the obvious fact that the Spirit of God was upon him in a doubly mighty way. The rest of 2 Kings 2 is filled with signs of his power as the prophet who succeeded Elijah.

By the time of our text, however, Elisha has finished his prophetic ministry. His last act was to prophesy that Jehoash the king of Israel would defeat the Arameans, at least partly. Then **"Elisha died and was buried"** (v20). That's where things get interesting.

Elisha's tomb

When the scripture says Elisha was buried, it doesn't say how. Interment in earth—six feet under, as we would say today—was not the commonest means of burial. Often people of some means would prepare their own tombs long in advance—we'd call it funeral pre-planning nowadays. These tombs were frequently little caves. They didn't have to be stone; they could be dug out of the dirt in a hillside. Inside the tombs they would build ledges of stone, on which the deceased would be laid after wrapping him or her in cloths. After a time the bodies would decompose leaving only bones. The bones were then put in jars or boxes (ossuaries) and kept there in the tomb, and the ledges or resting places would be used for other persons who died.

This author has been in one burial tomb in Israel. Rather than being in the side of a hill, it was dug into flatter ground, inside a clay brick structure like a house. There were several steps down into the tomb, where there were resting places dug into the walls. It wasn't a roomy place, but it was obviously enough for the dead.

Raiders

Our text tells us that sometime after the death of Elisha—probably more than a year or so—Moabite raiders who had developed the habit of carrying out their raids in the spring—springtime weather was nicer for raiding—came over into Israel to do a little damage—assault and battery, stealing, pillaging, plundering—the kind of things raiders usually do. They were headed into an area where there were some tombs, among them Elisha's. And another burial was going on, of some unnamed Israelite man.

When the burial detail of Israelites saw the raiding party in the distance come riding toward them, they panicked. They didn't want to be caught there, robbed and probably beaten. So they decided to head for the hills, or wherever they had to go to get away. But what to do about the body of the dearly departed? His tomb was not entirely ready for some reason, or perhaps he didn't rate a tomb and was, in fact, being interred.

But near them was another tomb, the cover of which could be removed quickly. We don't know whether they knew whose tomb it was, but when the tale was eventually told they had found out. It

296

was Elisha's tomb. They hastily carried their friend down probably a step or two into that tomb and tossed his wrapped body toward the ledge where the deceased prophet had been laid quite some time ago. They just wanted to get out and get away, before they themselves might need tombs.

Meanwhile, the raiders were coming closer. We don't know what happened to the raiding party or their planned mischief. The account doesn't say.

What it does say, however, is that when the dead friend landed in the tomb and fell on Elisha's bones, he had a change of mind. He got up, quite alive. No burial today!

The story ends there, but we can reasonably draw the inference that he joined his friends in running away from the raiders, and the friends may have been running away as much from their recently dead companion as from the approaching raiders.

Actually, we know that sometimes family members might visit graves a few days after entombment just to make certain the deceased had not revived. But to actually witness a dead friend or family member jump up in the tomb was to say the least surprising.

That's the story. Now, what did it mean at the time?

A word to Jehoash

When the startled grave detail had recovered their wits, gotten away from the Moabite raiding party, and let their blood pressure get back to normal, they put together what they knew and realized what had taken place was more than a fluke of sleeping sickness that turned out for the better. This man had really been dead. And the tomb they chose to uncover and throw him in was the tomb of Elisha. The only bones in there were Elisha's.

The message was first implicitly for Jehoash: the defeat of Aphek would take place as prophesied because the God of Elisha, who had prophesied it, was a miracle working God who would bring it about. If Elisha had needed any endorsement for Jehoash to believe his prediction (and he shouldn't have), this was it.

297

A *word to Israel*

The miraculous incident was a message not only to a king, but also to all Israel, which had known the ministry of Elisha and needed to be reminded that his preaching—both forth-telling as well as foretelling —should continue to be revered and followed.

Elisha had indeed received a double portion of what Elijah had from God. The Spirit of God was mighty in Elisha's life and ministry. Instead of forgetting the work of the prophets when they disappeared from the scene, the nations they prophesied to should have held them in continued respect and both hallowed and followed their preaching, *post mortem* for them.

We know that Israel didn't do that. The kingship passed from one to another, one bad king after another, in a procession of wicked men who to a greater or lesser degree reflected the monumental iniquity of Jerobam. Israel went down spiritually and morally, led by men who ignored and forgot the message of the prophets. Eventually, they were defeated and taken into bondage.

Learning the Lessons

This lesson to Israel has obvious application to us today. Is there anything else this startling little story has to say to modern Christians?

1. A *cautionary word*   A Truth to Believe ☑

There is no magic or automatic spiritual power conveyed by religious relics.

Perhaps most readers would not need this word of caution, but some might. Particularly in the Roman Catholic tradition there is the belief that some relic—a portion of a bone, a shard of pottery, a piece of cloth—connected by longstanding report to a long-deceased Christian leader, an Apostle, or even Christ himself—

might possess the power to heal or bless in some way if touched, etc. In fact, this very story about Elisha's bones has been used from time to time to support the notion of power in relics.

There is nothing in this story that legitimately teaches such a thing, and Christians need to stay away from this kind of superstition.

2. An inspiring word
A Truth to Believe ☑

God's power brings life out of death.

The lesson that lingers for God's people since the amazing story involving Elisha's bones took place is the truth symbolized in it. Elisha didn't bring the dead man to life; Elisha's body was dead and Elisha himself was in heaven. Rather, the power of God, which had dwelled in Elisha during his life, was symbolized in that miraculous event. The power of God brings life out of death for everyone who turns to him and by faith touches him.

Jesus Christ went to the cross willingly to pay the price of sin for every human being who would turn to him in repentance and faith. To demonstrate and also make possible what would happen to them, Jesus himself rose from the grave the third day, by the power of God: **"By his power God raised the Lord from the dead, and he will raise us also"** (1 Corinthians 6:14 NIV). **"It is the same power that raised Christ from the dead"** (Ephesians 1:20 NLV). Jesus Christ desires to touch us as we turn to him, that we might become eternally alive.

ALL THESE GIANTS!
1 Chronicles 20:4-8

Just about everyone who has even a modicum of knowledge of Christianity, Judaism or the Bible knows something about Goliath, the famous giant. David killed him with one rock, slung straight to the forehead. But Goliath was no anomaly. There were apparently quite a few giants in his day and previously. In the first chapter of this book, "Sons of God, Daughters of Men," we mentioned that the offspring of many, if not all, of the sexual unions of the spiritual beings who took on human form and the human women they had those children with, were Nephilim, which most interpreters say were giants.

We've already brought up this question: if the Nephilim appeared *before the flood* and the flood killed everyone except Noah and his family, how could there could be more giants *after the flood,* as all other biblical instances of giants were? Of necessity, we must return to that question in this chapter, because long after the flood, Babel, the call of Abraham, the enslavement of Israel in Egypt, and the deliverance by Moses, the Israelites encountered giants in the promised land—and had to defeat them in order to conquer it. But even several hundred years later when David came along, there was Goliath, a Philistine giant. And during David's reign, there were even more giants to be dealt with, which is the subject of this chapter's curious story from 1 Chronicles.

⁴ And after this there arose war with the Philistines at Gezer. Then Sibbecai the Hushathite struck down Sippai, who was one of the descendants of the giants, and the

Philistines were subdued. ⁵ And there was again war with the Philistines, and Elhanan the son of Jair struck down Lahmi the brother of Goliath the Gittite, the shaft of whose spear was like a weaver's beam. ⁶ And there was again war at Gath, where there was a man of great stature, who had six fingers on each hand and six toes on each foot, twenty-four in number, and he also was descended from the giants. ⁷ And when he taunted Israel, Jonathan the son of Shimea, David's brother, struck him down. ⁸ These were descended from the giants in Gath, and they fell by the hand of David and by the hand of his servants (1 Chronicles 20:4-8 ESV).

Where did all these giants come from? They seemed to have been a major impediment to the Israelites' conquering the promised land, and their significance is not usually dwelt upon in the Bible texts featuring them—directly, anyway. We'll try to uncover some of the answer to that query as we look more closely at the text.

Discovering the Text

A parallel story

First, we'll deal with the fact that this story as told in 1 Chronicles parallels the version of it told in 2 Samuel 21:15-22. There, a fourth giant is in the list of those killed: Ishbi-benob. He was actually the first one listed there as killed by David's men. The reason for the omission here in 1 Chronicles may be the Chronicler's not wanting to include the detail given in 2 Samuel about David's becoming exhausted in the battle with Ishbi-benob and his men's insisting that he not personally go into battle again. One writer suggests the Chronicler wanted to emphasize the main point of the story: "Thus are God's plans always brought to fruition, despite the frailties of those through whom he does his work."[205] Perhaps that's why the first giant is missing, but it's a matter of conjecture. The Chronicler had his reasons, as he did for numerous other interpretations of the same period of history that the writer of 1 Samuel recalled.

There are other differences in the two versions, some odd.

- In 2 Samuel the place of the first confrontation (discounting the confrontation with Ishbi-benob) was Gob; in 1 Chronicles it was Gezer.
- In 2 Samuel the name of this first giant was Saph; in 1 Chronicles it was Sippai.
- In 2 Samuel Saph was one of the sons of Rapha; in 1 Chronicles Sippai was one of the sons of the Rapha*im*.
- In 2 Samuel the warrior who killed the giant was Elhanan son of Jaare the Bethlehemite; in 1 Chronicles it was Elhanan son of Jair.
- In 2 Samuel—and this is the most troubling difference—the giant killed by Elhanan was Goliath the Gittite; in 1 Chronicles it was Lahmi *the brother of* Goliath the Gittite. In both versions, Goliath's spear was like a weaver's beam.
- In 2 Samuel and 1 Chronicles the details of the third giant and his defeat are agreed.

Storytellers often differ in what they include or omit, as is abundantly true in the Samuel and Chronicles versions of the history they record. But such conflict as in these different versions of the battles with the Philistine giants is rare. Scholars have looked carefully at the matter for a long, long time. The textual differences in the Hebrew and the interpretations suggested for solving them can be dizzying. We'll try to present a boiled-down version to avoid

---

[205] Roddy Braun, *1 Chronicles*, Word Biblical Commentary, (Waco, Texas, Word Books, 1986), 211.

drowning in the minutia.

The first giant

To begin with, the names Saph and Sippai are likely different only due to Hebrew linguistic changes over a quite a few years, just as other languages experience. Some English names have changed in spelling and pronunciation over five hundred years, as indeed the entire language has.

Similarly, the place this first giant was from, namely Gob or Gezer, was probably the same place, with a name that had changed between the times of the writer of 2 Samuel and the compiler of 1 Chronicles. "Gezeer, one of the walled cities of the area…also called Gob in 2 Sam 21:8, …is a place not otherwise known."[206]

The difference between the names of the places Saph or Sippai was from is due to the fact that in 2 Samuel the Hebrew word is *rāpāh,* a singular form, while in 1 Chronicles the Hebrew is $r^e p\bar{a}$ *'im,* a plural. Translators of either text vary in their decision to consider them both as singular or plural and whether to render the word "giants" or "Rapha." The point is that the giants were considered a class of people different from others. People knew that the giants among them had descended from other giants back to the time of the flood and even before. The difference between the Samuel and Chronicles versions is not therefore significant.

Second giant

Who was the second giant in this story?

The matter introduced above as the most troubling difference in the accounts is whether Goliath was killed by Elhanan or, as reported in 1 Samuel 17, by David, long before he became king. Scholars have long believed that the Hebrew text of 2 Samuel was

---

[206] J. A. Thompson, *1, 2 Chronicles,* The New American Commentary, Edited by E. Ray Clendenen, (Nashville, Broadman & Holman Publishers, 1994), 157.

corrupted by recopying somewhere along the way to read that Elhanan killed Goliath, and that the writer of Chronicles clarified the issue by reading the Hebrew sources a little differently. The simple version is this: a different division of words and association of those words in the Hebrew results in what 2 Samuel says was "son of Jaare-oregim the Bethlehemite" being in 2 Chronicles instead, "son of Jaire …Lahmi the brother of." The Tyndale Commentary takes this view with a very strong argument based on multiple sources.[207] The New American Commentary agrees: "We do not know the exact reading of the original, but it likely is to have been close to this text in Chronicles."[208]

In other words, the prevailing view is that the second giant killed in this story in 1 Chronicles was Lahmi, the *brother* of Goliath, the latter whom David had killed some years before. As Tyndale suggests, "It is therefore quite feasible to think of a confrontation between Elhanan and Lahmi…as a revenge for Goliath's death."[209]

Origin of the giants

Now that we've more clearly discovered the names of the giants we are back to our more pressing question: where did they come from?

The text, of course, tells us that they were from the region of the Philistines. But where they were *from* in the sense of ancestry is another matter. The vast number of the Philistines apparently were not giants. But the giants had found a ready home among them, as they all seemed interested in pursuing a warlike existence in the region. And the giants were treated like champions.

As we noted above, the first chapter of this book described the

---

[207] Martin J. Selman, *1 Chronicles*, Tyndale Old Testament Commentaries, Edited by D. J. Wiseman, (Downers Grove, Illinois, Inter-Varsity Press, 1994), 198.

[208] Thompson, 158.

[209] Selman, 199.

origin of giants in general as the progeny of the sexual unions of powerful fallen angels with beautiful human women. Genesis 6:4 calls them Nephilim, which the KJV, Websters, GNT, the Septuagint, and translations from the Aramaic all render as "giants." Modern translations probably use the word "Nephilim" because it embodies more than the idea of giantism, rather than to deny that "giants" is a legitimate interpretation of the Hebrew word.

The Old Testament doesn't give us more information about these giants *before* the flood. But they appear again *after* the flood, and, as we've said, that raises the question of whether they survived the flood or were, as everyone else but Noah's family, destroyed.

To posit that the giants survived the flood would be to opt for a flood that was not as extensive and deadly as the Bible clearly says it was, and we reject that view entirely. Accordingly, the obvious answer to where the post-flood Nephilim came from is that the fallen angels conducted some of their sexual activity after the flood, until divinely stopped. The flood destroyed all their giant-progeny born before it, but the flood did not destroy heavenly beings, including fallen angels, who normally existed in the heavenly realms and whose visits to humanity—as is clear from the totality of the Bible—were temporary, involving taking on human form to some degree and then abandoning that form to return into the spiritual realm or universe.

We concluded in the first chapter that: first, angels are capable of assuming human form and functioning in that role fully; and that, second, the purpose of the fallen angels (actually, "the sons of God" in Genesis 6:1) in pervasively corrupting many of the first generations of humanity was to defeat the plan of Yahweh to have a Savior come from a human family, purely conceived. The purpose of these angels did not disappear with the flood. But two things may have stopped them.

First, it is certainly probable that the sons of God or fallen angels, discovered that their children by these marriages were not going to be immortal as their angelic fathers were. Moreover, upon these children's deaths their spirits became demons (see footnote 19). That must have been a disappointment to the sons of God.

Second, it is likely that the Lord, Yahweh, simply prohibited any further sexual unions between the fallen angels and human women shortly after the flood and the re-expansion of humanity.

What Nephilim there were in those few years continued, themselves, to mate and reproduce. It is logical to conclude that at least some of their children carried on the traits of their Nephilim ancestors, such that many of them turned out to be giants. We may reasonably assume that the giants who settled with warlike peoples, such as the Philistines, were like the Nephilim in some ways— perhaps differing only in degree. While some interpreters believe the original Nephilim were twice or more than twice the size of normal human beings, by the time of the conquest of Canaan and our story about other giants from Philistia, their size had diminished to perhaps nine feet tall or so (see 1 Samuel 17:4). Some of them obviously also exhibited other abnormalities such as multiple fingers and toes.

We are led to believe that the giants defeated by David and his men were the last of their breed, the last remnants of the invasion of the sons of God into the multiplication of humanity.

Learning the Lessons

As always, we look for lessons in the story. A tale like this one makes it difficult to distill a practical application for Christians without resorting to what we call "spiritualizing"—to assume a direct, spiritual parallel to a historical account. A spiritualized "lesson" from this curious story might be simply that a Christian must defeat the giants in his life, the temptations or trials that would keep him from fulfilling God's will for him. That's not untrue, of course, but it may not be what God is trying to say through the inspired author of 1 Chronicles.

The Bible reader needs to try to understand the purpose of the writer of biblical history, and by extension the purpose of God for the ages of humanity to follow.

1. God preserved human generations   A Truth to Believe ☑

The defeat of the giants was crucial to eliminating the infiltration of fallen spiritual powers into humanity.

As we said in the introduction, we never planned to cover the story of the Great Flood in a chapter of this book. But if we had, we would have confronted a fascinating, and probably entirely correct, interpretation of the Bible's statement that **"These are the generations of Noah: Noah was a just man and perfect in his generations, and Noah walked with God"** (Genesis 6:9 KJV). A growing number of scholars think that the Hebrew of that verse does not refer to the generation—i.e. time—in which Noah lived, but his generations (note the KJV plural)—i.e. his ancestry. The point being made would be that while the fallen angels were trying to corrupt the generations, the family lines, of man, Noah's family so far had experience no such corruption. If he were the only family to be saved through the flood, he would have an uncorrupted, a *pure* line, from which the people of God would come.

It was this purely *human* ancestry God needed to use to bring forth eventually the Messiah who would be, as Luke says, "the son of Abraham…the son of Noah…the son of Adam…the son of God" (Luke 3:34,36,38). This is a foundational truth to be believed, as it helps to uncover the fundamental principles that underlie history.

2. Sovereign victory   A Truth to Believe ☑

God works sovereignly to bring about his purposes, through those fully committed to him, those not, and everyone else.

The comment above by one of our sources was well put in this matter: "Thus are God's plans always brought to fruition, despite the frailties of those through whom he does his work." In the text, those people with frailties included David, who at some point reached an age of diminishing powers, and had to stay out of battles and leave the final defeat of the giants to his mighty men. But in all of Jewish history, the list of human beings with serious frailties was immense, and of course, all human beings are frail. Throughout our lives, even those of us who want to be and try to be engaged in the will of God are imperfect performers and doers of it. God *always* has to override our failures and our mistakes—sometimes our stubbornness or rebellion—to carry out his plans in spite of us.

Obviously, we want to be the kind of children of God who love our Heavenly Father and walk with him faithfully and obediently. So, while we live against the background knowledge that he is not defeated or thwarted by our failures, we should strive to submit our frailties and weaknesses to him and operate in the power of the Spirit of God, the Spirit of Jesus. Paul wrote that God answered one of his prayers this way: **"My power is perfected in weakness"** (2 Corinthians 12:9).

A WHALE OF A TALE
Jonah

Before we even get underway with this chapter we'll say, "We know, we know—Jonah wasn't swallowed by a whale but by a *large fish*—Jonah 1:17. That will be one of the points of our discussion in this chapter.

A previous chapter, "Boiling Goat," was an exception to the 'rule' of curious stories because it wasn't a story. We've included this chapter on Jonah as another exception, because while every other curious story in this book comes *from* a Bible book, this one *is* a Bible book. But what distinguishes Jonah from all the other prophetic writings is that while all of them are records of the preaching of those prophets, Jonah is entirely a single story, containing a *one sentence* summary of his preaching. The only thing close to this "story" character among the prophetic books is Daniel, which includes several tales from his time in Babylon, as well as a lot of visions he received about the future.

Jonah is the tale of no doubt the most significant portion of Jonah's life, centering around that strange and remarkable incident involving the whale—sorry, "large fish." Since it would be impractical to quote the entire book as our scriptural basis for this story, we'll quote just the core of the part that certainly qualifies as curious:

> The LORD sent a huge fish to swallow Jonah, and Jonah was in the stomach of the fish three days and three nights (Jonah 1:17 NET).
> Jonah prayed to the LORD his God from the stomach

of the fish (Jonah 2:1 NET).

Then the LORD **commanded the fish and it disgorged Jonah on dry land** (Jonah 2:10 NET).

The entire story of Jonah is fascinating and the whole book contains many lessons for contemporary Christians. We may not get to them all, however, because doing so would make for a *very long* chapter. We'll cheat a bit, though, by hitting the high spots. After all, the character of Jonah is really what gives meaning to why he wound up inside the "great fish."

Discovering the Text

Overview

Let's begin with a brief summary of the book. God called Jonah to prophesy to Nineveh, capital of the Assyrian empire. Instead, he boarded a ship going the opposite direction, to Tarshish. During the voyage, a storm threatened the ship, and the sailors found out that Jonah was the cause. They threw him overboard, where God had appointed a great fish to swallow him.

While in the fish, Jonah repented and asked to be delivered. The fish spit him out, and he proceeded to Nineveh, where he preached that the city would be destroyed in forty days if the people there didn't repent. They did repent, and the city was spared.

Jonah was not expecting this turn of events and it made him extremely angry. He went outside the city and sat on a hill where he could watch to see if God would still send judgment. When he didn't, Jonah complained, and God chided him for his sore lack of compassion.

Jonah the man

This summary of the book shows a number of character descriptors of Jonah.

- *Hard spirit.* Jonah was obviously chosen for his task because he had a prophetic gift that God would use to bring repentance to Nineveh. But Jonah was a recalcitrant man who himself didn't learn the proper spirit of prophecy: he didn't learn the hope of mercy. He had a hard spirit toward those whom God wanted to be recipients of his grace.

  Jonah was like some preachers in eons since who took to their role as proclaimers of fire and brimstone eagerly, almost delighted with the prospect of witnessing the destruction of people for whom they had, let us say, a strong disaffection. But they were not as effective or even persuasive in their pleas for repentance or their descriptions of God's saving grace. They think God made them hammers and hammers they were going to be!

- *Fear.* Jonah's first response, to what he was obviously deeply convinced was a divine call to be a prophet, was disappointing. We read of the call of other prophets, often in the first verse or two of their books, and we're inspired by their conviction, their surrender, and their inauguration of their time of ministry where God planted them or sent them. Isaiah's call is described in chapter 6. Jeremiah's call is recounted in Jeremiah 1:2. Ezekiel's call is in chapter 2 of his work. —And so on. And then there's Jonah, who heard the voice of God in his heart just as clearly as the rest of them, and what did he do? He ran the other way. We can only conclude that this response was due to a fundamental fear of being God's emissary, a fear of the cost of obedience, or of the harmful opposition of those who would be the recipients of the message.

- *Lack of understanding.* In his response of fear we may be able to detect another characteristic of Jonah. He appears to have believed that God would let him out of the calling if he just resisted it firmly enough. This would show a lack of basic understanding of the character as well as the sovereignty of God —a lack that then showed up later in Jonah's attitude about

311

God's response to Nineveh's repentance.

- **Spiritual vulnerability.** While Jonah came with several deep-seated prejudices, he was capable of having, and expressing, a deep, life-changing encounter with God, and that's what took place in the belly of the great fish. Jonah 2:1-9 is written in poetry—obviously what Jonah later wrote down, not finding the interior of a great fish to be conducive to penmanship. At the end of that prayer-response to God, Jonah said, **"Those who worship worthless idols forfeit the mercy that could be theirs. But as for me, I promise to offer a sacrifice to you with a public declaration of praise; I will surely do what I have promised"** (Jonah 2:8-9 NET). Notice that he realized, at a deep level, that mercy was God's ultimate goal and that the message of judgment was the *means* to that *end*. This was an understanding that Jonah came by briefly, however, before it became subsumed again by his obsession with seeing Nineveh destroyed.

- **Impulsiveness.** The shifting attitude of Jonah throughout the book points to a basic impulsiveness about his personality, a fundamental tendency that affected his commitment to godly attitudes. Whether he learned later in life—after the events described in the book—to be more consistent spiritually, we have no idea.

Jonah's fish tale

As we said at the top of this chapter, it is the setting of Jonah's dramatic submission to God that qualifies the story as curious. There's really nothing else like it in the Bible. God sent (Heb. *wayman*—other versions have "appointed," "provided," or "prepared," etc.) a great fish to swallow him. The beast was specially located near the ship where Jonah was trying to make himself a martyr in a final attempt to get out of going to Nineveh. When the sailors reluctantly threw Jonah overboard because he insisted doing so would result in God's calming the storm, the fish shortly found him.

Jonah was in that fish for three days. No details are given us about his accommodations in the fish. Popular tales of Jonah have him comedically coming into Nineveh stinking of fish entrails and dragging seaweed. We just don't know what level of confinement there was or what extent of trauma he experienced. Obviously he was able to survive. But the point seems to be that this was no casual event that could have happened to anyone unlucky enough to fall overboard at sea and to encounter one of these unknown species of fish. No, this was a miraculous event. It is unique. No fisherman lost at sea—temporarily—has ever recounted another instance of what Jonah experienced.

The question always, *always* arises what kind of fish was Jonah's Motel 6 for those three days. The answer is impossible to give with any degree of certainty.

First, it's entirely possible that the fish existed at the time but not anymore—that it is extinct. We're not aware of many fishes that are extinct and that were of the size that would qualify. But one that does qualify was the Leedsichthys, which was fifty to a hundred feet in length. Of fish that still exist, we might include as possibilities the whale shark at sixty feet or so—capable of swallowing a person whole, and the basking shark at a little over forty-five feet. Various other sharks are large but not large enough.

It's interesting that even as smart as we are scientifically, we still give the label "*whale* shark" to a shark, a cartilaginous fish, not a mammal, which true whales are. What we really ought to study is just what we're dealing with in the original language.

First of all, there is a word the King James translated as "whales;" it's *tannin,* found in Genesis 1:21 and elsewhere. Without going on a long journey to every instance of this word, let us say that it was a general term for monstrous sea creatures, not limited to what we classify as whales today. The specific word for "fish" in Jonah 1:17 is the Hebrew *dāg,* along with an adjective for "great."

The Septuagint renders this phrase in Jonah as κητει μεγαλω

313

(kātai megalō), the same root words used in Genesis and translated "great whales." And in the New Testament, according to the King James version of Matthew, Jesus said that Jonah was "in the whale's belly" (κητους - *kētous*). Obviously, the idea that the great fish was a whale has its roots in very ancient sources.

Charles Ellicott wrote on this verse: "The Hebrew *dag* is derived from the prolific character of fish, and a great fish might stand for any one of the sea monsters. The notion that it was a whale rests on the LXX and Matthew 12:40. But κητος was a term for any large fish, such as dolphins, sharks, &c."[210]

It is highly worth considering that taxonomy in biology hasn't been around more than about three hundred years. Jonah was written some 2,800 years ago. People described what they saw. What was reported as swallowing Jonah was a good enough description for the purpose, and probably that should be good enough for us. The bottom line, in other words, seems to be that, the specifics of debatable linguistics aside, it may in fact have been a whale. It may not.

Jonah's story

We've already noted at the top of this chapter that Jonah differs from the other prophetic writings in that it is more the story of the significant part of Jonah's life, rather than a record of his preaching. But Jonah is very different in another way. It recounts his experience with God, with sailors, and with the people of Nineveh, in a very uncomplimentary way. None of the other prophets wrote about himself with such self-deprecation. We can almost believe that Jonah didn't write the story—wouldn't have written it.[211]

---

[210] Charles Ellicott, *Ellicott's Commentary for English Readers*, "BibleHub.com." October 25, 2024, https://biblehub.com/commentaries/jonah/ 1-17.htm.

[211] The traditional view is that Jonah wrote the book himself. Later scholars believe someone else penned the book based on the oral version circulating during the period of Israel's captivity.

But the uncomplimentary record of his running from the call of God, the shame he experienced, the discipline he endured, and the chiding he received may be exactly the reasons he wrote the little book. And it may indicate that he wrote it after some time had passed during which he had the opportunity to reflect, and the greater maturity to understand what God was doing with him during his time of prophesying. Perhaps later in life Jonah became confessional and tried to render an account that would both inform his readers of an important prophetic event and also share with them an illustration of the importance of loving mercy. Something about aging often makes people less defensive about their younger years and more inclined to both admit the lessons they learned and also to pass along these lessons to others.

Learning the Lessons

The lessons of Jonah for the modern Christian are several, and we've basically covered them in our perusal of the larger book. There is at least one lesson specifically derived from the core of the book, the text we quoted at the top. The heart of the book is Jonah's three days in the belly of the great fish.

The hard way   An Action to Take ☑

We may be able to avoid some hardship by resisting the sinful impulse to avoid doing God's will when we know very well what he wants.

Not all hardships in life are discipline for disobedience, but some of them are. Not all difficulties we run into are the result of having gone left when God said go right, but some of them are.

Many a preacher can tell the story of how he felt in his youth that God was calling him to ministry, and instead of yielding to that call, he ran from it. But it isn't just preachers who run from God's calling. Any Christian can sense something about the will of God that he or she then resists doing. It doesn't have to be a lifetime pursuit that's scary; it may be a little project God wants a Christian to pursue just for a day or a week, a person God wants a Christian to get to know and influence for Christ, or a place of service in a church. Sometimes it's something the individual believer is gifted for, but sometimes it's not. And because the Christian may think he's not the best person to be going, doing, or saying something for God, he excuses himself. He or she may have something else to do, even something he says to himself and to God, "is important, after all." He may, in fact, make himself unavailable (or so he thinks) by doing something else life-absorbing.

Who are we to tell God to get someone else? Remember that Moses did that, repeatedly. God finally got a bit perturbed with Moses. He didn't have a whale swallow him, but he let him know that he wasn't changing his mind and Moses wasn't going to talk him out of going to Egypt.

Jonah was in the same position. But his ticket to Tarshish was going to get revoked. He might—we can even say he *would*—have avoided the experience of spending days inside that fish if he had said Yes to God when he first heard him.

If we don't surrender to God's will when he first makes it known, we may have taken the road to hardship. God often prepares unexpected events, inconvenient circumstances or painful experiences to get our attention, reposition us, or bring about our surrender to his will. Such means on his part may not be necessary, if we just agree with him and submit to him when we hear him.

Practice saying Yes to the Lord.

- He's not going to lead you into something that isn't finally the best thing for your life.
- Even if what he tells you to do seems to require too much change on your part, too much sacrifice, or giving up other things you always wanted, you would find your other plans

finally unfulfilling if you miss God's plan.

- Even if what he wants of you sounds like danger, trouble and hardship, it's still the best plan. A life of ease and the safety of obscurity can be the most dangerous thing of all, if it is a substitute for your doing the will of God.

When you realize God is speaking, say Yes.

COUGH UP THE TAX
Matthew 17:24-27

A New Testament miracle account that isn't only curious but almost sounds whimsical is about Jesus, Peter, and a fish. Christ used it to plant the seed of a larger truth in Peter's mind and heart.

> [24] After Jesus and his disciples arrived in Capernaum, the collectors of the two-drachma temple tax came to Peter and asked, "Doesn't your teacher pay the temple tax?"
>
> [25] "Yes, he does," he replied.
>
> When Peter came into the house, Jesus was the first to speak. "What do you think, Simon?" he asked. "From whom do the kings of the earth collect duty and taxes— from their own children or from others?"
>
> [26] "From others," Peter answered.
>
> "Then the children are exempt," Jesus said to him. [27] "But so that we may not cause offense, go to the lake and throw out your line. Take the first fish you catch; open its mouth and you will find a four-drachma coin. Take it and give it to them for my tax and yours" (Matthew 17:24-27 NIV).

Like the Old Testament story of Elisha getting a student-prophet out of a jam by miraculously retrieving an ax head that fell in the water, this story about Jesus illustrates divine provision. But its meaning in context is greater than that.

Discovering the Text

Earthly obligations

Our story opens as the collectors of the temple tax catch up with Jesus' disciples and query Peter about Jesus' adherence to obligations. Apparently these disciples were on some sort of errand and were not with Jesus at the time. The collectors may have seen the absence of Jesus with this handful of disciples as a perfect opportunity to catch them in some way—easier than when asking Jesus directly, because his answers were always flawless.

They said, "Your teacher pays the double drachma tax, doesn't he?" (NET). The NIV's rendering makes the question seem just a little bit accusatory: "Doesn't your teacher pay the temple tax?" The CEV's rendering is completely neutral: "Does your teacher pay the temple tax?"

The underlying Greek doesn't contain any shades of meaning. It says these collectors of the *didrachma* (διδραχμα) just asked a simple question, setting up a possible "gotcha," which never came. The Greek word for "didrachma" doesn't specifically mean "tax." In fact, the Greek word for "tax," isn't even in v24. The three translations we've quoted above, and others, supply "tax" to clarify the fact that the word indicated the two-drachma tax for the support of the temple.

This was a Jewish tax only, which the Romans allowed them to collect as an exception to the usual rule in the Empire. Commentator Tasker notes that "Tribute renders κηνσον ... and here we have the origin of the English word 'census'."[212] This was a poll tax, not a property tax. It was charged simply because someone existed.

---

[212] R. G. V. Tasker, *The Gospel According to St. Matthew*, Tyndale New Testament Commentaries, Edited by R. G. V. Tasker, (Grand Rapids, Michigan, Wm. B. Eerdmans Publishing Company, 1975), 172.

Not paying it would have put Jesus and his disciples into the category of non-compliance, giving the temple authorities perfect justification for bringing charges against them. What charges or penalties there were for not paying it are uncertain.

Two kingdoms

After Peter answered the question put to him—we infer that he more or less *insisted* that Jesus was in compliance—the disciples rejoined him in "the house"—unidentified as to ownership.

Jesus knew about the scene with the tax collectors. The text is silent about whether he picked up on conversation between them as they neared and entered the house, or whether he knew the encounter supernaturally. But there's a clue in the Greek word *proephthasin* (προεφθασεν), which means "anticipated," and which the NIV renders, **"Jesus was the first to speak"** (v25). Peter didn't report on the conversation with the temple authorities; Jesus knew about it independently.

The Eternal Son set aside his omniscience while on earth, just as he wasn't omnipresent, either. Occasionally he did look inward and upward in perfect petition and knew instantly things that no one else did—Nathaniel under the fig tree, a Samaritan woman's having had five husbands, etc. But he didn't know when his second coming would be until he received the glory he had before Bethlehem with the Father (Matthew 24:36). It appears in this present story that Jesus did apprehend knowledge that others wouldn't have had.

The question Jesus asked Peter, prompted by the encounter he knew he had had with temple tax collectors, was premised on an imaginary but realistic scene where an earthly king was assessing taxes. Whether this king would require taxes of his own children was easily answered—of course not. Taxes were an obligation of subjects, not children. The Greek word for "others" in the NIV is *allotrion* (αλλοτριων). Classical translations render it "strangers," as does the modern CSB. Some versions say "foreigners." The point is that the people taxed were not the family of the king. With this obvious answer Jesus implied that neither were his disciples subjects of this figurative king. Somehow, in the analogy, they were sons, children of the king suggested by the brief illustration.

Jesus didn't offer any further details that would flesh out his illustration about kings and children and subjects and taxes. He left it to his disciples, and us, to make the connection to his other teaching themes.

Accordingly, we should note the context of this little story. Matthew's very next record of Jesus' teaching was about the kingdom of heaven (Matthew 18), specifically about children's being the quintessence of its members. He followed that with two teachings about those who will inherit heaven, and then a parable about the kingdom of heaven's being compared with an earthly king.

Clearly, Matthew was associating our curious story about the temple tax and the king's children with the whole subject of the kingdom of heaven—which features prominently within this gospel.

In fact, the point of Jesus' application of his analogy is that in a real sense the disciples—by extension all disciples of Jesus to come —were truly children of the Heavenly Father and only incidentally and provisionally subjects of earthly authorities. To be a "child of the king" was to be responsible to the Father in Heaven, certainly a far greater obligation in the way of obedience than owed to any earthly authority.

The larger implications of this pronouncement are staggering. "Jesus has freed them from obeying the law, both oral and written, except inasmuch as it is fulfilled and reinterpreted in his person and teaching."[213] Pauline teaching would later expand on that truth and principle in a remarkable way, when he said, "we are not under the law" (Romans 6:15).

But Jesus was not suggesting to his disciples that they thumb

---

[213] Craig L. Blomberg, *Matthew*, The New American Commentary, Edited by E. Ray Clendenen, (Nashville, Broadman Press, 1992), 271.

their noses at temple rulers, as he makes clear in the next sentence. He was telling them, however, to develop the conception of their new relationship to the God of the universe and to revel in the fact that they are his children, soon to be glorified in his presence, leaving the minor kingdoms of this world behind.

Avoiding offense

Having laid down the principle of the disciples' being children of the Father and therefore "free" of this obligation to the Temple, he said, **"but so that we may not cause offense…"** (v27). Lenski points out that "offense" in the Greek, which is *skandalisomen* (σκανδαλισωμεν), "goes beyond the idea of causing one to stumble." He says, "The refusal to pay this tax would be equal to baiting the crooked stick in a trap by which it is sprung; simple-minded people would bite at that bait and be hopelessly caught in the trap thus set for them."[214] In other words, Jesus didn't merely want to avoid upsetting them. He wanted to avoid confusing them further about his mission and its impact on the world.

God's provision

Against the backdrop of the question about the tax and Jesus' implicit teaching about God's kingdom, the way the disciples were to acquire the means of paying the tax on that occasion was to be a clear example of God's provision for man's need. It was another instance of Jesus' supernatural knowledge at a moment of opportunity. He told Peter to go throw a "line" (v27 NIV) in the sea, which would have been the Sea of Galilee. The Greek word is *ankistron* (αγκιστρον), which actually means "hook," as in the KJV and most other translations. While the fishermen among Jesus' disciples would have used a net when fishing for a living—to catch

---

[214] R. C. H. Lenski, *St. Matthew's Gospel*, (Minneapolis, Minnesota, Augsburg Publishing House, 1943), 675-676.

the most they could at one time—Jesus was specific about wanting Peter to throw *one hook*, and so to catch *one fish*, and to take that *first* fish and look in its mouth. This was no random sampling of dozens or even scores of fish, one of which *might* have gobbled up a shiny coin lost overboard by somebody in a boat. It was an example of provision for the need of the hour in a specific way that defied any attempt to explain it as anything but from God. And, it was not a single *didrachma* coin that Peter would find, but a four-drachma coin, as Jesus said, "for the temple tax for you and me" (v27).

Even more than providing for the *means* to pay the tax was the *reason* for paying it. The purpose of the miracle "was not to serve personal convenience but to set the stage for driving home a basic principle …his willingness to pay the tax in consideration of others."[215] He didn't have to do it. He did it to avoid adding more difficulty to their believing who he was.

The story ends there, not recording how Peter did what he was told to do, or his reaction when he did it. We are to assume that he carried through. The story actually has more impact as is, ending as it does with the remarkable words of Jesus rather than the amazement of Peter on the seashore when he found the coin.

Learning the Lessons

The contemporary lessons of this story are the same as those that Jesus taught his disciples.

1. Obey God supremely
An Action to Take ✔

When a Christian obeys God in everything, his just obligations on earth will be met.

---

[215] Frank Stagg, *Matthew*, The Broadman Bible Commentary, Edited by Clifton J. Allen, (Nashville, Broadman Press, 1969), 180.

As the story makes clear, Jesus' disciples are sons of the Heavenly Father. Their obedience to him is a superior obligation to any in this world. This relationship extends to every disciple of Jesus Christ—every Christian—since the time of Jesus' ministry on earth. In a profound way, we have been relieved of responsibility to obey the laws of man except as they are an expression of the law of God. And the law of God has been summed up in the statement in Romans: **"Love does no wrong to a neighbor. Therefore love is the fulfillment of the law"** (Romans 13:10 NET). As is attributed to St. Augustine in a sermon on 1 John 4:4-12, "Love God and do what you will." That's a bold way to put it, but it's biblically true.

This principle could be easily misused by someone wanting to escape responsibility to earthly government. Jesus did not give us an excuse to disobey whatever laws we choose *for any reason*. What he did was to put the authority of the King of Heaven over all earthly authorities, such that *if and when* human laws contradict God's law, the Christian must, under the lordship of Jesus Christ, obey God rather than man. Peter said this very thing to the Sanhedrin when they ordered the disciples to "shut up" about Jesus.

The flip side of that coin is that unless there *is* a conflict between God's law and man's, the default position of the Christian should be to obey the laws of man. Paul states this generality in Romans: **"Let everyone be subject to the governing authorities"** (Romans 13:1).

What Jesus did was to tell us one of the chief reasons for our general compliance with governmental obligations: to avoid giving government reason to consider Christians as rebellious. This is the upshot of what "giving offense" meant in the story.

So, should Christians be law-abiding citizens? Yes. Should they always place the will of God and the lordship of Jesus Christ above all human law? Yes. Will instances of necessary disobedience to human laws take place every day? Probably not, but such occasions will take place increasingly in these times of hostility toward Christianity.

2. The new temple

Jesus' life, death and resurrection brought an end to the need of the earthly Temple and set his followers on a new plane.

Beneath the mundane matters in this story of paying the Temple tax is a truth not elaborated upon, but which is powerfully encapsulated in what Jesus said. What he taught the disciples in about two dozen words wasn't just that human laws took a subsidiary position to the law of God. It was more importantly that the Temple was being rendered obsolete. Jesus' death would be the supreme sacrifice for sins for all time, and his resurrection would bring eternal life to all who claimed his blood for their salvation. The new temple would be the hearts and lives of all these believers.

3. God will provide

As Christians live in the lordship of Jesus Christ, God will provide for their earthly substance as needed to do his will.

This principle is one of the more difficult ones to internalize for the believer in Christ. Most of us have spent much time in prayer for things we think we need, only to sense silence from heaven. We try "claiming" the appropriate scriptures about prayer—having faith, confessing sin, praying without impure motives, praying persistently, praying in Jesus' name—and still heaven is silent. The one condition of prayer that is usually responsible for God's declining to give us what we want is asking for what is his will. 1 John 5:14 says, **"And this is the confidence that we have before him: that whenever we ask anything according to his will, he hears us"** (NET). If we sought the will of God exclusively, our success in prayer would improve.

In this fish tale involving Peter, he knew that going fishing was God's will because it was the direct instruction of Jesus. And earlier, in the first part of this same chapter of Matthew, Jesus had been transfigured before select disciples, including Peter; so they *knew* even more that he was God the Son. So, what he said was God's will.

We may not always know as clearly as Peter did that day that God wants to answer our prayers about specific needs. But the more we read the Bible, the more we ponder the things of God and study the purposes of the kingdom of God, the more we'll sense what God wants us to have. When we pray for *that,* the Heavenly Father will answer with joy.

SAINTS ALIVE!
Matthew 27:50-54

It's an old expression, now, but some readers' grandmothers or great grandmothers probably said it. When something extraordinary happened or they had some pleasant surprise, they might exclaim, "Saints alive!"

That's quite literally what Matthew's gospel tells us happened after Jesus died on the cross.

> **50 Then Jesus cried out again with a loud voice and gave up his spirit. 51 Just then the temple curtain was torn in two, from top to bottom. The earth shook and the rocks were split apart. 52 And tombs were opened, and the bodies of many saints who had died were raised. 53 (They came out of the tombs after his resurrection and went into the holy city and appeared to many people)** (Matthew 27:50-53 NET).

We've included vv50-51 in the story just for context. Matthew's version of the crucifixion records that Jesus called out in a loud voice—Matthew doesn't say what he said—and gave up his spirit—died. John 19:30 says Jesus said, "It is finished," and gave up his spirit. Luke 23:46 says Jesus said, "into thy hands I commend my spirit." Apparently Luke's version preserves the *very last* words.

At that point there was something akin to an earthquake (the Greek word, *eseisthe* is the root of our word "seismic") and rocks—in the vicinity of Golgotha? elsewhere?—were split. And then our curious story takes place. Saints alive!

Discovering the Text

Tombs opened

The reader who finds himself puzzled by this story and wonders if it is meant to be historical might be reassured to know that many scholars don't know quite what to do with it, either. In its twenty-eight words (in the Greek) are several logical and timing problems that don't seem to have a solution. Some interpreters throw up their hands and resort to labeling it as fictitious. As one writer puts it, "The *legend* is an extrapolation of Christian faith in the form of a story"[216] *(emphasis ours)*. Another commentator tries to bridge the gap between legend and history: "Matthew in these verses is making a theological point rather than simply relating history. This hardly means that the evangelist, or those before him with whom the tradition may have originated, is necessarily inventing all the exceptional events in his narrative."[217]

Nevertheless, we are faced with a statement by Matthew that these things happened, and it doesn't bear the marks of a parable or a fictitious story, except as a skeptic chooses to disbelieve anything that he thinks improbable.

We think that Matthew, who wrote his gospel likely somewhere between A.D. 55 and 65, had as one source multiple reports of these appearances in Jerusalem (and elsewhere?). We posit that he found them credible because they seemed to confirm each other independently, and he decided to include a short summary of these "sightings" of resurrected saints in his gospel, without further comment. Clearly he did have a theological purpose. Its "significance is found in the establishing of the basis of the future

---

[216] J. C. Fenton, *The Gospel of St Matthew*, The Pelican New Testament Commentaries, Edited by D. E. Nineham, (London, Penguin Books, 1973), 444.

[217] Donald A. Hagner, *Matthew*, Word Biblical Commentary, (Dallas, Texas, Word Books, 1995), 851.

resurrection of the saints."[218]

As to the account itself, one might reasonably conclude in reading v52 that the tombs were opened by the force of the quaking earth. Many tombs in Israel are underground or semi-underground structures and a few of them may have been so wrenched by the shaking ground that their doors or rock seals were twisted open or fell apart.

One can imagine the emotional response to such an event. It may be that families in Jerusalem were unaware at first that their loved ones' tombs might have been affected by the quaking. Many graves are in the Kidron Valley, on the east side of the city, and possibly families would have no immediate thought of their needing to go check on family tombs.

Appearances

Some scholars have suggested that this little story, which doesn't appear in the other three gospels, was inserted later into Matthew by someone other than the original author. There's no manuscript evidence to support that idea. Some scholars have also suggested that v52 was part of the original text but that someone added v53 to keep the resurrections and appearances from having happened until after Jesus was raised, so there would be no conflict with the statement elsewhere that Jesus was the "firstborn from the dead" (Colossians 1:18). There is likewise no textual evidence of such an addition. And further, this view overlooks the fact that the account says the resurrection of these saints took place Friday at the point of Jesus' death, irrespective of when they appeared to people.[219]

Our text as quoted above from the NET Bible proposes a simple solution to the confusion by adding parentheses around v53. The

---

[218] Hagner, 851.

[219] R. C. H. Lenski, *The Interpretation of St Matthew's Gospel*, (Minneapolis, Minnesota, Augsburg Publishing House, 1943), 1131.

Greek, of course, had no parentheses, nor periods nor commas, for that matter. Readers were left to their own understanding. Clearly, v53 intends to tell us that while the opening of the tombs in v52 was directly connected to the death of Christ, the appearance of those who were raised from the dead awaited the resurrection of Christ.

Frederick Bruner says on this passage, "Not only is Jesus' death strong enough to split the veil of the holy of holies and so to cancel sin; it is also strong enough to open tombs and so to cancel death. Sin and death are humanity's two main problems. Jesus' death conquers both and opens up a whole new way of facing the guilt of sin and the grief of death."[220]

Matthew's account includes no interpretation of this event. We are left to draw reasonable conclusions based on the other themes of Matthew and the whole message of the New Testament.

John A. Broadus offered a viewpoint in his commentary on Matthew:

> The conjecture of Plump concerning this matter is of some interest. He holds that the tombs opened by the earthquake were near Jerusalem, and as the term "saints" was almost from the first applied to Christians, he thinks that these saints were believers in Jesus who had died before his crucifixion. On this supposition we see some reason for their appearing to Christian friends and kindred, in order to show that they were not shut out from a share in the kingdom.[221]

While Broadus thought the "saints" were believers in Jesus

---

[220] Frederick Dale Bruner, *Matthew, a Commentary*, (Dallas, Texas, Word Publishing, 1990), 1060.

[221] John A. Broadus, *Commentary on Matthew*, American Commentary on the New Testament, (Philadelphia, American Baptist Publication Society, 1886), 576. (Broadus does not identify who "Plump" is. In his "Index I, Authors Quoted or Referred to," Broadus does not list anyone by this name.

during his ministry who had died already, others think they were Old Testament figures such as prophets. There's no way to know. The Greek word rendered "saints" here is *hagion* which simply means holy ones. In the New Testament, "saints" refers to all followers of Christ, made holy by his blood. In Old Testament references the corresponding word, *chasid*, means the faithful people of God. Here in this curious story in Matthew, it could mean either. We think it probably means people more recently deceased.

Our bottom line interpretation is this:

> **When Jesus breathed his last,** an earthquake took place, disrupting a number of tombs in the area. Nobody ventured into graveyards during the Sabbath, but on the first day of the week as the report of Jesus' resurrection began to spread rapidly among the network of Jesus' followers, startled disciples encountered appearances of deceased but risen friends or acquaintances. These saints may have done little but appear, confirm the reports of Jesus' own resurrection, and disappear again from view. They were not like Lazarus, who was raised only to die again. They had resurrection bodies like Jesus.

Learning the Lessons

Matthew's purpose for including this little story provides the basis for our applying its lessons to our lives.

1. *Death to life*   A Truth to Believe ☑

New and everlasting life comes from the death of Christ on the cross and his subsequent resurrection.

Contrary to what both Jewish and Roman authorities believed, the death of Jesus on the cross was not an end; it was just the beginning. On the cross, he died for the sin of mankind. When he said, "It is finished," he was proclaiming that the payment for sin was complete. The Father chose at the moment Jesus breathed his last to demonstrate his power to bring life out of death.

If you have become a follower of Christ through repentance and believing in him as crucified and raised, you have come from death into life (John 5:24 NIV). Count on this truth and be confident of your future!

2. A *substantive eternity*   A Truth to Believe ☑

God plans for us to have a bodily existence in heaven, like the one we have now but glorified and perfected for eternity.

The idea of some religions is that people join a great spirit beyond and lose their identity. Others have people floating around in a sort of spiritual cloud forever. It's no wonder some people aren't very excited about eternal life. But the Bible teaches that what lies ahead for the Christian is a new, perfected, bodily life. "Matter matters. God made it in creation, took it on in incarnation, and raises it again in resurrection. Bodies are not 'immaterial' or unimportant to the biblical God; they matter so much that God raises them."[222]

The Bible further gives us a hint about the nature of those bodies. John wrote that "we will be like him, because we will see him just as he is" (1 John 3:2 NET). As we grow older, become more frail, or experience disease, injury, or incapacity, the more we think of the glory of having a perfect body, and of being able to experience God's creation in power and great mobility, for eternity. That's what's coming for the born-again believer in Jesus Christ!

---

[222] Bruner, 1061.

NAKED IN THE GARDEN
Mark 14:51-52

All four gospels record most of the incidents of the night when Jesus was arrested and tried. Some details are in only one gospel or the other, such as the identity of the man who tried to prevent Jesus' arrest by slicing off the ear of the high priest's servant Malchus. (It was Peter, John tells us.) In Mark there is also a little snippet of fascinating information. It seems that somewhere near the disciples and Jesus in the Garden of Gethsemane that night was an unidentified young man who was not properly clothed:

> 51 **A young man was following him, wearing only a linen cloth. They tried to arrest him,** 52 **but he ran off naked, leaving his linen cloth behind.** (Mark 14:51-52 NET).

The natural first question in the reader's mind is Who was this young man? The next question, if we're thinking correctly, is Why is this curious story in the Bible?

Discovering the Text

The boy's identity
It should be noted from the outset that while readers of the Gospel of Mark were never explicitly let in on the secret of who the young man was, there are pretty obvious clues.

First, in the Greek language of the account, the unknown person is described as *neaniskos tis* (νεανισκος τις), which the KJV and some other word-for-word translations render as "a *certain* young man." His identity may not have been known to the reader, but the writer is tipping us off that he knew very well who he was.

Second, it was common among writers during that time, if they wished to include themselves in historical narratives, to do so without stating their names. In the New Testament we have other obvious examples. The Gospel of John includes three references to "the disciple Jesus loved" (John 13:23, 21:7, 21:20), which virtually all scholars agree was John himself. The Book of Acts is universally agreed to have been written by Luke the Physician, and at one point he abruptly changes voices in his narrative from the third person— "Paul," "they," etc. —to "we" —inclusive of the author, Luke. It's obvious the writer, who was part of Paul's missionary group, was Luke. But he never puts his name into the work.

On the basis of these clues in Mark, we can determine with a fair degree of certainty that the young man was the author, John Mark.

Some scholars, particularly early in Christian history, argue against the identification of Mark, saying that he didn't know or follow Jesus during his ministry. But the image we get of the young man in Gethsemane is that he was not actually with the disciples or part of them. The few details we have, and the inferences we might reasonably draw, suggest that he was acquainted with who Jesus was, though he may never have met him, and that he found out where Jesus and the disciples were headed that night and followed them. This author develops that theory in a work of fiction, *The Evangelist: a Story of John Mark.*

We put forward a further theory that the upper room where Jesus and the disciples had just been was owned by a woman who lived in Jerusalem and was one of his supporters. This woman may also have been the mother of John Mark.

Why he was there

Closely related to the matter of who the young man was is why he was there. We've hinted at it already in the paragraph above: he had an interest in Jesus. It's possible that he knew one or more of the disciples. And the fact that he is described as being in the Garden of Gethsemane, at night, apparently by himself, and wearing nothing but a linen undergarment—the underwear of the day— suggests strongly that he had rushed to Gethsemane specifically to see and perhaps warn them all of the approach of the Temple guards. If so, he was apparently too late.

If the foregoing guesses are on target, the question would remain as to how he knew where the disciple group was going, and how he knew the Temple authorities were headed to Gethsemane as well. This author's novel takes a stab at these questions in a logical way, but his version of what might have happened just barely exceeds the necessities of this book.

Attempted arrest

It appears that the young man—Mark, as we believe—had not planned well ahead of time to be in the Garden that night, as he had rushed there barely clothed. But he was apparently close enough to the disciples when the Temple guards burst into Gethsemane for them to see him and assume he was one of Jesus' followers. On that basis they tried to arrest him, apparently before they decided to let everyone but Jesus go.

But the lithe young man was faster than a soldier in light armor, and he got away—without his linen underwear. The account is insistent that he was naked. The author used the Greek word *gumnou* (γυμνου), which means just that: naked. The word is part of where we get "gymnast," which originally mean "to train naked," which the Greeks did. The fact that the author of Mark—and as we think, the person being described here—writes that the boy had a linen garment "about his naked body" (the literal Greek), suggests not only knowledge that perhaps no one but Mark would have had, but also emphasizes that he was intensely aware that he didn't have anything but underwear on, and was embarrassed about it.

So, when Mark then writes that the young man left his linen cloth behind, we know he really was naked. In an earlier chapter about King Saul's having fallen into an ecstatic experience of prophecy, we suggested that while the Bible says he lay there naked all night, he may not have been stark naked. (See the chapter, "Saul Gets in the Spirit.") There was reason to believe that, in that specific case. In the case of this story in Mark, however, the author has left us with no choice but to realize that the young man got away only because he was willing to part with his clothes in the grasp of the Temple guard.

Why include the story?

Is there any indication in the story itself as to why Mark included it in his gospel?

The most obvious reason was that it constituted a sort of signature on his work, as suggested above. When an author included himself as a character in a historical narrative, his declining to identify himself was an implicit signature: I wrote this.

Merely identifying oneself anonymously might not seem to have been a particularly useful message, but if Mark intended it to be understood by the Christian community as his "mark" of authenticity, it would be useful to the church in the Christian era to come. In addition to the church's early knowledge on other bases that this gospel account came from the pen of Mark, this "signature" in his work was added evidence of who wrote it. And since it was known that Mark was a frequent companion of Peter's, the assumption has long been made that the gospel that now bears Mark's name was the product, in part, of his preserving the memories and preaching of Simon Peter.

Contemporary authors suggest other possibilities for Mark's purpose in telling this curious story. Some think the unidentified young man was emblematic of all the disciples, who shamefully deserted him and fled (Mark 14:50). Others suggest there is a connection symbolically between the linen garment the young man left and the linen cloth covering Jesus in the tomb. This latter idea is a stretch, we think.

Learning the Lessons

Is it possible to derive some kind of application of this story to a Christian's life today? We suggest some possibilities:

1. *Bible truth* A Truth to Believe ☑
You can believe the truth of the gospel accounts in part because of the willingness of their authors to be self-effacing.

People doubt the gospels for mostly the same reasons—their antiquity, perceived "conflicts" with other gospels or writings, etc. But a number of internal elements in these accounts argue for their being truthful. One is the occasional willingness of their authors to include details about themselves—supposedly anonymously!—that aren't very complimentary. It's pretty clear that the "young man" in our story was Mark, the author of the gospel. If he had told his story of what happened that night to friends and neighbors, it would have been with a red face. He probably ran quickly in the dark hoping that no one would recognize him. We suggest he didn't go back home naked and talk about it. He chose to put it in his book years later, when by that time he had gotten over his embarrassment.

For the rest of us, his little scribble about his dangerous venture the night of Jesus' arrest is a mark of authenticity. We can believe his story about Jesus.

2. *Be faithful* An Attitude to Develop ☑
In the quest to follow Jesus, be faithful to the end, whether pursued and persecuted or not.

The young man in the story almost certainly tracked the

disciples to Gethsemane, for whatever purpose. We cannot blame him for trying his best to escape arrest when he was discovered. But in the modern Christian's discipleship to Christ, somewhere there is a line or a point at which eluding persecution becomes simply avoiding witness.

An old hymn by George Duffield, Jr., says, "Stand up, stand up for Jesus!" Sometimes our stance needs to be more than just neutrality—not hiding our faith but not exactly displaying it, either. Sometimes we need to take a positive stand. Speak out. Do something. Be counted.

For instance, in order not to draw attention to ourselves we may avoid participating in something designed to confront sin—demonstrating against abortion outside a clinic, for instance. But sometimes the need of testimony to the truth of the word of God becomes so vital that we *shouldn't* avoid such activities. That may be the line or point where our avoiding persecution becomes hiding our witness.

This line or point is something every believer must decide for himself, under the leading of the Holy Spirit. What makes you decide to flee the grip of the soldiers of the spiritual enemy, or to not resist them so you can represent Jesus instead, is up to you.

TONGUES OF FIRE
Acts 2:1-4

The Christian era began with a curious story. Some 120 followers of Jesus were together in Jerusalem, no doubt in secret, following the crucifixion of their leader, Jesus of Nazareth. Though he had been crucified, he had appeared to many of them the third day *after* his death and burial, both in Jerusalem and in Galilee. And then, while with his core eleven disciples[223] on a mountain, he had disappeared into heaven after commanding them to go tell the world about everything that had happened.

In another week or so the twelve and numerous others were together again in Jerusalem, praying. And waiting. And praying. And waiting. And then, something happened.

> [1] **Now when the day of Pentecost had come, they were all together in one place. [2] Suddenly a sound like a violent wind blowing came from heaven and filled the entire house where they were sitting. [3] And tongues spreading out like a fire appeared to them and came to rest on each one of them. [4] All of them were filled with the Holy Spirit, and they began to speak in other languages as the Spirit enabled them** (Acts 2:1-4 NET).

Any reader with only a little knowledge of Christianity will recognize this as the signal event that inaugurated the Christian

---

[223] Plus one, Matthias, we presume.

church. For those who were part of that group and those who witnessed what was happening among them, the event must have been the most startling, amazing, surprising, strange, and fascinating thing that had ever taken place in their lives—or ever would.

Discovering the Text

Pentecost

The term "Pentecost" appears here for the first time in the Bible. While it is primarily a Christian celebration now, it was a Jewish feast during Bible times. It took place seven weeks after Passover.

Technically, as one commentary points out, Pentecost (which comes from the Greek word for "fifty") was "exactly fifty days after the first day of the Passover."[224] Or, as another commentator puts it, Pentecost was the fiftieth day from the second day of the passover."[225] Confused? It depends on whether you were a Pharisee or a Saducee, and whether you were counting inclusively or not, but it wound up being the same day. Most people just say Pentecost was/is fifty days after Passover. If you look it up online you'll usually find it connected instead to Resurrection Day[226] since it's now principally a celebration of the Christian church.

Various references in the Old Testament spoke of Pentecost: Deuteronomy 16:9-10, Exodus 34:22 *et al.* It was called the Feast of Weeks and the Harvest Festival. "Pentecost" (πεντηκοστης in Greek) appeared in the Septuagint in the books of Tobit and Maccabees in reference to this feast. Jews looked forward to it and

---

[224] John B. Polhill, *Acts,* The New American Commentary, Edited by David S. Dockery, (Nashville, Broadman Press, 1992), 97.

[225] Horatio B. Hackett, *Acts of the Apostles,* An American Commentary on the New Testament, Edited by Alvah Hovey, (Philadelphia, American Baptist Publication Society, 1882), 41.

[226] Most people call this "Easter." This author hasn't, since his first years in ministry.

celebrated it with holy gusto.

It was certainly fitting that what happened at Pentecost immediately following the death, burial, resurrection and ascension of Jesus Christ should take place on the day of Pentecost, since it started the great spiritual harvest in response to the preaching of the gospel message. By the time of Jesus, Pentecost was reckoned by many Rabbis "to be the anniversary of the giving of the law at Sinai—a reasonable deduction from the chronological note in Ex. 19:1."[227] Thus the coming of the Spirit would parallel the coming of the law.

In one place

The disciples were together at Pentecost, as they had been with each other regularly since the weekend when Jesus had died and then risen. They were still generally hunted people. Probably the initial inclination of the Jewish authorities to round them up and prosecute them had died down a bit since the crucifixion of Jesus; the Jews thought they had succeeded in stopping a "dangerous" movement. But the disciples had been cautious. The twelve had been together in Galilee for a time, perhaps a number of days. Now, they were back in Jerusalem with the larger group of faithful followers. On this Pentecost day they were **"together in one place."**

Where was this place? First of all, it was a **"house"** as v2 says (Greek *oikon*). Hackett thinks it was the house referred to in Acts 1:13, because the term "house" doesn't elsewhere ever refer to the Temple or any part of it.[228] F. F. Bruce says it was probably the Temple, but we disagree and hold with the American Commentary. We are unable to be dogmatic, but it seems very likely that it was where they had been before the crucifixion and probably repeatedly

---

[227] F. F. Bruce, *Commentary on the Book of the Acts*, The New International Commentary on the New Testament, Edited by F. F. Bruce, (Grand Rapids, Michigan, Wm. B. Eerdmans Publishing Co., 1971), 54.

[228] Hackett, 41.

until the resurrection: the Upper Room.[229] They were huddled in this room, perhaps a venue built into a house somewhere in Jerusalem, probably very near the Temple. They had been there at various times over the seven weeks since Passover.

They had been obeying the instruction of Jesus that he gave them at the point of his ascension just a little more than a week before:

> **"Do not leave Jerusalem, but wait there for what my Father promised, which you heard about from me. For John baptized with water, but you will be baptized with the Holy Spirit not many days from now"** (Acts 1:4-5 NET).

As they prayed and fellowshipped and then began to privately observe Pentecost, the fire fell.

Sight and sound

Two things happened that gave the disciples a fantastic sensory experience inaugurating their new, transformed lives.

The first thing was audible. **"[A] sound like a violent wind blowing came from heaven"** (v2). Polhill says that "Luke was well aware that he was using metaphorical language in these verses."[230] It wasn't wind: it was *like* a mighty wind. But it sounded like wind.

In 1989 this author was living in Charlotte, North Carolina, when Hurricane Hugo swept up from the coast of South Carolina and stayed strong as it rushed across the state, hit Charlotte, and didn't wane until it had gone through the mountain area around Boone. In the middle of the night, the author's family was awakened

---

[229] This author advances this theory in his work of fiction, already cited, *The Evangelist: A Story of John Mark.*

[230] Polhill, 98.

by a "violent wind" shaking the windows, roaring through trees, and demanding the attention of all.

This was something like what the disciples experienced—though no doubt it wasn't something they interpreted as dangerous. There was no actual wind. Luke wrote what he was told by those who witnessed the event, and what the disciples told him was simply an attempt to describe what they experienced. "God has often been pleased to reveal himself to men in conformity with their own conceptions as to the mode in which is it natural to expect communications from him."[231]

The second thing that happened was visual, as **"tongues spreading out like a fire appeared to them and came to rest on each one of them"** (v3). Again, the language is metaphorical. What they saw *looked like* tongues of fire. Picture a roaring bonfire, where thick, rising smoke ignites, licking the air above and darting skyward. What the disciples saw looked something like that, and then it spread out among them all, a vision of what was happening invisibly in a movement of God in that room.

In the film "National Treasure" starring Nicolas Cage, his character Ben Gates and his little team have finally found the treasure room they've hunted, in a cave deep beneath a Boston church. Their torches illuminate what they think is a small room with a few ancient artifacts. But Gates peers into the darkness of the room and with his torch he touches a nearby reservoir of lamp oil. Instantly the oil blazes up, and then spreads into a channel of oil that branches into more channels as the flames catch and run outward throughout what turns out to be an underground chamber a hundred feet or more long, packed with treasure of all kinds. The lamps finally illuminate the entire room and its priceless contents.

What exactly did the disciples see in that room in Jerusalem? The scripture gives a simple and profound description. The mind of

---

[231] Hackett, 42.

each reader will try to envision it. In the end, it's impossible because we weren't there. But that's hardly the point. What it meant is what's important. The audible and visual signs meant that the Holy Spirit was coming upon them in power. "These audible and visible signs were but passing phenomena; the presence and power of the Holy Spirit was the permanent and important reality."[232]

Languages

As the sound of something like wind and the sight of something like fire took place, what happened then was that **"All of them were filled with the Holy Spirit"** (v4). This expression is used in the New Testament to indicate the special enlargement of the Spirit of God in a believer's life enabling him to perform the will of God in power. The study of the ministry of the Holy Spirit and what is meant by "baptism with the Holy Spirit" and "filling of the Holy Spirit" etc. is complex and we won't attempt to conduct or even summarize it here.

What is important for this chapter is to say that the Holy Spirit—whom Jesus had already conferred upon his disciples much earlier (John 20:22)—has now, in this unique event at the birth of the church, come in power upon them all. Frank Stagg writes that "[t]his coming of the Holy Spirit upon the Christian community on the day of Pentecost parallels the coming of the Holy Spirit upon Jesus at his baptism."[233] (Perhaps we would say, "the appearance of the Holy Spirit upon Jesus" instead.)

And as the Spirit filled them all, suddenly they broke forth in praise and worship, speaking what they were feeling. And they were speaking in other languages, which they had never learned.

Kudos to the NET Bible and a few other translations for rendering the Greek words *heterais glossais* as "other languages"

---

[232] Frank Stagg, *Acts*, (Nashville, Broadman Press, 1985), 50.

[233] Stagg, 50.

rather than "other tongues." The word *glossa* (γλωσσα) does mean "tongue," either the bodily part or a human language, and in the days of the King James translation it was the commonest term to refer to English, French, Spanish, etc. —a foreign *tongue*. However, the use of "tongue" for "language" has diminished over the past few hundred years, used in mostly formal or poetic writing now. And a confusion has arisen since 1906 with the Azuza Street Revival and the rise of the Pentecostal and Charismatic movements. Adherents to these movements have re-interpreted "tongues" to mean not just languages, but *ecstatic utterance:* human speech that *does not* conform to any known language but constitutes a kind of *heavenly language* or spiritual language, not something spoken on earth.[234]

As with the matter of Spirit baptism or filling, we cannot discuss this subject of "tongues" in this book. Our focus is on the clear language of Acts 2:4 and the following verses. The disciples—we think that included all 120 or so occupants of that Upper Room— began to speak in actual human languages they had not learned. The proof of that is that foreign Jews in Jerusalem for the Feast of Weeks were hearing **"the great deeds God has done"** (2:11) in their own languages. This was an astounding miracle.

Some interpreters over the years have come to believe, however, that the miracle was one of hearing rather than speaking. They would be equally miraculous events, but we think the language of Luke is abundantly clear. The speakers spoke in foreign languages, **"as the Spirit enabled them"** (v5), and were understood by native speakers of those languages.

Learning the Lessons

What did this event mean—to the people who witnessed it and

---

[234] This author has written extensively on this subject in his commentary, *1 Corinthians: Teachings for a Typical Church*, available from lulu.com.

to us? The lessons of Pentecost are fundamental to the Christian church.

1. Jesus with us
A Truth to Believe ☑

In the Holy Spirit, Jesus is with his followers until he returns.

Just before he ascended, Jesus told his disciples, **"I am with you always, to the end of the age"** (Matthew 28:20 NET). In the Pentecost event, the Spirit of Jesus came in the fulness of his power to be with *all* his disciples for as long as this age lasts.

Philippians 1:19 expressly calls the Holy Spirit the Spirit of Jesus Christ. 2 Corinthians 3:17 says **"The Lord is the Spirit."** There are other scriptures that make very clear the truth that the Holy Spirit is the person of God who makes Jesus real to the Christian and transmits the presence, peace, and power of God to every believer. While we are trying to find and follow the will of God, the Holy Spirit is Jesus in us. While we are obeying his command to spread the gospel, the Spirit of God is the power of Jesus in us to do it. As we face the struggles, the problems, the conflicts of life, squaring off against temptation, dealing with obstacles, enduring difficulties, Jesus himself is with us through the Holy Spirit. He came to his church at Pentecost, and he has not left us. His power is in us to enable us to live faithfully for him.

2. Commissioned to tell
A Teaching to Obey ☑

The church is empowered by the Holy Spirit to fulfill the Great Commission to go into all the world with the gospel.

When the disciples spoke the languages of the world around them the Spirit was sending them a message that the church was to advance quickly, first to the Jews dispersed in various parts of the world and then to others—to cover the known world with the message of Jesus Christ. But the gift of languages was not a permanent gift, and it didn't equip the church for any substantial time beyond that particular day of Pentecost to tell people about the gospel. The significance of the gift of other languages was symbolic. The church was "destined to break through social, racial, and religious barriers with a message of light and life for all mankind."[235]

Modern Christians are to believe this truth and to obey its mandate. It is not enough for us to find a warm, happy church to attend and to sing and feel inspired. We are to reach our world and the world beyond with the message that Jesus Christ died for our sins, rose from the grave to bring us new life, and commands people everywhere to repent and believe on him!

---

[235] T. C. Smith, *Acts*, The Broadman Bible Commentary, Edited by Clifton J. Allen, (Nashville, Broadman Press, 1970), 25.

SLEEPING DURING CHURCH
Acts 20:7-12

We close this book with a little chapter about a miracle story, part of the missionary travels of the Apostle Paul. The setting was Troas on the Asian continent, just across the Aegean Sea from Greece. Paul was returning to Syria from Greece and sailed into Troas where there was a church.

> [7] On the first day of the week we came together to break bread. Paul spoke to the people and, because he intended to leave the next day, kept on talking until midnight. [8] There were many lamps in the upstairs room where we were meeting. [9] Seated in a window was a young man named Eutychus, who was sinking into a deep sleep as Paul talked on and on. When he was sound asleep, he fell to the ground from the third story and was picked up dead. [10] Paul went down, threw himself on the young man and put his arms around him. "Don't be alarmed," he said. "He's alive!" [11] Then he went upstairs again and broke bread and ate. After talking until daylight, he left. [12] The people took the young man home alive and were greatly comforted (Acts 20:7-12 NIV).

This delightful tale took place during Paul's third missionary journey. It appears from the change of pronouns from third person to first person plural in this chapter that Paul had just been joined by Luke the physician, probably in Philippi. Luke's being with the group plays into the story as we shall see.

Discovering the Text

One night in church

The text tells us the event took place in a meeting of the church: v7 says it was the **"first day of the week,"** which was Sunday, and that they had met to **"break bread."** Virtually all commentators agree this was a gathering of the church where they celebrated the Lord's Supper. "Break bread" is a regular expression for the Lord's Supper and less often refers to the "love feast," which was more like present day "covered dish" suppers. In fact, we think many commentators are overly concerned with *when* this event took place, probably because nailing down exactly when it was might help determine just when Christians shifted formally to Sunday as their day of worship.

But Luke has set the scene for us as a writer. 'Picture this,' he says. 'It's Sunday and the church is together to hear Paul preach.' This is Luke the doctor plying another of his gifts, that of writing. The reader is invited to imagine a large room where many people could meet. It was an **"upstairs room"** (v8) on the **"third story"** (v9).

A long winded preacher

Previous verses in this same chapter informed us that Sopater, Aristarchus, Secundus, Gaius, Timothy, Tychicus, and Trophimus had all sailed ahead of Paul to Troas and were waiting for him, Luke, and anyone else who was with them to arrive. Presumably these men had alerted the church in Troas to be ready for Paul's arrival and make preparations. It was a highly anticipated gathering.

Paul wasn't going to be long in Troas, so the meeting on that Sunday night (all the "lights" were on in the room—v8) was expected to be long. "Church meetings were not regulated by the clock in those days, and the opportunity of listening to Paul was not one to be cut short: what did it matter if he went on conversing with them until midnight?"[236]

In the present day, in some "country" churches, in particular, it has often been said, especially by older worshipers, that the preacher should "preach on!" as long as he is led by the Spirit to do so. If many were expecting Paul to "preach on!" in Troas that night long ago, they were not disappointed. He **"kept on talking until midnight"** (v7). We don't know when he got started. But he was leaving the following day, and it was likely they would not see him again, so the consensus was that the floor was his as long as he wanted it.

A stuffy room

Luke gives us a clue as to what complicated the matter of paying full attention to the long-winded Paul. **"There were many lamps in the upstairs room where we were meeting"** (v8). This sentence is inserted all by itself with no explanation, but apparently Luke knew his readers would understand what was going to happen:

- The lamps provided nice lighting for the meeting, but as we know today, they burned oxygen—they made the room stuffy.
- There were windows, but there may not have been much cross breeze, and the multiple lamps meant the air still wasn't fresh.
- Likely the meeting room was packed, adding to the stuffiness.
- A lot of nodding was probably going on.

A sleepy boy

On the edge of the room, sitting in a window, was a boy named Eutychus. It's possible he had retreated there to get a breath of fresh air, but more likely it was one of the only seats left when he arrived at the meeting, and he was glad to have it.

The New American Commentary opines that possibly the hour

---

[236] Bruce, *Commentary on the Book of Acts*, 408.

was "past the lad's normal bedtime;"[237] but the hour was late for everyone, and in due time the boy succumbed to the circumstances. He nodded, then dozed, and then went soundly to sleep (v9). The Greek says literally that he was overpowered by sleep (ὑπνῶ - *hypnō*).

A deadly fall

Eutychus may have been propped against a side of the window, but once he went to sleep fully, his body relaxed and he fell out of the opening. It was three stories down, probably not much different in height from our average story height today, though the third story room itself may have had a higher ceiling. Eutychus probably fell twenty to thirty feet to the street below, possibly stone-paved.

People rushed down and out of the building and no doubt crowded around the still figure. Luke doesn't say who picked him up; possibly it was his parents. No EMS crews were in existence to warn people about moving a fall-victim. There were no neck-stabilizing braces to prevent further spinal cord injury. There were just distraught family and friends, hoping he was alive, picking him up, probably calling his name.

But he was **"picked up dead"** (v9). Here's where we must recall that Luke the doctor had joined Paul's entourage just prior to coming to Troas. It is entirely likely that Luke was asked to confirm what everyone feared. Probably the fall had produced what we call today "blunt force trauma," perhaps to his head and torso as well. He wasn't breathing. There was no pulse. Everyone there knew death. Eutychus was dead.

Some Bible readers doubt every miracle, and this one is no exception. Many believe Eutychus only appeared to be dead, and when they read, "was picked up dead" they read it as, "was picked up *as* dead," or some such re-phrasing. But the Greek doesn't allow

---

[237] Polhill, 419.

it and Luke didn't write it that way. He is crystal clear. The boy was killed in the fall.

An apostolic miracle

Perhaps Paul was on the periphery of the crowd around Eutychus by the time he could get out of the building. The account says **"Paul went down,"** suggesting everyone else was ahead of him to the scene. But he broke his way gently through the crowd and got to Eutychus.

Paul didn't deny that Eutychus was dead. In fact, it was because he knew, as did everyone, that the boy was dead, that Paul did what he then did. He **"threw himself on the young man and put his arms around him"** (v10). In an action reminiscent of both Elijah (1 Kings 17:17-24) and Elisha (2 Kings 4:8-37), who each had raised boys to life from the dead, Paul embraced Eutychus's dead body, possibly praying aloud for his resuscitation. Luke provides no details other than the sudden and decisive embrace of the lifeless lad.

And then, apparently very quickly, he released him and told everyone not to worry, that Eutychus was alive (v10). Again, Luke does not burden the story with details—whether the boy suddenly sprang to life, bones healed, head injuries gone, any cuts having disappeared—nothing but the basic fact that one moment everyone was groaning over a dead boy and the next moment he was alive and well. In a while, his family would go home with him.

Meanwhile, however, the church meeting resumed. Paul went back in, **"broke bread and ate."** The group had already had the Lord's Supper, probably at the beginning of the evening. Possibly they had eaten a meal before beginning a time of worship. But that had probably been hours ago, and it was now after midnight, and Paul was hungry. He had something to eat, likely joined by others.

And then Paul finished his sermon. He went on until daybreak! No doubt, nobody was sitting in the windows for the remainder of the service!

Learning the Lessons

Paul's gospel

Though repeated miracles, the Holy Spirit continually validated the Christian faith as preached and taught by Paul.

Paul sometimes referred to the content of his ministry as "my gospel" and "the gospel that I preach." He was describing the whole of his preaching and teaching ministry everywhere he went. In Galatians 1 he told how he had gone to Arabia shortly after his conversion, and then back to Damascus, before going to Jerusalem. In his first few years as a believer in the Jesus whose followers he had tried to stamp out, Paul learned from God what he was to teach and preach.

Some people claim that the Jesus of the gospels and the Christ of Paul's letters are essentially different people, that what Jesus taught and what Paul taught were not the same—that Paul created a new body of teaching that wasn't authentic. This is a false analysis that doesn't match up with the unified picture the New Testament gives us.

The principal lesson of this little story about Eutychus seems to be one that was meant for the witnesses of his coming back to life that night, and for everyone since who has read about it. Paul was again attested to be the divinely commissioned apostle that he had shown himself to be since his dramatic conversion on the road to Damascus. Repeatedly, his missionary efforts had been punctuated by miraculous events. The Holy Spirit enabled Paul to do mighty things: to demonstrate to his hearers that he was divinely sent; to show that his gospel message had the power to save; and to verify that his teaching of Christian doctrine was authoritative for the church.

BIBLIOGRAPHY

Baldwin, Joyce G. *1 Samuel.* Tyndale Old Testament Commentaries. Edited by D. J. Wiseman. Downers Grove, Illinois: Inter-Varsity Press, 1988.

Barnes, Albert. *Notes on the Bible.* Grand Rapids, Michigan: Baker Books, 2001.

Benson, Joseph. *Benson's Commentary.* New York: Carton & Porter, 1825.

Bergsma, John and Scott Hahn. *Noah's Nakedness and Curse on Canaan.* Accessed March 10, 2022. https://www.godawa.com/chronicles_of_the_nephilim/Articles_By_Others/Bergsma-Noahs_Nakedness_And_Curse_On_Canaan.pdf, the Internet, accessed March 10, 2022.

Bible Hub. "Exodus 4." Cambridge Bible for Schools and Colleges. Accessed June 14, 2024. https://biblehub.com/commentaries/exodus/4-24.htm.

Bible Hub. "Numbers 22:5." *Matthew Henry's Concise Commentary on the Whole Bible.* Accessed August 25, 2024. https://biblehub.com/ commentaries/numbers/22-5.htm.

Block, Daniel I. *Judges, Ruth.* The New American Commentary. Edited by E. Ray Clendenen. Nashville: Broadman & Holman Publishers, 1999.

Blomberg, Craig L. *Matthew.* The New American Commentary. Edited by E. Ray Clendenen. Nashville: Broadman Press, 1992.

Bodoff, Lippman. *The Binding of Isaac, Religious Murders & Kabbalah:*

Seeds of Jewish Extremism and Alienation? New York: Devora Publishing / Urim Press, 2005.

Braun, Roddy. *1 Chronicles.* Word Biblical Commentary. Edited by David A. Hubbard and Glenn W. Barker. Waco, Texas: Word Books, 1986.

Bruckner, James K. *Exodus.* Peabody, Massachusetts: Hendrickson Publishers, 2008.

Bruce, F. F. *Commentary on the Book of the Acts.* The New International Commentary on the New Testament. Edited by F. F. Bruce. Grand Rapids, Michigan: Wm. B. Eerdmans Publishing Co., 1971.

Bruner, Frederick Dale. *Matthew, a Commentary.* Dallas, Texas: Word Publishing, 1990.

Butler, Trent C. *Joshua.* Word Biblical Commentary, Edited by David A. Hubbard and Glenn W. Barker. Waco, Texas: Word Books, 1983.

Butler, Trent C. *Judges.* Word Biblical Commentary. General Editors Bruce M. Metzger, David A. Hubbard and Glenn W. Barker. Nashville: Thomas Nelson, 2009.

Ryle, Herbert E. *Genesis.* The Cambridge Bible for Schools and Colleges. Edited by A. F. Kirkpatrick. London: Cambridge University Press, 1914.

ChaimBenTorah. Accessed June 5, 2024. https://www.chaimbentorah.com/2020/07/ hebrew-word-study-donkey/.

ChurchMyWay. Accessed June 30, 2024. https://churchmyway

.org/the-origins-and-lessons-of- the-nephilim/.

Clarke, Adam. *Commentary on the Holy Bible.* Kansas City, Kansas: Beacon Hill Press, 1972.

Clements, Ronald E. *Exodus.* The Cambridge Bible for Schools and Colleges. Cambridge, England: Cambridge University Press, 1972.

Coffman, James Burton. *Commentary on 1 Kings 13.* Accessed May 24, 2024. https://www.studylight.org/commentaries/eng/bcc/1-kings -13.html.

Connectusfund. Accessed May 17, 2024. https://connectusfund.org /exodus-4-24-meaning-of-the-lord-met-moses-and-was-about-to-kill-him.

Cosby, Bill. "8:15, 12:15." January 12, 1969. Tetragrammaton, 1969, LP.

Craghan, John F. *Exodus.* Collegeville, Minnesota: Liturgical Press, 1985.

Cundall, Arthur E. *Judges.* Tyndale Old Testament Commentaries. Edited by D. J. Wiseman. Downer's Grove, Illinois: Inter-Varsity Press, 1968.

Dalglish, Edward R. *Judges.* The Broadman Bible Commentary. General Editor Clifton J. Allen. Nashville: Broadman Press, 1970.

Deffinbaugh, Bob. *Genesis: From Paradise to Patriarchs.* Accessed June 15, 2024. https://bible.org/seriespage/ 10-nakedness-noah-and- cursing-canaan-genesis-918-1032.

Delitzsch, Franz. *A New Commentary on Genesis*. Edinburgh, Scotland: T&T Clark, 1889.

DeVries, Simon J. *I Kings*. Word Biblical Commentary. Edited by David A. Hubbard and Glenn W. Barker. Waco, Texas: Word Books, 1985.

Driver, S. R. *Cambridge Bible for Schools and Colleges*. Cambridge, England: Cambridge University Press, 1929.

Durham, J. I. *Exodus*. Word Biblical Commentary. Edited by David A. Hubbard and Glenn W. Barker. Dallas, Texas: Word Books, 1987.

Egypt Museum. "Circumcision in Ancient Egypt." Accessed May 17, 2024. https://egypt-museum.com/circumcision-in-ancient-egypt/.

Ellicott, Charles John. *Ellicott's Commentary for English Readers*. Accessed June 9, 2024. https://biblehub.com/commentaries/judges /21-25.htm.

Ellicott, Charles John. *Ellicott's Commentary for English Readers*. At "BibleHub.com." Accessed October 25, 2024. https://biblehub.com/commentaries/jonah/1-17.htm.

Ellison, Henry L. *Exodus*. Philadelphia: Westminster Press, 1903.

EnduringWord. Accessed April 25, 2024. https://enduringword.com / bible-commentary/exodus-4/.

EvidenceUnseen. Accessed June 10, 2024. https://www.evidenceunseen.com/bible-difficulties-2/ot-difficulties/joshua/josh-1013-how-could-the-sun-stand-still-without-destroying-life-as-we-know-it/.

Fenton, J. C. *The Gospel of St Matthew*. The Pelican New Testament Commentaries. Edited by D. E. Nineham. London: Penguin Books, 1973.

Fleming, Don. *Fleming's Bridgeway Bible Commentary*. Brisbane, Australia: Bridgeway Publications, 2005.

Francisco, Clyde T. *Genesis*. The Broadman Bible Commentary. Edited by Clifton J. Allen. Nashville: Broadman Press, 1973.

Geisler, Norman L. and Frank Turek. *I Don't Have Enough Faith to Be an Atheist*. Wheaton, Illinois: Crossway, 2004.

Gispen, W. H. *Exodus*. Grand Rapids, Michigan: Zondervan, 1982.

GotQuestions. Accessed May 10, 2024. https://www.gotquestions.org/kill-Moses.html.

Hackett, Horatio B. *Acts of the Apostles*. An American Commentary on the New Testament. Edited by Alvah Hovey. Philadelphia: American Baptist Publication Society, 1882.

Hagner, Donald A. *Matthew*. Word Biblical Commentary. Edited by David A. Hubbard and Glenn W. Barker. Dallas, Texas: Word Books, 1995.

Hamilton, Victor P. *The Book of Genesis: Chapters 18-50*. The New International Commentary on the Old Testament. Grand Rapids, Michigan: Wm. B. Eerdmans Publishing Company, 1995.

Heiser, Michael S. *Demons*. Bellingham, Washington: Lexham

Press, 2020.

Heiser, Michael. *Naked Bible Podcast #062*. Accessed June 15, 2024. https://nakedbiblepodcast.com/podcast/naked-bible-62-qa-5/.

Heiser, Michael S. *The Unseen Realm*. Bellingham, Washington: Lexham Press, 2015.

Henry, Matthew. *1 Kings 13*. *Complete Commentary on the Bible*. Study Light. August 21, 2024. http://www.studylight. org/ commentaries/eng/mhm/1-kings-13.html.

Henry, Matthew. *Commentary on the Whole Bible, Vol. II, Joshua to Esther*. McLean, Virginia: MacDonald Publishing Company, 1985.

Henry, Matthew. *Commentary on the Holy Bible*. Brattleboro, Vermont: Fessenden, 1834.

Henry, Matthew. *Concise Commentary on the Whole Bible*. Accessed May 15, 2024. https://www.studylight.org/ commentaries/eng/ mhn/numbers-22.html.

Hobbs, T. R. *2 Kings*. Word Biblical Commentary. Edited by David A. Hubbard and Glenn W. Barker. Waco, Texas: Word Books, Publisher, 1986.

House, Paul R. *1, 2 Kings*. The New American Commentary. Nashville: Broadman & Holman Publishers, 1995.

Howard, Jr., David M. *Joshua,* New American Commentary. Edited by E. Ray Clendenen. Nashville: Broadman & Holman Publishers, 1998.

Jamieson, Robert, A. R. Fausset and David Brown. *A Commentary, Critical, Practical, and Explanatory on the Old and New Testaments.* Hartford, Connecticut: S. S. Scranton and Company, 1878.

Keil, Carl Friedrich and Franz Delitzsch. *Vol 1, Genesis to Judges 6:32. Biblical Commentary on the Old Testament.* Lafayette, Indiana: Associated Publishers and Authors, 1960.

Keil, Carl Friedrich and Franz Delitzsch. *Vol 2, Judges 6:33 to Ezra. Biblical Commentary on the Old Testament.* Lafayette, Indiana: Associated Publishers and Authors, 1960.

Kidner, Derek. *Genesis.* The Tyndale Old Testament Commentaries. Edited by D. J. Wiseman. Downers Grove, Illinois: Inter-Varsity Press, 1967.

Klein, Ralph W. *1 Samuel.* Word Biblical Commentary. Edited by David A. Hubbard and Glenn W. Barker. Waco, Texas: Word Books, 1983.

Lias, J. J. *Deuteronomy, Joshua and Judges.* The Pulpit Commentary. Edited by Joseph S. Exell and Henry Donald Maurice Spence-Jones. New York: Funk & Wagnall's, 1919.

Lenski, R. C. H. *The Interpretation of St. Matthew's Gospel.* Minneapolis, Minnesota: Augsburg Publishing House, 1943.

Mathews, Kenneth A. *Genesis 11:27-50:26.* The New American Commentary. Edited by E. Ray Clendenen. Nashville: Broadman & Holman Publishers, 2005.

McNeile, Alan H. *The Book of Exodus.* London: Methuen Publishers, 1908.

Meyer, F. B. *Our Daily Homily: Samuel-Job, Volume 2*. Westwood, New Jersey: Revell, 1966.

Mikkelson, David. *NASA Discovers a 'Lost Day' in Time?'* Snopes. https://www.snopes.com/fact-check/the-lost-day/.

Pevney, Joseph, dir. *Star Trek*. Season 1, Episode 28, "The City on the Edge of Forever." April 6, 1967 on NBC.

Philbeck, Ben F., Jr. *1-2 Samuel*. The Broadman Commentary. Edited by Clifton J. Allen. Nashville: Broadman Press, 1970.

Polhill, John B. *Acts*. The New American Commentary. Edited by David S. Dockery. Nashville: Broadman Press, 1992.

Poole, Matthew. *A Commentary on the Whole Bible*. "BibleHub." July 15, 2024. https://biblehub.com/commentaries/exodus/23-19.htm.

Pray, L. (2008) Discovery of DNA structure and function: Watson and Crick. Nature Education 1(1):100.

Rawlinson, George. *Exodus, Vol. II*. The Pulpit Commentary. Edited by Joseph S. Exell and Henry Donald Maurice Spence-Jones. New York: Funk & Wagnall's, 1897.

Rawlinson, George. *Genesis - Numbers*. A Bible Commentary for English Readers. Edited by Charles John Ellicott. London: Cassell and Company, LTD, n.d.

Ramm, Bernard L. *The Christian View of Science and Scripture*. Grand Rapids, Michigan: W.B. Eerdmans Publishing, 1954.

Sasson, Jack M. *Circumcision in the Ancient Near East*. Journal of Biblical Literature, 85.4 (1966). Society of Biblical Literature, 1966.

Sedley, David. "'Joshua stopped the sun' 3,224 years ago today, scientists say." *The Times of Israel*. Accessed June 18, 2024. https://www.timesofisrael.com/3224-years-later-scientists-see-f irst-ever- recorded-eclipse-in-joshuas-battle/.

Selman, Martin J. *1 Chronicles*. Tyndale Old Testament Commentaries. Edited by D. J. Wiseman. Downers Grove, Illinois: Inter-Varsity Press, 1994.

Shakespeare, William. *Macbeth.*

Simms, Robert. *Where Did I Come From?* Greer, SC: Robert F. Simms, 2011.

Skinner, John. *A Critical and Exegetical Commentary on Genesis.* New York: Scribner, 1910.

Smith, T. C. *Acts.* The Broadman Bible Commentary. Edited by Clifton J. Allen. Nashville: Broadman Press, 1970.

Soggin, J. Alberto. *Joshua, A Commentary.* Philadelphia: Westminster Press, 1972.

Stackexchange. "What is the meaning of 'sought to' in Exodus 4:24?" Accessed May 2, 2024. https://hermeneutics. stackexchange.com/questions/68942/what-is-the-meaning-of-sought-to-in-exodus-424.

Stagg, Frank. *Acts.* Nashville: Broadman Press, 1985.

Stagg, Frank. *Matthew.* The Broadman Bible Commentary. Edited by Clifton J. Allen. Nashville: Broadman Press, 1969.

Stuart, Douglas K. *Exodus.* The New American Commentary,

Edited by E. Ray Clendenen. Nashville: Holman Reference, 2006.

Tabor, Greg. "God Means What He Says." Accessed May 1, 2024. https://www.sermoncentral.com/sermons/sermons-about-1-kings-13/?searchPhrase=1%20kings%2013&searchPhrase=1%20kings%2013.

Thompson, J. A. *1, 2 Chronicles*. The New American Commentary. Edited by E. Ray Clendenen. Nashville: Broadman & Holman Publishers, 1994.

Tsumura, David Toshio. *The First Book of Samuel*. The New International Commentary on the Old Testament. Edited by R. K. Harrison and Robert L. Hubbard, Jr. Grand Rapids, Michigan: William B. Eerdmans Publishing Company, 2007.

Waller, C. H. *Joshua*. Ellicott's Commentary on the Whole Bible. Accessed Jun 10, 2024. https://biblehub.com/commentaries/habakkuk/3-11.htm.

Walsh, Jerome T. *1 Kings*. Collegeville, Minnesota: Liturgical Press, 1996.

Wenham, Gordon J. *Genesis 1-15*. Word Biblical Commentary. Edited by David A. Hubbard and Glenn W. Barker. Waco, Texas: Word Books, 1987.

Whitcomb, John C. *Solomon to the Exile: Studies in Kings and Chronicles*. Winona Lake, Indiana: BMH Books, 1971.

Whitelaw, Thomas. *Genesis*. The Pulpit Commentary. Edited by H. D. M. Spence and Joseph S. Exell. New York: Funk & Wagnalls Company, 1950.

Wikipedia. "History of Circumcision." Accessed May 17, 2024. https://en.wikipedia.org/wiki/History_of_circumcision.

Wilson, Ralph F. *Jesus Walk Bible Study Series.* Accessed May 15, 2024. https://www.jesuswalk.com/ moses/appendix4.htm.

Woudstra, Marten H. *The Book of Joshua,* The New International Commentary on the Old Testament. Edited by R. K. Harrison. Grand Rapids, Michigan: William B. Eerdmans Publishing Company, 1981.

Abbreviations Used

AMP	Amplified Bible
ARA	Aramaic Bible Translated
ASV	American Standard Version
BSB	Berean Study Bible
CEV	Contemporary English Version
CSB	Christian Standard Bible
ERV	English Revised Version
ESV	English Standard Version
GNT	Good News Translation
GWT	God's Word Translation
HCS	Holman Christian Standard Bible
ISV	International Standard Version
KJV	King James Version
NAS	New American Standard Bible
NET	New English Translation
NIV	New International Version
NKJ	New King James Version
NLT	New Living Translation
YLT	Young's Literal Translation

www.ingramcontent.com/pod-product-compliance
Lightning Source LLC
Chambersburg PA
CBHW070403100426
42812CB00005B/1616